The French Connection in Criminology

Rediscovering Crime, Law, and Social Change

BRUCE A. ARRIGO

DRAGAN MILOVANOVIC

ROBERT CARL SCHEHR

State University of New York Press

Published by
State University of New York Press, Albany

© 2005 State University of New York

For information, address State University of New York Press,
State University Plaza, Albany, NY 12246

Production by Kelli Williams
Marketing by Michael Campochiaro

Library of Congress Cataloging-in-Publication Data
Arrigo, Bruce A.
The French connection in criminology: rediscovering crime, law and social change/Bruce A. Arrigo. Dragan Milovanovic, Carl Schehr.
p. cm.—(SUNY series in new directions in crime and justice studies)
includes bibliographical references and index.
ISBN 0-7914-6355-9 (alk. paper) —ISBN 0-7914-6356-7
(pbk.: alk. paper)
1. Crime—Sociological aspects. 2. Criminology. 3. Sociology—France.
I. Schehr, Robert C. II. Milovanovic, Dragan, 1948– III. Title. IV. Series

HV6025.A677 2005
364'.01—dc22

2004045403

10 9 8 7 6 5 4 3 2 1

The French Connection in Criminology

SUNY series in New Directions in Crime and Justice Studies
Austin T. Turk, Editor

DEDICATION

———————————————

For all those students and educators, researchers and activists who theorize the possible in the face of human struggle. You live the challenge of
social change deeply, daily, and directly.

Contents

Introduction

OVERVIEW

Post-Enlightenment thought in the social sciences brought with it a set of core assumptions that too often have remained unexamined. Modernist thought has both advanced and placed limitations on critical inquiry. In its most celebrated form, modernism has contributed profoundly to fundamental insights about the human condition and to potential emancipatory practices. However, the emerging postmodern society has demanded alternative theoretical analyses in understanding its political, economic, and cultural potential, its repressive and liberating tendencies, and its possible directions. Postmodern thought, traced to many of the "first wave" French scholars of the last four decades, has ushered in a new era of scholarly inquiry. This book traces some of the key contributions to the evolving postmodern perspective, especially as they apply to a rediscovery of crime, law, and social change.

In this introduction, we briefly delineate several of the more prominent conceptual and organizational components informing, or otherwise contributing to, this text. Indeed, *The French Connection in Criminology*, and its application to crime, law, and social justice studies, emerges from a number of factors that warrant some general comments. Accordingly, we draw our attention to four concerns. First, we situate this book within its relevant historical context. Along these lines we provide some background material on the emergence of postmodernist thought and its development in the areas of law, crime, and social change, noting especially some of the more virulent criticisms that challenge its place in the academy today. Second, we identify the need for *The French Connection in Criminology*, highlighting what this work endeavors to accomplish. Third, we review our own presuppositions about theory and method, suggesting to readers how they might interpret our analysis. Fourth, we outline the organization of the book, providing a chapter-by-chapter summary.

THE EMERGENCE OF POSTMODERNISM:
THE HISTORICAL CONTEXT

During the past twenty or so years, much has been made of French post-modern social thought and its capacity to inform cultural theory and contemporary media, art, and society. Academic disciplines as broad ranging as politics, history, literary criticism, philosophy, architecture, gender studies, and anthropology have seized upon the insights of many postmodern concepts, and have articulated new methods and strategies for understanding the social world and people in it. The disciplines of law and criminology are no exception to this trend. Indeed, during the 1980s and 1990s, many "second wave" socio-legal researchers appropriated the tools of the postmodern sciences in order to deepen our regard for crime and justice controversies. Regrettably, however, little attention has been given to the consolidation and coordination of this scholarship in any systematic fashion. Thus, our appreciation for French postmodern social theory, and its impact for socio-legal studies, remains uneven, fragmented, and disorganized at best.

In part, this lack of systematic and integrative thought is traceable to how postmodern sensibilities have been interpreted and appropriated by other scholars. Indeed, we recognize that not all the theoretical or applied research in law and criminology has been supportive of the postmodern enterprise. For example, Martin Schwartz and David O. Friedrichs (1994, 221–222) suggest that not only is this orientation outside the mainstream of legal and criminological thought but that it rests at the fringe of the critical tradition itself. In addition, Joel Handler (1992) argues that discourse analysis, a component of postmodern conceptual inquiry, is not in any way theoretically based. "Rather, it is a method or process for raising questions and criticizing the presumptions of theory" (1992, 723). According to some observers, these and other similar criticisms cast doubt on the efficacy of the postmodern sciences to inform and advance our appreciation for such matters as crime and its control, violence and victims, punishment and correctional practices, deviance and delinquent behavior. However, we note that our task in this book is not to directly challenge these sorts of reservations; rather, we merely wish to draw attention to where and how the postmodern critique has been and can be significant for advancing our knowledge of law, crime, and social justice.

We do not totally dismiss modernist's claims, assumptions, or theories, nor do we want to reestablish dualisms and clear-cut polarities that become the basis of dogmatic defense; rather, we look forward to ongoing dialogue with modernism's adherents. In this spirit, we do challenge any tendencies toward stasis and closure. In the affirmative postmodern perspective, the search is not for definitive conceptualizations, theories, and solutions, but for approaches to understanding meaning that ensure openness, reflexivity, transparency, and sensitivity to the multifaceted nature of being human in society.[1] It is a search for possible relatively stabilized configurations in which harms of reduction and harms of repression diminish, while personal and social growth expand. It is a call for what chaologists refer to as "dissipative structures" in which institutions and structures remain criticizable, responsive, and transparent. It is a call for "far-from-equilibrium" conditions rather than a privileging of homeostasis, structural functionalism, and linear developments. It is a recognition of nonlinearity, dialectics, irony, spontaneity, flux, flow, the unexpected, and rhizomatic development. It valorizes the notion of Julia Kristeva's "subject-in-process." In this context, we seek to establish transpraxis rather than praxis; a method in which critique is combined with visions of the possible.

Moreover, we regard the above stated cavils and cautions as the anticipated fall out of a more nihilistic, pessimistic, and fatalistic approach to postmodernist thought. It may very well be that the early form of postmodern analysis was merely an adolescent stage of development; a reaction-negation praxis to various repressive activities without an affirmative vision of the possible. As we explain in chapter 3, while a skeptical line of inquiry can be traced to this heterodox intellectual tradition, there also is an affirmative reading located within it. This replacement approach to postmodern thought offers new insights about the human condition and about social life, potentially yielding new vistas of meaning that promote transformative and emancipating social change.

One way to appreciate this more liberating version of postmodernism, especially as developed throughout this book, is to situate it within its appropriate historical context. French postmodernism was fueled by many intersecting events: rapid economic modernization in the wake of World War II; new forms of mass culture, technology, consumerism, and urbanization that concealed psychological alienation and social oppression; the conceptual demise of Marxism, existentialism, and phenomenology and the intellectual birth of structuralism and poststructuralism; and several new theories about writing and discourse as developed by philosophers, psychoanalysts, and linguists of the infamous *Tel Quel* group. All of these events contributed to the riots of 1968, in which students and workers momentarily brought the political economy of France to a halt. Although short-lived, the uproar of 1968 inaugurated a new historical epoch, a postmodern era, in which an epistemological shift was given life (Best and Kellner 1991, 16–20; Best and Kellner 1997).

Figured prominently in this epistemological transition was the role of language and its capacity to shape our understanding of social phenomena and human behavior.[2] Central to this exploration of language was the psychoanalytic formulations of Jacques Lacan, particularly his insights on the relationship between discourse and subjectivity. His novel and groundbreaking observations on language and identity were presented in seminar form throughout the 1950s to 1980 in Paris, France. Lacan was to take the early Freud (1900–1920) and integrate and synthesize various theorists: Ferdinand de Saussure provided the theoretical statement for his nonreferential semiotics; Alexandre Kojeve offered the interpretations of George W. F. Hegel's notion of desire; Emile Benveniste specified the nature of the personal pronoun and how "I" is a shifter, that is, a stand in for the subject; Roman Jakobson, through his studies on speech disorders, developed the idea that metaphor and metonymy are the two organizing principles of semiotic production; and Claude Levi-Strauss elaborated on the nature of the Symbolic Order.

Lacan, too, was to be inspired by the works of a number of mathematicians, especially topologists (quite early in his career in the 1950s by Georges Guilbaud). In his late works of the 1970s, Lacan turned even more to the works of mathematicians, especially topologists (e.g., Pierre Soury, Michel Thomé), in developing his theory on the use of the Borromean knots and *le sinthome*. Several contemporary mathematically oriented Lacanians such as Jean-Michel Vappeareau were to assist this integration in the 1970s. These syntheses were the basis of Lacan's seminars, most of which have yet to be translated into English; many still await even French publication (for a detailed application of Lacan's contributions in law, crime, and justice see, Milovanovic 1997, 2002).

THE POSTMODERN ENTERPRISE IN CRIME, LAW, AND JUSTICE

Despite its considerable relevance throughout and application to various academic disciplines, the development of French postmodern thought has not been consolidated in the legal and criminological research. *The French*

Connection in Criminology: Rediscovering, Crime, Law, and Social Change aims to remedy this deficiency. Although in a previous article (Arrigo, Milovanovic, and Schehr 2000), we attempted this very exercise, the limits of that scholarship did not permit us to develop more fully many of the important thinkers and themes explored in the pages of this text. Accordingly, this book represents the first comprehensive, accessible, and integrative overview of postmodernism's contribution to the field. More specifically, this text draws attention to where and how the more affirmative and synthetic approach to postmodern inquiry has been and can be significant for advancing our knowledge of and response to law, crime, and justice, particularly in relation to an array of social problems society confronts today.

The *French Connection in Criminology* also is written principally as a "primer" and a pedagogical tool for the field. As such, it endeavors to reveal the utility of postmodernism's diverse theoretical and methodological underpinnings, especially in relation to more liberating prospects for social change. Moreover, this text represents a rallying cry for future research. Indeed, the taken for granted conceptual prisms and methodological tools through which most criminological and legal investigations unfold must be de-centered and displaced if meaningful, sustainable, and structural change is to occur. With this in mind, *The French Connection in Criminology* seeks to fan the flames of alternative, provocative, and novel lines of socio-legal scholarship; approaches that simultaneously identify the limits of existing research while charting new directions that provisionally, positionally, and relationally advance the interests of citizen well-being, collective humanism, and social accord. Finally, this text stands as a challenge to the modernist tradition in crime, law, and social justice. We invite our colleagues to rethink how such phenomena as identity, social structure, cause and effect logic, time and space configurations, deductive and syllogistic reasoning, role formation, knowledge, truth, and progress, and so forth, are all based on implicit assumptions and concealed values anchored in dominant discourses with their corresponding alienating and marginalizing effects. To this end, *The French Connection in Criminolgoy: Rediscovering Crime, Law, and Social Change* endeavors to establish a vision not of what is but of what could be. Consequently, this book signifies a search for transpraxis (Henry and Milovanovic 1996), particularly in the way we think about, talk about, or otherwise engage in criminological and legal *verstehen*.

A COMMENT ON PRESUPPOSITIONS

No piece of scholarship is without its presuppositions and this book is no exception. In our case, we understand theory and method to be intertwined.

For example, there are multiple theoretical variants to postmodernism (e.g., poststructuralism, discourse analysis, chaos theory, dialogical pedagogy) just as there are different methodological approaches to it (e.g., narrative jurisprudence, semiotics, deconstruction, constitutive). However, in the topography of postmodernism, theory and method converge: language becomes method and method becomes theory; conceptualizing the linguistic turn in crime, law, and social justice becomes a new approach for conceiving, interpreting, and knowing phenomena; "doing" an affirmative and integrative postmodern analysis represents theoretical and methodological reformulation. Our regard for postmodern inquiry unfolds with these presuppositions in mind.

Given our understanding of the relationship between theory and method, the applied investigations that follow (chapters 4–8), signify attempts at crafting novel lines by which to engage in research. This observation should not be underestimated or dismissed. Indeed, what this book attempts to accomplish is to dramatically reframe many of the existing debates in law, crime, and justice studies by drawing from the provocative insights of first and second wave French postmodern social theorists. Thus, we neither presume to offer any definitive truths on the subjects canvassed, nor do we propose that our inquiries represent the final word on the topics investigated. Instead, what we assume is that our observations—incomplete, provisional, and suggestive—signify some of the possible ways in which we can rethink law, criminology, and social justice.

Finally, we assume that readers will be somewhat unfamiliar with several of the ideas, lines of analyses, terms, and algebraic formulations discussed or presented throughout this book. We do not wish this unfamiliarity to harbor resentment or to promote confusion for the uninitiated. Accordingly, several theoretical and methodological themes reemerge, especially in the application chapters. This is deliberate. Our efforts here are designed to encourage novice readers of postmodernist thought to become increasingly comfortable with the alternative conceptualizations proposed. For those readers more informed about postmodern analysis, the book provides an accessible collection of various potential applications and suggestive integrations for further research in these areas and beyond.

ORGANIZATION OF THE BOOK

During the past two decades, several noteworthy texts and edited volumes have relied upon selected insights contained within the domain of French postmodern social theory, and have applied these notions to relevant themes in law, criminology, and social justice (e.g., Smart 1989; Manning 1988;

Milovanovic 1992; Henry 1983; Arrigo 1993, 2002a; Butler 1990; Young 1996). Today, this body of scholarship, although far from exhaustive, is voluminous. What each of these works shares is a genuine commitment to the power of postmodern thought to provide different lenses that establish new meanings for complex problems in crime, law, and social justice. However, these texts are neither specifically designed to explain, nor are they intended to unify the strains of thought encompassing French postmodern social theory. More recently, however, a few attempts at theoretical synthesis and/or consolidation have materialized (e.g., Henry and Milovanovic 1996; Milovanovic 2002). Although more mindful of the conceptual and historical origins of postmodern theory, these efforts do not directly address who the key first wave scholars were, nor how their coordinated insights represent a conceptual framework of sorts for social science inquiry, subsequently appropriated by second wave legal and criminological researchers.

 The French Connection in Criminology: Rediscovering Crime, Law, and Social Change contributes to the existing body of postmodern work by squarely attending to the limitations identified above. Specifically, the text reviews and consolidates the unique contributions of eleven first wave French postmodern luminaries, mindful of the more affirmative and liberating dimensions of their scholarship. These prominent thinkers include Roland Barthes, Jean Baudrillard, Hélène Cixous, Gilles Deleuze and Felix Guattari, Jacques Derrida, Michel Foucault, Luce Irigaray, Julia Kristeva, Jacques Lacan, and Jean-François Lyotard. Certainly there could be a claim for the inclusion of others in this group; however, we wish to limit our coverage to those who have had the most direct influence in law, criminology, and social justice. To be sure, the scholarly work of some of the less exposed and less translated French scholars will be the basis of important insights in the coming years. Their "discovery" will certainly contribute more momentum to the body of literature supportive of a more postmodern understanding. In addition, the text documents where and how the theorists' respective insights have been extended into the legal and criminological realm through the application work of second wave scholars. Relatedly, in order to demonstrate the future utility for engaging in an affirmative and integrative postmodern investigation, a number of crime and justice application chapters are presented.

 Accordingly, in chapter 1, we present the insights of Jacques Lacan, Roland Barthes, Gilles Deleuze and Felix Guattari, Michel Foucault, and Jean François Lyotard. Each of these first wave luminaries has passed way; however, the vitality of their insights endures. Along these lines, we briefly draw attention to the applied research generated by second wave scholars who have appropriated and extended the contributions of French postmodern social theorists as linked to law, crime, and justice studies.

In chapter 2, we sustain our presentation of first wave French postmodern thought. In particular, we review the work of Jean Baudrillard, Hélène Cixous, Jacques Derrida, Luce Irigaray, and Julia Kristeva. Similar to our exposition in chapter 1, where useful and appropriate, we summarize several of the second wave studies that have applied first wave insights to pressing issues in law and criminology.

In chapter 3, we explore what is meant by "doing" affirmative and integrative postmodern research. In order to accomplish this task, we first review the more nihilistic, skeptical, and antifoundational forms of postmodern inquiry. Next, we explain several theoretical and methodological aspects of our affirmative and integrative enterprise. The comments that follow in this section are not exhaustive; rather, we identify several robust areas where promoting a transformative agenda in socio-legal studies is not only possible but also realizable. Finally, we suggestively propose several areas in which postmodern syntheses are discernible. With this thrust, we conclude the chapter by specifying a number of attempts at affirmative and integrative postmodern research relevant to crime, law, and justice studies (e.g., edgework, constitutive criminology, chaos theory, and psychoanalytic semiotics).

The balance of *The French Connection in Criminology* (chapters 4–8) demonstrates how the insights of the first wave social theorists can be applied to relevant and topical themes in crime, law, and social justice research. Again, our analysis in these chapters is suggestive of what an affirmative and integrative postmodern exposition might encompass.

Accordingly, in chapter 4, we examine confinement law and prison resistance. In this chapter, we first look at persons identified as competent but mentally ill and indicate how an affirmative and integrative postmodern approach to confinement, competency, mental illness, and treatment would offer alternative and more liberating practices. In the second part of this chapter, we focus on four areas of prisons resistance: poststructuralist feminist critiques; agency and resistance in women's prisons; jailhouse lawyers (primitive rebels or revolutionaries?); and constitutive penology. In each case, we summarize some of the central ideas and then follow with how first and second wave French postmodern insights could further contribute to an even greater understanding of these phenomena.

In chapter 5, we highlight critical race theory and a jurisprudence of color. We first indicate one of the main reservations presented by critical race theorists—that because of compelling, daily, and systematic repressive practices CRT researchers do not have the luxury to engage in highly theoretical, abstract, and esoteric discourses. Therefore, some critical race theorists contend that they must be more pragmatic in using law as one of the few weapons available to correct wrongs. We describe how postmodern analysis could provide some critical tools for a jurisprudence of color. Indeed, an alliance between the two would enhance both. Accordingly, we engage three areas: storytelling and narrative constructions; the wherewithal of intersectional subjectivity; and an alternative methodology rooted in transpraxis.

In chapter 6, we explore the relationship between media/cultural studies and feminism. We first develop the Lacanian cinema model. In this model the "spoken subject" is developed; a subject who identifies with the discursive subject positions offered and begins to see the world as the director suggests. Underlying this model is a reliance on the oedipalization of the subject; a passive notion of desire as a response to lack; the mirror stage of ego development; and the tendency toward the development of a readerly text. We provide several examples of this application. We then move to revisionist and integrative Lacanian models and explain how women and other disenfranchised persons are denied voices and how they may find expression. Here, the work of Kristeva on the "abject" provides an alternative perspective on how subjectivities and realities are constructed. We provide some applications to filmic and literary texts. A revisionist and integrative perspective is subsequently developed drawing from Norman Denzin's postmodern ethnograpy, Minh-Ha Trinh's critical observations, and the suggestive theoretical work of Deleuze and Guattari on the body without organs. The central notion developed here is the idea of an "intersectional standpoint" which goes beyond mere "standpoint epistemology."

In chapter 7, we assess restorative justice initiatives and victim offender mediation practices. We first summarize victim offender mediation (VOM) and note that contrary to its main defenders it very much can be likened to legal formalism whereby a dominant discourse in a disciplinary mechanism functions to co-opt discussion in restricted ways. We then offer first and second wave theorizing to not only critique, but also to suggest future directions. We describe a more progressive version of VOM; one that endorses transformation through transpraxis rather than a mere "restoration." We conclude with a discussion of restrictions concerning the viability of VOM, given the existence of a hierarchical political economy.

In chapter 8, we investigate the phenomenon of social movements, drawing attention to the manifestation of innocence projects and intentional communities. We explain that conventional theorizing about social movements privileges large-scale organization of assumed rational calculators who mobilize resources, build coalition networks, and engage in long-range planning. However, we demonstrate that challenges to dominant cultural institutions and practices operate at subaltern levels and in nonlinear ways. As such, we delineate a fourth approach to movement potential; a paradigm that relies on the insights of chaos theory. To substantiate our position, we explore the manifestation of innocence projects as a response to wrongful convictions and the presence of intentional communities as a strategy designed to house the homeless. As these illustrations reveal, postmodern social movements argue for the privileging of nonlinear dynamics, framing processes, structural dislocations, sensitivity to the reemergence of the discourse of the *master*, intersectional standpoints, and shifting coalitions. The examples signify a persistent resistance bubbling beneath the surface of dominant culture, and they hold the potential for stimulating nonlinear, but nonetheless manifest, institutional changes. Very central, then, to the new social movements are ideas emerging from chaos theory and first and second wave French scholars.

The French Connection in Criminology: Rediscovering Crime, Law, and Social Change is a timely invitation to the reader. More than critiquing how things are and more than proposing how things could be, this book challenges those who wrestle with its contents to rethink the way in which teachers, researchers, policy analysts, practitioners, and activists can promote, establish, and sustain much needed reform in the every day world of criminal justice. If change is to successfully resist the dust heap of abject idealism, if transpraxis is to avoid the charge of intellectual abstraction, and if humanism is to transcend the confines of false sentimentalism, than the future of socio-legal studies must reconcile itself to the postmodern era. This is the invitation we lay before the reader.

CHAPTER 1

Establishing the First Wave:
The Linguistic Turn in Social Theory

INTRODUCTION

In this chapter, we succinctly describe the contributions of several prominent first wave thinkers whose work has contributed substantially to our understanding of postmodern thought.[1] These authors include Roland Barthes, Gilles Deleuze and Felix Guattari, Michel Foucault, Jacques Lacan, and Jean-François Lyotard. We note that while each of these luminaries has passed away, they individually and collectively helped to establish the first wave's agenda endorsing social and political change. In chapter 2, the insights of those first wave thinkers, who have sustained the postmodern project, are likewise delineated.

Chapter 1 also summarizes where and how the inroads of the identified social theorists have been utilized by various second wave authors, especially those commenting on different facets of law, crime, and social justice. This related and secondary task is important to the text's overall purpose. As the subsequent application chapters make evident, embracing a postmodern attitude need not produce a nihilistic, fatalistic, or pessimistic worldview. Indeed, the linguistic turn in social theory can also lead to affirmative, transformative, and emancipatory praxis. Thus, the aim of the following exposition on postmodernism, the first wave architects of this heterodox perspective, and the crime and justice scholars who have since then appropriated many of their insights, is to suggest that "doing" affirmative and integrative analysis of the sort proposed here dramatically moves us beyond our conventional understanding of criminological and legal research, to a place in which transpraxis and social justice can thrive.

FIRST WAVE CONTRIBUTIONS

Jacques Lacan

Jacques Lacan (1900–1981) arguably is the key figure in the development of French-inspired postmodern analysis.[2] Lacan's (1977) main contribution was that the subject is intimately connected to discourse. This subject, or "speaking" (*parlêtre*) being, is a de-centered rather then centered subject offered by Enlightenment epistemology.

Lacanian thought undermined the concept of the "individual," captured in the notion of the juridic subject in law or the "rational man" assumption contained in rational choice theory in criminology. Rather, the speaking being was depicted in a more static form in Schema L, and in a more dynamic, topological form in the Graphs of Desire, Schema R, Schema I, the Cross-Cap, and the Borromean Knots (Lacan 1977, 1988). His topological constructions also included the Mobius Band and the Klein bottle. What he showed was that there were two planes to subjectivity: the subject of speech, and the speaking subject (Lacan 1981). The former included the deeper unconscious workings where desire was embodied in signifiers that came to "speak the subject"; the latter was the subject taking a position in various discourses, identifying with an "I" as a stand in for her/his subjectivity, and engaging in communication with the other. He was to show that three intersecting spheres existed in the production of subjectivity: the Symbolic (the sphere of the unconscious, nuanced discourse and the "law-of-the-father"), the Imaginary (the sphere of imaginary constructions including conceptions of self and others), and the Real Order (lived experience beyond accurate symbolization). Since the Symbolic Order is phallocentric, all is tainted with the privileging of the male voice. According to Lacan (1985), women remain left out, *pas-toute*, not-all. However, they have access to an alternative *jouissance*, which remains inexpressible in a male-dominated order (Lacan 1985). Hence, the basis for the call for an *écriture féminine* (i.e, women's writing) to overcome *pas-toute*.[3]

Lacan's attention to discourse and subjectivity includes a dynamic understanding of speech production and its psychic mobilization (Lacan 1991). Interested in both the inter- and intra-subjective plane of human existence and development, Lacan graphically depicted what he termed the "four discourses." These included the discourse of the *master, university, hysteric*, and *analyst*. Each of these organizing schemas, as distinct mechanisms for understanding speech production and its psychic configuration, explained how desire did or did not find expression (and legitimacy) in discourse, and what sort of knowledge was privileged (or dismissed) when one of these specific discourses was in use.

Briefly, each of the four discourses includes four main terms and four corresponding locations. These terms are *S1* or the master signifer; *S2* or knowledge; *$* or the desiring subject; and *a* or the *objet petit (a)* understood by Lacan to be *le plus de jouir* or that excess in enjoyment left out (*pas-toute*) in the discursive arrangement of the particular discourse (e.g., *university, master*) in operation.

Master signifiers are primordial, originate through our childhood experiences, and form the basis for how speech production typically unfolds. In the United States, the examples of "due process" in law or "just deserts" in criminology are master signifiers. The meanings assigned to these phrases are anchored in ideologically based contents, consistent with a materialistic political economy, established during one's formative development. For Lacan (1991), the knowledge term, *S2*, is a part of a chain of signifiers where meaning always and already insists. To illustrate, the circumscribed meanings for the master signifier "due process" are linked to other signifiers such as "equity," "fairness," "reasonableness," and these signifiers form the basis of or become the subject for yet other key signifiers in law. The divided or slashed subject is depicted by the *$* term. The subject is divided because his or her *jouissance* is not fully embodied in the words or phrases used to convey speech or to invite action. All linguistic coordinate systems are specialized grammars where communicating effectively means that one must insert oneself and/or be positioned within the discursive parameters that give that language system coherence. What is lost in this process, however, is the subject's being; his or her interiorized self (Lacan's lack, *pas toute*, or *a*) that slumbers in despair because the subject's true words cannot find anchorage in prevailing modes of communicating and interacting.

Lacan also identified for structural positions corresponding to the four terms. These four locations can be depicted as follows:

<u>agent</u>   <u>other</u>
truth   production

The left side of the formulation represents the person sending some message. The right side of the formulation symbolizes the receiver of the message. The upper left hand corner or *agent* signifies the enactor of the message. The upper right hand corner or *other* signifies the receiver of the message. The activity of the agent and other occurs above the bar thereby representing that which is more active, overt, or conscious in speech production. The lower left hand corner or *truth* signifies what is unique to the person sending the message to another. The lower right hand corner or *production* represents the unconscious effects following the communication from sender to receiver. The activity that occurs below the bar is more passive, covert, and latent.

The four terms and four locations were integral to explaining the operation of Lacan's four discourses. The discourse of the *master* is as follows:

$\underline{S1} \rightarrow$	$\underline{S2}$	The person sending the message invokes master signifiers,
$\$$	a	yielding circumscribed knowledge based on what is implicit in the sender. This exchange produces incomplete understanding.

The discourse of the *university* is as follows:

$\underline{S2} \rightarrow$	$\underline{a}$	Some form of knowledge is activated by the agent,
$S1$	$\$$	resulting in *pas toute* for the other. Although this body of knowledge is based implicitly on the enactors truth, it renders the other a divided subject.

The discourse of the *hysteric* (hysteric read more broadly as not only clinical but also those opposing in some form) is as follows:

$\$ \rightarrow$	$\underline{S1}$	The slashed subject or the oppressed, alienated subject,
a	$S2$	attempts to convey his/her desire, lack, and suffering to the other who only responds through master signifiers. These signifiers produce a reconstituted version of the slashed subject's desire, transforming the divided subject's desire into acceptable (though circumscribed) knowledge.

The discourse of the *analyst* is as follows:

$\underline{a} \rightarrow$	$\$$	The analyst (read as a reformist or healer) conveys infor-
$S2$	$S1$	mation to the alienated subject (the hysteric as other). The hysteric as divided is exposed to new data about his/her being and, consequently, produces new, alternative, and

> replacement anchorings of signifieds to signifiers. This is
> because the slashed subject realizes his/her despair and
> longing for change, reform, revolution.

Lacan's work has been influential with a number of second wave theorists. In law we note: Judith Butler (gender construction, 1990, 1993, 1997a; injurious speech, 1997b); Dracilla Cornell (critical feminist analysis, family law, sexual freedom, 1991, 1993, 1998a); David Caudill (subjectivity in law, 1997); Peter Goodrich (legal speech production, 1990); Pierre Legendre (development of doctrines of the sacraments in the twelfth and thirteenth centuries, 1996); Renata Salecl (fantasy, repression, and justice, 1994); Philip Shon (on police-citizen interactions, 2000); Helen Stacy (aboriginal women's denial of voice in law, 1996); Bruce Arrigo (the insanity defense, 1997a; the guilty but mentally ill verdict, 1996a; desire in the psychiatric courtroom, 1996b); Louise Halper (use of metaphor and metonymy in law, 1995); Marty Slaughter (fantasy and the single mother in family law, 1995); Jeanne Schroeder (property contract and subjectivity, 1995 and on legal advocacy and the hysterical attorney, 2000); Milovanovic (integration of Lacan and chaos theory, 1992, 1996a); Veronique Voruz (psychosis and legal responsibility, 2000); and Christopher Williams and Bruce Arrigo (on forensic mental health intervention, 2000). In criminology we see: Allison Young (detective fiction, 1996); Renata Salecl (crime as a mode of subjectivization, 1994); and Bruce Arrigo (criminal and civil confinement, 1996c, 1997b). In social justice we find: Mark Bracher (culture and social change, 1993); Arrigo (liberating pedagogy in the classroom, 1995a, 1998; ethics in crime and justice; 1995b); Bruce Arrigo and Robert Schehr (victim offender mediation and restorative justice for juveniles, 1998); Butler (undermining traditional repetitive discursive production, 1993); Cornell (reimagining of our world through myth, 1993; protecting the imaginary domain, 1998b); Ernesto Laclau and Chantal Mouffe (development of alternative discursive forms, 1985; see also Laclau, societal dislocations and the possibility of new, liberating articulations, 1996a, 1996b); and Milovanovic (critical legal practices informed by a Paulo Freire, Jacque Lacan, and chaos integration, 1996a).

Roland Barthes

The contributions of Roland Barthes (1915–1980) were exhaustively developed in his postmodern literary critiques of reading texts.[4] Barthes (1974, 35–41) recognized that all texts were constituted by a "galaxy of signifiers" that when minimally and provisionally decoded would "explode and scatter." Elsewhere, this approach to interpreting meaning led him to speak of enjoyment and pleasure (*jouissance*) as the object of textual analysis (Barthes 1973b). Indeed, "the subject gains access to bliss by the cohabitation of languages [different modes of discourse] working side by side" (Barthes 1973b, 4). In addition, Barthes (1988) maintained that the truth of a text was never an arrival in sense making but was always a departure from it. And finally, the activity of ascertaining the message of a text included "forgetting meaning" [as an integral dimension] to reading" (Barthes 1988, 264).

These later works and observations by Barthes emphasized the creative role of the reader (Berman 1988, 147; see also Velan 1972, 328, on Barthes and the mix of structure, language, and desire in literary interpretation). For Barthes, the person interpreting textual meaning was so profoundly significant to the process, that he was led to conclude that the reader could "make anything signify" (as cited in Culler 1975, 138). As Berman (1988, 148) puts it, "the reader naturalizes, seeks and, sure enough, finds meaning" (also see, Culler 1981, 1982, for more on semiotics, deconstruction, and literature).

A key development in Barthes' literary criticism was the distinction between the "readerly" versus "writerly" text. The readerly approach reproduces the classic text's ideals. The organizing principles of this reading (and viewing) are primarily noncontradiction, coherency, and consistency. The reader/viewer is encouraged to accept "as truth" the words themselves. Thus, there is nothing behind or underneath the words. What the text means is direct, without question, on the surface. Missing from the readerly approach is the sphere of the text's production; that is, its connection to the political economy and to cultural inequalities that remain concealed. The reader/viewer experiences fulfillment. The text promises a coherent narrative and the reader/viewer interprets the text accordingly. Thus, in this reading, subjects reconstitute and revalidate the dominant understandings of reality embedded in the text. The readerly approach emphasizes the manifest content of the narrative. Missing from this rendition, however, is the deep structure of the text that often represents a more cloaked reality affirming certain power relationships and a certain understanding of the person in the social order.

Conversely, the writerly approach is a subversive and insurgent method of reading a text. It emphasizes a multitude of interpretations that validate an array of truths and knowledges. Unlike the readerly approach that tends toward closure or the text's finiteness, the writerly approach resists structure and a definable, singular product. In the writerly method the process is central. The underlying structures of signification, of meaning, are unearthed. The text is understood to contain an explosion and scattering of meaning. Rather than privileging one interpretation, one voice, through the text, the reader/viewer is encouraged to discover the multiple and repressed voices embedded in the words. Familiarity and coherence, cornerstones of the readerly approach, are resisted and supplanted with displacement and ambivalence. This is an active deconstruction (i.e., de-centering and destabilizing) of sedimented and privileged interpretations. It is also an active reconstruction of alternative truths and replacement ways of knowing.

The distinction between the writerly and readerly approach is perhaps best exemplified in works such as *Elements of Semiology* (1968b) and *S/Z* (1974). The former project synthesized Barthes' views on semiotics as the science of signs, utilizing Sassure's (1966) interpretation of language and his assessment of myth and ritual. The latter text was a compelling application of structural linguistics to Honoré Balzac's short story, "Sarrasine." By methodically reviewing this story according to phases, Barthes examined the phenomenon of reading, its relation to the reader, and the way the reader contributes to or otherwise participates in the language of the text. Investigations of this sort led Barthes to conclude that the unity of a text was not situated in its origin but in its destination. Indeed, ". . . the birth of the reader must be at the cost of the death of the Author. . . ."

Direct applications of Barthes' ideas in law, criminology, and social justice have been somewhat modest. This notwithstanding, his insights have been suggestive for several second wave theorists. Thus, in law we note: Susan Tiefenbrun (exploring approaches to legal semiotics, 1986); and Arrigo (on narratives in mental health law, 1993). In criminology we see: Stuart Henry and Dragan Milovanovic (establishing a constitutive criminological praxis, 1996); and Arrigo (integrating postmodern theory, 1995c). In social justice we find: Gilles Deleuze and Felix Guattari (describing the operation of "minor" literatures and rhizomatics as dimensions of social change, 1986); and Dawn Currie, Brian MacLean, and Dragan Milovanovic (redefining the administration of critical social justice, 1992; see also Milovanovic 1995).

Gilles Deleuze and Felix Guattari

Although Deleuze (1925–1995) and Guattari (1930–1992)[5] did not themselves position their work in the realm of the postmodern, their ideas represent a wholesale critique of the emblems of modernist thought.[6] Similar to Karl Marx, Deleuze and Guattari identified the ultimate state of human oppression as a product of capitalism. Their prime objective was to free the realization of human desire from the artificial and subjugating constraints imposed upon it by capitalist social relations and normalizing techniques of domination. Deleuze and Guattari distinguished themselves from other social commentators (e.g., Hegel, Freud, and Lacan) who viewed the desiring subject as "lacking" wholeness or completeness. They articulated a theory of desire as "technology" that was a productive force (Best and Kellner 1991, 86–87). It is the unpredictable, ambulant, chaotic, and unstable aspect of desire that stimulates cultural change and creativity.

Deleuze and Guattari's vision of the subject is one of a "desiring machine." It is a body composed of various energies in movement, in various speeds and intensities where tentative linkages are established, but always in a process of reconfiguration. In this regard, they follow much of what has been said by Spinoza and Nietszche. Indeed, in this construction, desire is seen as ever active, affirming, bringing things together, producing "reality." It assembles and breaks things down; it knows only proliferation and actualization. It is not essentially connected to "lack." Desire takes on organization at two levels: the "molecular" level is where it is in maximal deteritorializing form. Here, only multiplicities are produced; it knows only flows, intensities, various speeds, and singularities. It is nomadic, unpredictable, meandering, spontaneous, and creative. The "molar" level is where more permanent configurations of energy are crystallized. It is the plane where unity, stability, stasis, and divisions prevail. It knows the laws of homeostasis, repetition, functionality, hierarchy, stratification, unification, fixity. It is the basis of categorizations such as class, gender, race, and so forth.

Borrowing from Antonin Artaud, and stimulated by Spinoza, the body, in its most free state, can be seen as a Body without Organs (BwO). "The full body without organs," they tell us, "is a body populated by multiplicities" (Deleuze and Guattari 1987, 30). It is a body of continuous becomings. It knows only continuous variation, intensities, proliferations, momentary understanding (as in epiphanies), assemblages, and disassemblages.

The "empty" BwO, on the other hand, is one where stasis and repetition have been established; where flows and intensities have been subjected to the dictates of molar forces. They identify the drug addict, paranoid, masochist, and hypochondriac as examples. The empty BwO has been emptied of molecular flow. In the process, it has disconnected itself from other BwO. However, the "full" BwO, is completely connected to the affirmative energies of desire: it is nomadic, proliferating, spontaneous, flowing. It is characterized as a "becoming-something."[7] There are infinite becomings: becoming-child, becoming-poet, becoming-comedian, becoming-woman, becoming-other. There are also other forms of becoming: becoming-dog, becoming-horse, when a person becomes one with the animal world. Becoming-dog, for example, means developing a profound understanding of dog!

The highest state that can be attained is a "becoming-imperceptible" (Deleuze and Guattari 1987, 279). Here, all identities are traversed, both molar and molecular. It is the realm of "the immanent end of becoming"

(1987, 279). As Elizabeth Grosz (1994, 178) explains, it is "the most micro-scopic and fragmenting of becomings . . . the freeing of infinitely microscopic lines, a process whose end is achieved only with complete dissolution, the pro-duction of the incredible ever-shrinking 'man.'" Moreover, "indiscernibility, imperceptibility, and impersonality remain the end point of becoming, their immanent orientation or internal impetus, the freeing of absolutely minuscule micro-intensities to the nth degree" (1987, 179).

Deleuze and Guattari (1983) promoted a new form of political activism referred to as "schizoanalysis."[8] In order to establish smooth functioning social relations in the capitalist political economy, efforts are made to "territorialize" and "code" all behaviors as appropriate for or inconsistent with meritocracy and the preservation of commodity production. The purpose of the schizo is to "deterritorialize" behavioral expectations, "destroying beliefs . . . , represen-tations, [and established] theatrical scenes" (Deleuze and Guattari 1983, 314). Once the schizo initiates deterritorialization, s/he becomes a "body-without-organs." This is a state of being that is fluid, fractured, and unbounded by the discursive constraints imposed by dominant cultural expectations. This ambulant and deterritorialized movement promotes the reconstitution of subject-positions in relatively new and previously unmanifested ways. While the emphasis is on the perpetual reconstruction of the individual based on the appropriation of political, economic, and cultural space, Deleuze and Guattari recognized that there were limits to this kind of activity. When schizoanalysis is effective in realizing deterritorialization, individuals experience a "break-through." However, when subjects encounter accidents and relapses that hinder breakthrough, they experience "breakdown" (Deleuze and Guattari 1983, 278). The latter condition is not in a position to reclaim desire for the body-without-organs. Thus, schizoanalysis is a strategy by which we de-oedi-palize; that is, we release ourselves from the imposition of a capitalist oriented form of internal economy of desire, and return to the molecular level of con-tinuous variation and multiplicities.

What Deleuze and Guattari intimated was the need for a certain, methodical, and vigilant deterritorialization process. Radical transformations of culture and self may lead to breakdown. Consequently, as a matter of political praxis, Deleuze and Guattari championed social movements that combined micro and macro levels of analysis and action. For example, they believed that the core of fascism resided, not only in the manifestations of state inflicted oppression and violence, but also at the level of the unconscious. Thus, in order for any real political, economic, or cultural change to occur, subjects were encouraged to perpetually revisit their own oppressive and alien-ating tendencies, their molar organizations. According to Deleuze and

Guattari, social movement organizations need to remain reflexive, constantly challenging instances of marginalization and hierarchical developments within their ranks, a sign of molar forces in dominance.

Deleuze and Guattari (1986) applied their schizoanalytic method to the literary work of Kafka and developed the concept of "minor literatures." They demonstrated how disruptions and departures from conventional interpretations of the written (or spoken) word produced opportunities for deterritorialization; that is, alterative and new forms of reading texts. Again, consistent with their critique of capitalism, minor literatures create an effusive and mobile space for alterity, multiplicity, and fluidity.

Deleuze and Guattari (1987) also argued for a rhizomatic politics of desire. Rhizomatics represent the dislodging of "root" or essentialist philosophical and political systems. Rather than moving on striated space, with carefully defined rules for engagement, Deleuze and Guattari envisioned a politics where space was smooth (i.e, plateaus) and movement was fractured and unpredictable. One of the most relevant aspects of their work on the rhizome was their contention that it simultaneously encourages segmentation *and* lines of escape. What this suggests, consistent with the science of chaos theory, is the presence of orderly and disorderly movement accounting for the behavior of complex systems.

A politics inspired by rhizomes anticipates the perpetual, though not necessarily overt, nature of "nomadic" struggle. Rhizomatic movements are like "weeds," impossible to completely eliminate. Deleuze and Guattari (1987, 15) suggested that, "to be rhizomorphous is to produce stems and filaments that seem to be roots. . . . We're tired of trees. We should stop believing in trees, roots, and radicals. They've made us suffer too much." Deleuze and Guattari maintained that American culture benefited most from subterranean, rhizomatic, and nomadic activities that stimulated the realization of desire. In contemporary culture, we note that alternative and underground music, art, film, poetry, other literary genres, stand as ongoing examples of these theoretical observations.

The final book by Deleuze and Guattari, *What is Philosophy?* (1994, orig. 1991), extends their revolutionary work to scholarly genres, in particular, the difference among philosophy, science, and the arts. Philosophy, they tell us, is not purely logic, but is connected with the pursuit of becoming-imperceptible. They see science, art, and philosophy as the three "chaoids"—forms of thought—about chaos. Chaos is defined "not so much as disorder as [it is] by the infinite speed with which every form taking shape in it vanishes" (1994, 118). As Deleuze and Guattari (1987) explain, it is not a void but a "virtual," "containing all possible particles and drawing out all possible forms, which spring up only to disappear immediately, without consistency or reference, without consequence" (1987). "Science," they tell us, is much like a "freeze-frame" which imposes structure on this virtual. Philosophy attempts to provide some consistency to this space, but ever recognizing the inability to frame it in any long-term symbolic representations. And, the artist attempts to produce affects reflecting this virtual. All three are engaged in creating new conceptions and perceptions about the virtual.

For the philosopher, thinking involves confronting the world and her/himself and de-stratifying and reconstructing the world and oneself. It is thought rooted in the molecular, not molar. It is similar to their notion of schizoanalysis, in that the person returns to the premolar flows, intensities, singularities, speeds, and becomings. Through this practice, new molecular possibilities are released. The immanent principle is consistency. Concepts are related to various intensities existing in the virtual. They are inseparably related to other concepts, are not based on individual attributions, find themselves in various overlapping zones of intensities, and are constituted by rules of consistency related to ever becoming. A philosopher's task is to create concepts: "they must be invented, fabricated, or rather created and would be nothing without their creator's signature" (Deleuze and Guattari 1994, 5). Concepts are always in the state of becoming. Borrowing from chaos theory, they are "always fractal" (1994, 36–40), not whole dimensional as in modernist thought rooted in Cartesian geometry.

Thus, for Deleuze and Guattari, the critical philosopher is constantly engaged in deconstruction and reconstruction of concepts, which are themselves in constant movement. One can provide only temporary discursive representations of these concepts. To do more is to place them within the constraints of molar processes.

The insights of Deleuze and Guattari have recently been applied to selected areas in law, crime, and social justice. The field of law includes: Ronnie Lippens (nomadic subjective states and radical democracy, 1998a; legal thought and hybrid hopes for rhizologists, 1998b; postcolonial and feminist legal theory, 1999). In criminology we note: Lippens (critical criminology and utopia, 1995; rhizomatics and the establishment of a border-crossing criminology, 1998c; see also Giroux, 1992). In social justice we find: R. Young (hybridity in theory, race and culture, 1995); Christopher Williams (the Self and Other in mental illness, 1998); Milovanovic (understanding edgework experiences and their seductions, 2002: chapter 10).

Michel Foucault

It is difficult to locate with precision the place of Michel Foucault (1926–1984) in the pantheon of postmodernism.[9] Without question, Foucault's insights have substantially informed notable debates in the disciplines of history, sociology, political theory, feminism, linguistics, cultural studies, and psychoanalysis (e.g., Couzens 1992). Among Foucault's most significant contributions was his relentless effort to understand and document the historically variable but, nonetheless, normalizing techniques of power, social control, and domination, characteristic of European and North American culture.

The breadth of Foucault's intellectual life was distinguished by three relevant periods pertinent to this theme: (1) the archeological, (2) the genealogical, and, as an aspect of his genealogical analyses, (3) techniques for constituting the self (Dreyfus and Rabinow 1982; Best and Kellner 1991, 1997).

Foucault (1973) claimed that contemporary and inventive mechanisms of disciplinary control originated in discourse. Discursive techniques of power activated by language, displaced the rational, reasonable, self-same subject of modernity. "Power [expressed through words] produces; it produces reality; it produces domains of objects and rituals of truth" (Foucault 1977, 194). Foucault's archeology of knowledge manifested itself in hermeneutic interpretations of individual experiences. Directing attention to micrological manifestations of power and social control meant confronting modernity's totalizing essentialisms. According to Foucault, no "grand theory" of human nature could explain "particularisms" that flourished at the level of the individual, the group, or the community. Consistent with his analysis of biopower is Foucault's articulation of *dispositif* (1980a, 134–145). *Dispositif* refers to normalizing projects characteristic of a concrete social apparatus. Specifically, a *dispositif* refers to a "thoroughly heterogeneous ensemble' of discursive and material elements—for example, discourses, institutions, architectural forms, regulatory decisions, laws, administrative measures, scientific statements, philosophical, moral and philanthropic propositions, and the system of relations established between these elements" (1980a, 194). Together with Foucault's concept, "normalization," *dispositif* can be applied to studies of positive power (Brigg 2002).

Foucault acknowledged the contributions of Marx and Freud; however, he found himself more closely aligned with German philosophers, such as Frederick Nietzsche and Martin Heidegger. In opposition to a belief in a certain, but repressed, human essence, Foucault articulated an antifoundational theory of agency constituted by and through discourse. As he explained: "man is cut off from the origin that would make him contemporaneous with his own existence: amid all the things that are born in time and no doubt die in time, he, cut off from all origin, is already there." (cited in Dreyfuss and Rabinow 1982, 38). Elsewhere, for Foucault (1972), this move toward anti-essentialism and away from grand theory was described as the play of unpredictability, fissures, ruptures, and multiplicity. In these observations, Foucault (1973) advocated an analysis of discontinuity that focused more on ambulant patterns of behavior. In other words, he maintained that the seeds for change were located in the current epoch as reconceptualizations of preexisting discursive stock.

Foucault initiated his genealogical attempt to provide specific institutional support for the historical transformation of modes of domination and control, conveyed through discourse, with the publication of *Discipline and Punish* (1977) and *The History of Sexuality* (1980b). Institutions like the prison, the school, the hospital, the workplace, and the military, were noteworthy for their complicity in encouraging the production of docile bodies through inventive mechanisms of control. Established through technologically evolving facets of everyday life, the functioning of these structures demonstrated how power productively inserted itself into discourse. Indeed, the "power/knowledge" techniques used to probe the inner secrets of subjects' lives proved an invaluable source of information for institutions seeking to enhance the predictability and regulation of behavior. Clearly, as Foucault described, advances in the social and natural sciences were critical to the task of acquiring these data. He argued that the metamorphosis of disciplinary techniques was driven by the desire for better punishment and/or disciplinary control.

In Foucault's (1986a, 1988) later works, he shifted his analysis toward the constitution of the self. Foucault sought an articulation of the person, particularly as a political entity, that celebrated the expression of desire. Moreover, since power was expressed through the effusive "carceral archipelago," Foucault called for the cultivation of multiple sites of political contestation. According to Foucault, given the diffusion of power, a single, monolithic political strategy was doomed to fail. Thus, as Foucault argued, "a plurality of autonomous struggles [was needed] waged throughout the microlevels of society: in the prisons, asylums, hospitals, and schools" (Best and Kellner 1991, 56).

In scholarly lectures, interviews, and published articles, Foucault spent the last five years of his life exploring three important concepts—problematization, curiosity, and pleasure. Foucault begins with an understanding of freedom as the ontological condition of ethics (as cited in Rabinow 1997, 284). Freedom provides the necessary environment conducive to the realization of these three concepts. Foucault's notion of problematization can be traced to his admiration for quality journalism. In fact, many of Foucault's most lucid conceptual innovations were either first delineated in journalistic format or were subsequently elaborated there. Foucault was impressed with the ability of journalists to provide thoughtful and insightful analyses of pressing events while remaining relatively objective in order to avoid imposing a vantage point. It was Foucault's belief that "in order to establish the right relationship to the present—to things, to others, to oneself—one must stay close to events, experience them, be willing to be effected and affected by them" (Rabinow 1997, 18). Foucault argued that true self-knowledge was acquired through both experience and engagement. Problematization, then, consists of the practice of coming to know who human beings are through experience and engagement with political, economic and cultural institutions, practices, and actors.

Often overlooked in Foucault's work is the emphasis he placed on curiosity. This is an important idea because Foucault is typically viewed by his critiques as an apolitical and disengaged intellectual. In a 1980 interview published in the French daily, *Le Monde*, Foucault appears anonymously as the "Masked Philosopher." When asked by *Le Monde* interviewer, Christian Delacampaigne, whether our historical epoch lacked the great minds needed to help explain and offer solutions to global problems, Foucault responded by suggesting there is a great curiosity among people to know about the machinations of the world around them. In opposition to science and the church—which have in their unique ways denigrated the act of curiosity—Foucault places this concept at the center of his effort to explain the "knowing self." Curiosity signifies care. Specifically,

> It evokes the care one takes of what exists and what might exist; a sharpened sense of reality, but one that is never immobilized before it; a readiness to find what surrounds us strange and odd; a certain determination to throw off familiar ways of thought and to look at the same things in a different way; a passion for seizing what is happening now and what is disappearing; a lack of respect for traditional hierarchies of what is important and fundamental. (Foucault 1980a, cited in Rabinow 1997, 325)

In this same interview, Foucault's emphasis on curiosity creates the foundation for promoting destabilizing knowledges produced through multiple media sites. As he states, "I dream of a new age of curiosity. We have the technical means; the desire is there; there [are] an infinity of things to know. So what is the problem? Channels of communication that are too narrow . . ." (1997, 326). Finally, and related to problematization and curiosity, Foucault articulates the primacy of pleasure as a route to self-knowledge. His articulation of pleasure appears in the concept *homosexual ascesis*. Ascesis refers to the practice of transforming the self through a state of perpetual reflexivity.

Foucault wrote with a specific attention to gays who, he believed, should strive to attain greater pleasure as a way to self-knowledge. According to Paul Rabinow (1997), Foucault appears to be distinguishing pleasure from desire where the former refers to the body and the latter to the person. This is an important distinction for Foucault who is attempting to articulate acknowledgement of a moment (pleasure) that will instigate greater introspection thus producing greater self-awareness. Foucault believed that pleasurable experiences provided actors with increasing opportunities to reflect, experiment, and reformulate (Rabinow 1997, 37).

The application of Foucault's work in law, criminology, and social justice has been considerable. Thus, the field of law includes: Carol Smart (feminism and the discursive power of legal thought, 1989); Douglas Litowitz (describing the inadequacy of the law to protect individual rights, 1997); M. Thornton (creating a feminist jurisprudence, 1986); and Alan Hunt and Gary Wickham (exploring the sociology of law as governance, 1995). In criminology we note: Vicki Bell (describing the desexualization of rape, 1991; and interrogating police practice, 1993); David Garland (examining subjugation and punishment in modern society, 1990); Winifred Woodhull (exploring power, sexuality, and rape, 1988); and Adrian Howe (detailing a feminist, non-androcentric assessment of penality, 1994). In social justice we find: Iris Young (interpreting the tension between individualism and community, 1990); T. Wandel (Foucault and critical theory, 2001); D. Dupont and F. Pearce (on Foucault's articulation of power, security, population, and governmentality, 2001); M. Brigg (on Third World colonization and Foucault's "*dispositif*", 2002); A. C. Besley (narrative therapy, 2002); Sara Cobb (explaining how the discourse of violence in mediation is domesticated, 1997); Stanley Cohen (commenting on the phenomenon of "net widening" producing a disciplinary society in which subjects regulate themselves, 1979); and George Pavlich (critiquing community mediation and self-identity, 1996).

Jean-François Lyotard

Jean-François Lyotard (1924–1998)[10] was engaged in a political practice that sought to uncouple modernist notions of the just and the true.[11] Like Jacques Derrida, Lyotard acknowledged the embeddedness of the postmodern in the modern.[12] Influenced by Kantian exposition of the sublime, and Nietzschian emphases on the "will to power," Lyotard viewed modernist versions of ethics and epistemology (based on reason) as foundations for justice and truth as a totalizing logic (Drolet 1994).

For Lyotard, modernity's tendency to marginalize through the presence of a meta-narrative, a comprehensive articulation of justice and truth, should be confronted with a postmodern emphasis on *pagan justice* (Drolet 1994;

McGraw 1992). Pagan justice privileges the *Différend*, or phrases in a dispute (Lyotard 1984). To promote justice, interlocutors must remain open to "continual renewal" (Britt 1998). Like Derrida, Lyotard viewed negotiating the poles between totalitarian meta-narratives and pluralistic heterogeneity to be the postmodern project leading to justice.[13]

Lyotard's primary emphasis was to avoid declarations of utopian ideals, or arguing from historically generated positions. Rather, a truly revolutionary politics would encourage destabilization of meta-narratives by emphasizing attention to "*signs*" of history. Following Immanuel Kant, signs signify phenomenal levels of experience not easily rendered through cognitive historical accounts. Specifically, Lyotard advocated a "politics of feeling" akin to an ethics of care. By placing "feelings" at the locus of his theory of postmodern politics, Lyotard sought to insert aesthetic immediacy, receptiveness of changing conditions, suspension of judgment, and, ultimately, an openness to the Other as those qualities most likely to promote justness. By privileging the heterogeneous and multiple universes of activities and beliefs (McGraw 1992), Lyotard articulated a vision of greater equity and participation in those decisions directly affecting conditions promoting justice. There is no "once and for all" in Lyotard's taxonomy; every circumstance must be responded to based on subjective feelings. Remaining open to multiple renderings of political, economic, and cultural events promotes "judicial plurality," thus leading to greater experimentation and creativity (1992, 267).

Lyotard (1984), then, is best known for his exposure of instability rather than consensus as underlying modernist thought. His "paralogy" considers quantum mechanics, chaos theory, catastrophe theory, Gödel's theorem, and the celebration of the small narrative (*petit récit*) over the grand narrative (*les grande récits*). His expressed emphasis and rallying cry was: "wage war on totality." Quantum mechanics questions linear, predictable, continuous pathways. Contrary to Einstein, it informs us that "God does play dice" (Stewart, 1989). Chaos theory offers the idea of fractal geometry, fractal spaces, attractors, bifurcations, and dissipative structures. Catastrophe theory provides the notion that discontinuities can exist in otherwise deterministic and continuous systems. Gödel's theorem represents the idea of "undecidability:" all cannot be subsumed under any generalized system of rules; exceptions shall *always* exist. *Petit* narratives cannot be subsumed under some consensus, nor is it desirable to do so. Thus, in Jürgen Habermas's (1984, 1987) communication theory, the goal of dialogue (i.e., consensus for Lyotard) is not a desirable end for developing notions of justice. The linkage between consensus and justice is broken. Language games necessitate sensitivity to various truths. Consensus is only a momentary state in dialogue and cannot be an end in itself. It is paralogy that underlies the search for genuine dialogue.

Much of Lyotard's work has had an indirect influence in law, crime, and social justice; however, postmodern theory has benefited considerably from his ideas of paralogy. Thus, in law and chaos we note: Dennis Brion (legal reasoning, 1991); Taylor (critical hermeneutics in legal analysis, 2000); T. Britt (narrative and law, 1998); William Conklin (legal discourse and how suffering is concealed through its specialized vocabulary and grammar, 1998); Caren Schulman (critical legal studies, 1997); and Bruce Arrigo and Christopher Williams (civilly confining the mentally ill, 1999c). In criminology and chaos we find: T. R. Young (describing various attractor basins that arise from the political economy, 1997); Allison Forker (revising Quinney [1977] indicating the usefulness of nonlinear dynamics, 1997); George Pavlich (using Lyotard's idea of paralogy to sensitize critical criminology's need for expanding boundaries, 1999); and Stuart Henry and Dragan Milovanovic (developing constitutive criminology, 1996). In justice studies and chaos theory we note: T. R. Young (outlining how justice may arise from nonlinear dynamics, 1992, 1999); R. Schehr (devising an alternative model of social movement theory, 1997); Robert Schehr and Dragan Milovanovic (critiquing mediation programs, 1999); McGraw (feminism and justice, 1992); M. Drolet (postmodern politics, 1994); and Christopher Williams and Bruce Arrigo (integrating anarchist thought and chaology as an alternative approach to social problems research, 2001). Relatedly, in the domain of catastrophe theory, Lyotard's postmodern epistemology, although minimally employed in the crime, law, and justice literature, has been useful. Thus, for example, in peace studies and catastrophe we note Milovanovic (developing a "third way" in deescalating conflict situations, 1999, 2002).

CHAPTER 2

Sustaining the First Wave:
More on the Liniguistic Turn in Social Theory

INTRODUCTION

In this chapter, we extend our analysis of postmodern social theory, high-lighting the contributions of those first-wave thinkers who have sustained this intellectual and practical movement's agenda, endorsing wholesale political and social change. The authors reviewed in this chapter include Jean Baudrillard, Hèléne Cixous, Jacques Derrida, Luce Irigaray, and Julia Kristeva. What distinguishes these thinkers from those canvassed in the previous chapter is that they continue to wrestle with and write about sundry themes germane to social theory and the postmodern enterprise.

Similar to the exposition found in chapter 1, we summarily present the key insights of each luminary. In addition, we identify the work of several second-wave scholars who have appropriated their insights and have applied them in the areas of law, crime, and justice studies. This commentary is useful as it demonstrates the vitality and utility of postmodern social theory, especially when investigating complex and enduring problems in contemporary society.

FIRST WAVE CONTRIBUTIONS: SUSTAINING
THE POSTMODERN AGENDA

Jean Baudrillard

Jean Baudrillard (1929–) is recognized as a postmodern luminary par excellence.[1] The early work of Baudrillard (1968) examined mass consumption in advanced monopoly capitalism where objects or commodities "devoured" the consumer's "perception, thought, and behavior" (Best and Kellner 1991, 113). This theme is renewed in Baudrillard's (1970) next work where he more closely studied the manner in which conspicuous goods, as sign objects, formed the basis of our everyday reality, organizing and constituting our existences into a mass-mediated consumer culture. In his subsequent work, Baudrillard (1981) attempted to integrate the political economy of Marxism with structuralism and semiotic theory, mindful of his previously articulated insights. As a trilogy, these tracts represent an outline for a developing neo-Marxian social theory in which semiotics and sign systems theory assume an important role in explaining the process of symbolic exchange in a consumer-oriented society (e.g., Poster 1988; Best 1989; Kellner 1989).

It is not until Baudrillard's later works, however, that a social theory is posited considerably removed from the political economy of Marx. In these and other texts, Baudrillard claims that we live in a computerized and digitized world in which mass-mediated information and cybernetic control systems simulate reality and displace production as the organizing principle of society (Best and Kellner 1991, 118). Simulation entails the use of models, signs, and codes in which a "semiurgic society" dominates social life (Baudrillard 1981, 185). The semiurgic society Baudrillard has in mind symbolically produces mass-mediated and conspicuously consumed images (e.g., the image of soap opera doctors receiving fan mail requesting medical consultation, the image of television lawyers inundated with petitions for legal advice). These simulations, as counterfeits of the real, as images of the factual, are more authentic than the "real" physicians and lawyers for whom such services might otherwise be solicited. Indeed, for Baudrillard (1983a, 23), these simulations are "hallucinatory resemblances," that are more real-than-the-real. This is what Baudrillard means by the *implosion of reality*. These are moments in which the boundary separating form and substance, fact and fiction, reality and appearance, collapse and collide producing an implosion, "and with it the very experience and ground of 'the real' disappears" (Best and Kellner 1991, 119).

The disappearance of the real, as a process of social entropy (Gane 1991), makes possible the proliferation of increased symbolic exchanges and the circulation of multiple simulations, where codes of technology, sophisticated advertising, and computerized information produce a virtual authenticity, a hyper-reality, a world that is based on models of the real (e.g., the O. J. Simpson double-murder trial as simulated on *Entertainment Television*). According to Baudrillard, though, these representational, hyper-real forms become a determinant of the real; that is, the replica informs the authentic and the reality-appearance divide vanishes (Poster 1988). In obliterating this boundary, however, not only does Baudrillard (1983a) remind us how the foundation of the real is undone (i.e., image and simulation displace it), he cautions that the foundation of the counterfeit is itself equally unstable. In other words, the counterfeit, although seemingly more real-than-the-real, is nothing more than illusion. Thus, it cannot signify factual existence. In short, simulation, implosion of reality, and hyper-reality leave nothing behind but a vacuous cybernetic state in which simulacra (i.e., words, extra-verbal cues, gestures) abound. These simulacra are floating, pseudo-sign images, without definite referents and are unable to be tangibly anchored, signifying (hyper)reality, disseminating simulated media messages, and conveying the illusory other worldliness of our postmodern condition (Kellner 1989).

Applications of Baudrillard's work in the areas of law, crime, and social justice have been limited. In part, second-wave scholars recognize that Baudrillard's critique arrestingly demonstrates that "we have no way to experience or conceptualize relationships between people except as these are defined by the exchange of [consumer sign image] commodities" (Willis 1991, 162). The effect is a nihilistic, fatalistic, antifoundational critique, lacking an identifiable substitute for progressive social change (Palmer 1990, 199). This notwithstanding, several important efforts are discernible. In law we note Arrigo (exploring the double-murder trial of O. J. Simpson, 1996d). In criminology we find: Stephen Pfohl (investigating social problems in an ultramodern environment, 1993); and Jeff Ferrell, Dragan Milovanovic, and Steven Lyng (indicating the ways ephemeral and ineffable emotional states are given meaning in situated contexts of media practices, 2001). In social justice, we recognize: Gregg Barak and Stuart Henry (describing mass-mediated imagery and its relationship to developing an integrated, critical criminological understanding of social justice, 1999); Mark Gottdiener (suggesting a strategy that reverses the one Baudrillard describes by reclaiming or restoring lost, repressed, and stripped signifieds in a cultural criticism that returns to "roots," 1995)[2]; and Stuart Henry and Dragan Milovanovic (integrating the mass consumption of societal images, their symbolic meanings, and prospects for a radical pluralism, 1996).

Hélène Cixous

Perhaps Hélène Cixous's (1937–)[3] *oeuvre* can be prefaced with her words: "Write yourself. Your body must be heard" (Cixous 1976, 875). For all her writing,[4] perhaps the one concept that remains most prominent is her notion of *écriture féminine* (woman's writing). She works through the seminars of Lacan in arguing that the phallocentric Symbolic Order and the law-of-the-father create a deprivileged space for woman. Woman is *pas-toute*, not-all, in this Order. But following Lacan, they do have access to a different form of *jouissance*, the *jouissance* of the body.

Cixous shows how, precisely because women are less fixed in the Symbolic Order, they have a greater capacity to be otherwise. Men, on the other hand, according to Mary Klages's, (1997, 4) reading of Cixous, "haven't yet discovered the relation between their sexuality and their writing, as long as they are focused on writing with the penis . . . men will be prisoners of a Symbolic order which alienates them from their bodies."

Both men and women are constrained by the phallocentric Symbolic Order in repressive binary structures. Cixous has extended this notion to understanding racial issues, such as in apartheid. Following Lacan, the subject, in order to speak, must assume a traditional position of an "I" which can be inserted in discourse. But women, in situating themselves in a male-defined discursive subject-position, deny themselves even as they speak of themselves. It is in poetry that *l'écriture féminine* finds best expression: here, language is set loose—the chains of signifiers flow more freely, meaning is less fixed; poetry . . . is thus closer to the unconscious, and thus to what has been repressed" (Klages 1997, 4). Consequently, women must insist on writing themselves, writing their own bodies, about their form of *jouissance*; it is only through this activity that a new language—new signifying practices—will emerge and take on relatively stable form as *l'écriture féminine*. This language will be more dynamic, less static, more fluid, less linear, more playful, where the subject is more active than passive (1997). Inherently, it will be a deconstructive discourse, not to be objectified, always in process. Cixous (as cited in Sellers 2000, xvii) dismisses the "I" form of modernist discourse: ". . . I never ask myself 'who am I?' (*qui suis-je?*) I ask myself 'who are I?" (*qui son-je*)—an untranslatable phrase. Who can say who I are, how many I are, which I is the most I of my I's? . . . We: are (untranslatable)."

Cixous acknowledges in particular the Brazilian author, Clarice Lispector, in influencing her as to the relationship between writing and life. In Cixous's view, hers is the closest example of a feminine writing. Verena Conley's (1994, vii) introduction to the text, *Reading with Clarice Lispector*, argues that the latter's prose "suggests a writing, based on an encounter with another—be it a body, [a portion of text], a social dilemma, a moment of passion—that leads to an undoing of the hierarchies and oppositions that determine the limits of most conscious life." It is *l'écriture féminine*, she adds, that is both disruptive and reconstructive. Cixous also has had a strong ongoing relationship with Jacques Derrida, notably expressed in her *La Venue a l'écriture*. He wrote the foreword to her work, *The Helen Cixous Reader* (2000). In this book, Cixous argues against the boundaries placed between fiction and theory, and argues that *l'écriture féminine* is not necessarily confined to women, but can be employed by male writers. She uses the example of James Joyce and Jean Genet.

Repressive binary structures are traced by Cixous to the oedipalization of the drives. It is the inauguration to the Symbolic that imprisons subjects in discursive positions. Thus, it is to the pre-oedipal, prior to this binary system, that we must look for liberating potentials. Women, then, contrary to Lacan's position of being lacking, should be seen as "women as excess." They have an access to the *jouissance* of the body. But we are all inherently bisexual; we potentially may identify with male and female characters (Cixous 2000, xxix; see also Sellers 1994, 83, 142). But again, it is women who are more uniquely situated in the pre-oedipal, to a feminine economy, to a bodily *jouissance* and, hence, they have the greater potential for reconstruction in discourse.

The feminine discursive subject-position resists destroying the other's differences in its self-constitution of subjectivity. In the feminine register "one is no longer in the economy of opposition, one is in the economy of the gift. And of love. Of how to give" (Cixous 2000, 40–45; see also Cixous cited in Seller's introduction, 2000, xxx). Thus, we find in her text, *The Newly Born Woman* (1986), Cixous arguing that in contemporary society the masculine position is supported by relations to property; the gift only reinforces his position of power; it always has strings attached. For women, the gift is not meant to be "recovered"; it is freely given (1986, 65). She does not try to "recover her expenses" (Cixous 2000, 44). In Susan Seller's (1994, 17) reading, Cixous "sees the new 'feminine economy' as engendering a love relation in which 'each one would keep the other alive and different': 'each would take the risk of other, of difference, without feeling threatened by the existence of an otherness, rather, delighting to increase through the unknown that is there to discover.'"

Cixous has more often been an indirect influence in criminology, law, and social justice. The understanding of her notion of *l'écriture féminine* is widespread in critical analyses and has reached the level of a take for granted concept, although debated sharply and cogently within feminist circles. In postmodern analysis of law, Drucilla Cornell (1998b, 1993, 1999) is arguably the leading figure (see also Spivak 1987, 1992; Frug 1992; Delphy 1995). In law and justice, see Tracey Higgins (1995) and Katherine Sheehan (2000). For a critique of postmodern feminists, see Catherine MacKinnon (2000).

Jacques Derrida

Jacques Derrida (1930–) is often regarded as the leading exponent of French deconstructionist philosophy and social theory.[5] He is not and never has been a postmodernist (Critchley 2000). Self proclamation, however, is belied by the free play of the text which has propelled his writings onto center stage in post-modern thought. According to M. Calarco (2000), Derrida positions himself at the fulcrum of modernist and postmodernist conceptualizations of identity, ethics, and politics. In both "The Ends of Man" (1968) and *The Other Heading* (1991), Derrida stresses commitment to *responsibility* as a way to cultivate radical democracy. In "Force of Law" (1992), *Spectres of Marx* (1994), and *Politics of Friendship* (1994), Derrida assumes a Habermasian articulation of the incompleteness of the Enlightenment. This is especially true as it relates to the European search for identity. Rather than posit, as postmodernists do, a rejection of a totalizing European identity to celebrate difference, or rather than asserting the more essentialist and modernist vision; namely, an irrefutable European identity, Derrida locates radical democracy in the center of this debate. For him, radical democracy can be realized through the for-mulation of a series of techniques that promote, temporally and spatially, bounded political decisions.[6] Thus, this notion is akin to the concept "nodal points" as found in Jaques Lacan (1977, 1991) or "liquid identity" as found in Z. Bauman (2000). Again, consistent with Habermas, Derrida emphasizes the creation of "gestures, discourses, and politico-institutional practices" (Calarco 2000, 54) to promote a temporally and spatially bounded unity of opposites.[7] Derrida's vision of radical politics, then, seeks to avoid total denunciation of history and tradition, while also avoiding a totalizing Eurocentrism.

Among his many contributions to deconstruction, ten themes appear most relevant: (1) the Principle of Differentiation, (2) the Principle of Iterability, (3) the Principle of Rhetoricity, (4) the Concept of the "Trace", (5) the Principle of Unbounded Textuality, (6) the Critique of Closure, (7) the Critique of "Presence", (8) the Critique of Dualism, (9) the Critique of

Narrative, and (10) the Critique of Figuration (Binder and Weisberg 2000, 381–383). While it is true that many of these themes signify a reworking of antiessentialist pragmatism (Patterson 2001), Derrida's interpretation is noteworthy. Below we consider just a few of the themes developed by Derrida that appear to have had the greatest influence on scholars applying his work to the study of crime, law, and social justice.

A key proposition within Derrida's epistemology is the "metaphysics of presence" (Derrida 1977). The metaphysics of presence exposes the hierarchical positions (e.g., "straight" over "gay," "white" over "black," "objective" over "subjective," "reality" over "appearance," "man" over "woman") embedded in the words or phrases we use to communicate (shared) meaning. In each cited instance, the first term is privileged and rendered as presence. Conversely, the latter term is de-valued and rendered as absence or lack. According to Derrida (1977), the concept that explains this notion of "privileging" the first term in the binary opposition is "logocentrism."[8] Logocentrism indicates that the implied centrality of the first or dominant term masks and conceals the interdependence of both values. In Western thought, there is "a hidden premise that what is most apparent to our consciousness (i.e., what is most simple, basic or immediate), is most real, true, foundational, or important (Balkin 1987, 748). Thus, Derrida's deconstruction entails a reflexive explication of those encoded hierarchical terms that conceal entrenched "value positions that need to be brought to light" (Agger 1991, 121). This process reveals the "logic of supplementality." Marginalized political, economic, and cultural ideas and activities, though absent from manifest discourse, appear as *supplements to* manifest discourse by virtue of their juxtaposition to them. It is by establishing the binary hierarchy characteristic of logocentrism that Derrida proclaims the impossibility of essential identity.

The metaphysics of presence and the critique of logocentrism are further delineated by Derrida's use of three interrelated principles. These precepts include: (1) the reversal of hierarchies, (2) the concepts *différance* and trace, and (3) arguments that undo themselves. Inverting privileged values allow us to consider what new or different insights might be contained within the words in binary opposition. In addition, the reversal demonstrates how the terms are mutually interdependent, displacing the notion that the first (or second) value is foundational.

The concept of *différance* (with an "a") conveys three interrelated meanings for Derrida. As Balkin (1987, 752) describes it:

> *Différance* simultaneously indicates that (1) the terms of an oppositional hierarchy are differentiated from each other (which is what determines them); (2) each term in the hierarchy defers to the other (in the sense of

making the other term wait for the first term); and (3) each term in the hierarchy defers to the other (in the sense of being fundamentally dependent upon the other).

Différance, however, is significant to Derrida's deconstructionist agenda for a related reason. The idea of trace implies that the two values in binary opposition rely for their clarity and cohesion on the differentiation between them. In other words, each term contains the vestige of the other within it, and it is this lingering trace that anchors difference making the deconstruction of hierarchical oppositions possible.

The related concepts of *différance* and trace give rise to Derrida's logic of justification that is ungrounded through deconstruction (see e.g., Derrida 1977, 34–43 critiquing the privileging of speech over writing). In short, arguments supporting the privileging of the dominant term may be the reasons for endorsing the other value. The task of deconstructionist analysis, then, is to identify the play of differences and the mutual interdependencies between terms in a hierarchical opposition, as a way of demonstrating the positional, relational, and provisional nature of all phenomena. In this context, meaning is "inexhaustible" (Sarup 1989, 36), and what is spoken or written is liberated from the author. We note, too, that the concepts of *différance* and trace are not essentialist terms in Derrida's epistemology. This thinking is antithetical to the deconstructionist project. Indeed, as Richard Rorty (1978, 153) contends, such notions cannot be "divinized." *Différance* and trace fleetingly capture the "foundationless, provisional . . . , or reversibl(e)" nature of meaning in human affairs (Balkin 1987, 752).

Application of Derrida's epistemology to law, criminology, and social justice have been considerable. In law, much of the Critical Legal Studies movement was inspired by his philosophical and political insights (e.g., Kairys 1982; Tushnet 1986; Russell 1986; Unger 1986; Kelman 1987; see also the special issue of the *Stanford Law Review*, 1984). More recent connections between Derrida's thought and law include: Drucilla Cornell, M. Rosenfeld, and D. Calrson (legal decision making and feminist jurisprudence, 1992); John Caputo (legal reasoning and the [im]possibility of justice, 1997; see also the Special Issue of the *Cardozo Law Review*, 1991); Drucilla Cornell (feminist legal theory, the possibility of justice, and the feminine over the masculine voice, 1992); D. Manderson (transgendered jurisprudence, 2002); J. Cummins (fragmented self and legal culpability relating to Disparate Impact Doctrines, 1998); G. Binder and R. Weisberg (law as literary interpretation, 2000); G. Shreve (on fact, value and action through deconstruction, 2002); and Stephen Fuchs and Steven Ward (an analysis of building cases in law,

1994). In criminology we note: Martin Schwartz and David Freidrichs (understanding metaphors of violence, 1994); K. L. Scheppele (definitions of rape, 1987); Bruce Arrigo and Christopher Williams (execution of psychiatrically disordered prisoners, 1999a); and Bruce Arrigo (investigating the criminal law doctrine of competency to stand trial, 2003b). In social justice we find: Roshan D. Wijeyeratne (exploring linkages between semiotics and justice, 1998); John Caputo (questioning the relationship between justice, law, and equality, 1997); R. Schehr (analysis of employee drug testing, medicalization, and social control, 1995), and Bruce Arrigo (investigating the metaphors of war and peace in medical justice, 1999b).

Luce Irigaray

Iris Irigaray (1930–),[9] philosopher, psychoanalyst, and linguist, has reflected on her work and sees three distinct stages: first where she argued that the world had been constructed by the masculine subject; second, how alternative spaces could be developed for feminine subjectivity; and third, a new model of how men and women could relate to each other without either one being in the position of subordination to the other (Hirsch and Olson 1995). She also has had an ongoing debate with Lacan and Lacanian thought. She both draws from it and refutes it.

Her agreements with Lacan include the following: (1) the primacy of language; (2) the linkage of the psychical structure and linguistic processes in the construction of the subject; (3) the sexualized positions assumed in the symbolic by the subject; and (4) a common lineage to Freud's analysis of the pre-oedipal and oedipal, the unconscious and its logic and economy, but qualified with extensive criticism. She distances herself from Lacanian thought, however, in several important respects. These include the following: (1) in the importance of the mother-daughter relation and its ability to undermine patriarchal ideology; (2) in the pre-oedipal source for subversion; and (3) in the libidinal drives and sources of pleasure which can resist the dictates of the dominant patriarchal Symbolic Order and offer an alternative form; namely, the *jouissance* of the body. In short, Irigaray's project is in constructing an alternative theory of linguistic production that makes visible women as speaking subjects (Grosz 1990, 149).

For Irigaray, the crystallization of the significance of the phallus develops after the umbilical cord; thus, the womb is the first instance for the plenitude and the development of the child. It is a space within which all needs are met. Consequently, it provides the primordial paradigm preceding any discussion of the Oedipus complex. According to Irigaray (1993c, 14), "all takes place within an originary womb, the first nourishing earth, first waters, first sheaths, first membranes in which the *whole* child [is] held, as well as the *whole* mother, through the mediation of her blood." And, "mother and child are linked in a way that precedes all dissociations, all tearing of their bodies into pieces" (1993c). The break, the "cut," from this sheltered, nourishing space and its effects has not been fully investigated in terms of its contribution to subsequent symbolization. Freudian theory, therefore, in its neglect of the mother is based on matricide. According to Tamsin Lorraine's (1999, 222) reading of Irigaray, "the phallus is a displaced symbol of desire veiling the lost umbilical cord, the lost place of wholeness of intrauterine experience in which the whole child was sheltered in the womb of the mother." And, "the intrauterine space is an anoedipal space, a space of plenitude rather than lack, singularity rather than universality . . ." Thus, the first "cut," the birth of the child, symbolizes the first separation from what Deleuze and Guattari (1987) have referred to as "molecular processes" (see Lorraine 1999, 226).

Irigaray shows how discourse itself privileges one sex over another. In this context, she is not suggesting any form or essentialism. However, Irigaray does argue for an understanding of power rooted in patriarchal discursive practices and for how women may resist these everyday occurrences. Her work is directed toward developing better representations of women. As Elizabeth Grosz explains (1990, 169): "Irigaray is interested in developing accounts of subjectivity and knowledge that acknowledge the existence of two sexes, two bodies, two forms of desire and two ways of knowing." Thus, as Irigaray argues, psychoanalysis can only provide a depiction of the imaginary and symbolic from boy's/man's position; it is hard pressed to explain both from a girl's/woman's position (1990, 170). Moreover, since psychoanalysis and capitalism are so intimately synchronized, Freudian models also are based on possession rather than enjoyment or pleasure (Sellers 1994, 54).

Irigaray also argues for the existence of an excess of psychical energy that has up until now been mined by one sex. It is the phallocentric psychical economy that allows for the hierarchical development of the sexes. She advocates the importance of the speculum, a mirror, which provides an alternative basis of reflexivity and centeredness in the construction of the ego. This mirror would not represent the man as the other, but a woman as the other. It is only in this way that an alternative subject may emerge. She does not necessarily advocate the development of a new woman's language; rather, she implores the use of existing texts, meanings, and symbolizations, thereby forcing the overflow of the already existing tensions within.

Irigaray argues that women are other for the male in the Symbolic and Imaginary Order. She is only defined secondarily in relation to the primacy of the male. The fixation of the libidinal economy, its territorializations, is such as to privilege male discourse and embodiments of desire, while de-privileging female voices. Irigaray contends that language maintains the patriarchal system. Following Lacan, woman is *pas-toute*, not-all, lack. Whereas the stabilized male discourse privileges possession, "singular meanings, hierarchical organization, polar oppositions, the division into subject-predicate form" (Grosz 1990, 17), and subject-object relations in hierarchical and dualistic forms, the unarticulated forms of the female privilege enjoyment, unadulterated pleasure, fluidity, and relations that are without bounds or hierarchies. Women's identities remain outside of contemporary male-ordered representative schemas. Moreover, since they do, these feminine identities pose an ongoing potential for undermining the phallocentrically organized society.

Irigaray suggests the strategy of "mimesis" which involves production rather than passive imitation of imaginary and symbolic forms. Mimesis is a rhetorical tactic of converting subordination into affirmation. "To play with mimesis is thus, for a woman, to try to recover the place of her exploitation by discourse, without allowing herself to be simply reduced to it" (1985b, 76). Specifically, Irigaray suggests that mysticism has come closest to offering an alternative articulatory practice. According to Susan Seller's (1994, 137) reading of Irigaray, "mysticism offers a means of escape from the 'disciplines' of knowledge, philosophy and science, since [their] tenets involve a 'flowing out' in which subject and other 'mingle,' and in which 'consciousness is no longer master'." The basis of this orientation is a "surrendering of self," a "self-loss" whose language has yet to be developed. This orientation defies full capture in dominant discourse. It entails an overflowing of boundaries, an excess, a "feminine poetics," open-ended possibilities, exploiting blanks and ambiguities in phallocentric discourse. In short, Irigaray argues for new spaces, an alterity, outside the male economy of representation, within which feminine desire may be articulated, producing new articulations without subjection of one sex by another. "It will be an economy based on pleasure, on reciprocal living, on the sharing and overflowing of the boundaries between yours and mine" (Sellers 1994, 138). And "it will be an economy in which power is abolished, a constant (r)evolution in which nothing is ever repeated or the same" (1994). The new poetics will be based on an alternative (to male) "economy of representation." The emerging discourse will be more intuitive and relational, connected with myth, magic, nature, feelings, enjoyment, fluidity, and multiplicity.

Irigaray's influence has been substantial in law, less developed in criminology, and substantial in theorizing social change. Second wave theorists in law include: Drucilla Cornell (developing an "ethical feminism," 1991; critiquing sex-discrimination law, formal equality, and laws of equivalence,

1992, 1993; rethinking family law, 1998a); Judith Butler (focusing on exclusionary and binary practices in the phallocentric order, 1993; suggesting strategies of subverting repetition as the basis for the development of new subjectivities, 1990); Gayatric Chakavorty Spivak (developing a place from which to speak, 1991); and Judith Grbich (describing the female body in taxation laws, 1996). In criminology we note: Ngaíré Naffine (developing a feminist histiography of criminology, 1996); and Spivak (developing strategies by which the "subaltern" can speak, 1991). In social change we find exemplary: Cornell (turning subordination into affirmation through mimetic practices, 1999; transcending "sameness ideology," 1993; cultivating the sanctity of the imaginary domain, 1998b); Naffine (delineating imaginative parody and mimicry, 1996); Lorraine (who traces the possible development of a new "corporeal cartography" where ever-becoming based on the "intrauterine metaphor and an "anoedipal space" are more apparent, not the Oedipus complex which privileges the male, 1999); and Grosz (who begins with not lack, absence, rupture, but plenitude, becoming, fullness, 1994).

Julia Kristeva

Julia Kristeva (1941–) arrived in Paris for her formal studies in 1966,[10] and attended Jacques Lacan's seminars on a regular basis. She has written several Lacanian inspired, though revisionist, works focused on linguistics and psychoanalysis. Some (Oliver 1993, 1998) have argued that her work could be seen as focused on three areas: (1) bringing back the body in scholarly investigations in the social sciences; (2) highlighting the importance of the pre-oedipal and the importance of the maternal in the development of the subject; and (3) explicating the notion of "abjection" in its contribution to various forms of domination. We would include a fourth area: "semanalysis"—the study of the production of meaning and its disruptions, subversions, and dislocations of subjectivity in discourse.

The first area focuses on the mind-body reconnectedness. Much of modernist analysis privileges the mind over the body. This dualism represents a hierarchy with the dominance of one term. Kristeva (1984) shows how the maternal body operates with tones, rhythms, movement—all found in the pre-oedipal stage of development as part of the "semiotic." These bodily drives, in turn, are provided signification in the "symbolic" (dominant discourse with its grammar, semantics, and semiotic codes). As Kelly Oliver (1998, 2) summarizes, "words give life meaning (nonreferential meaning) because of their semiotic content. Without the symbolic, all signification would be babble or delirium. But, without the semiotic, all signification would be empty and have no importance for our lives." Thus, Kristeva shows how the body and mind are intimately connected, even at the level of bodily functions. Freudian analysis, she argues, especially with the positing of the Oedipus complex which privileges the male, represses this alternative loci of signification (Kristeva 1982, 1995) and, in the process, also privileges the (masculine) mind over the (feminine) body.

Her work indicates how women are denied expression (following Lacan, *pas-toute*, not-all) in the dominant patriarchal order (the law of the father), yet have access to a primordial place, the semiotic chora, which threatens disruptions in the conventional Symbolic Order (Kristeva 1980, 1984). Kristeva revised Lacan's analysis of the Imaginary and Symbolic Order. She argues that prior to the Oedipal phase of Freud and the development of the Imaginary and Symbolic Orders of Lacan, the child already has her/his drives organized in the semiotic sphere where the primary process (i.e., unconscious thoughts, feelings, impulses) are ubiquitous. This sphere is more rhythmic, disordered, energy in movement, and a maternally structured space. For Kristeva, the imaginary domain goes beyond Lacan's focus on the visual, to include touch, taste, smell, and vocalizations that are preconditions for the acquisition of language and for discursive production. As Kristeva explains, the semiotic undergoes an oedipalized, territorialized structuration (akin to the work of secondary process described by Freud) by the *symbolic* transmitted through the mother: it is the discursive sphere responsible for the coherent, ordered, unified speaking subject governed by the law-of-the-father.

The symbolic is always subject to the disruptions of the semiotic chora. These disruptions can be engendered by a "poetic language." The poetic transgresses the semiotic codes and allows the reemergence of the semiotic, the sphere of the maternal. Kristeva cites authors who take full advantage of this disruptive style (i.e., Mallarme, Joyce, Artaud) (cf. the section of this chapter on Barthes for a description of the "writerly text").

The second area of her work, and related to the first, deals with the pre-oedipal and the maternal in the development of the subject. She questions both Freudian and Lacanian analysis of castration and the fear generated that was said to underlie the "correct" identifications of the girl and boy. As Kristeva contends, prior to "paternal law," there was already a "law" operating, the maternal "law." As Oliver (1998, 1) summarizes, we do not have a viable "maternal discourse;" rather, the dominant discourse of maternity is found in religion (e.g., Catholicism, see Kristeva, 1977) and science. This is not necessarily to argue for an *"écriture féminine"* as a replacement to the phallic Symbolic Order, but only to underscore how discursive constructions are constrained within the framework of the paternal. What this more maternal discourse would include is the idea that the maternal function does not necessarily reside only with the woman. "Kristeva's analysis suggests that to some extent anyone can fulfill the maternal function, men or women" (Oliver 1998, 1).

In Kristeva's view, the maternal side always is present, even if in subdued form, always threatening to disrupt the conventional order founded on the Oedipus complex. Human beings, because they constantly are balancing the various forces of the body and mind, are always in process. Thus, for Kristeva (1984), the person is always a "subject-in-process."

The third area of Kristeva's (1982) work concerns her use of the notion of "abjection." *Webster's* dictionary meaning is: "a low or downcast state; meanness of spirit; degradation." And for "abject": "a person in the lowest and most despicable condition; a castaway . . . to cast off, or down; prostrate; reject; degrade."[11] According to Barbara Creed (1993, 1):

> The place of the abject is where meaning collapses, the place where I am not. The abject threatens life, it must be radically excluded from the place of the living subject, propelled away from the body and deposited on the other side of an imaginary border which separates the self from that which threatens the self.

Kristeva argues that we first experience abjection at birth, at the separation of the child from the mother. Thereafter we experience numerous possible abjections. Abjection stands for the idea that we strongly revolt against the very thing that provides us with our very existence.[12] It is a dialectic by which we both attempt to distance ourselves from but yet embrace the abject. We both fear it and identify with it; are attracted to it and repelled by it. Since it is first experienced in association with the maternal function, it is thereafter primarily a derivative of this sphere. According to Samantha Pentony (1996, 1), "it provokes us into recalling a state of being prior to signification (or the law-of-the-father) where we feel a sense of helplessness. The self is threatened by something that is not part of us in terms of identity and nonidentity, human and nonhuman." Confronting abjection produces crises: a profound disruption of identity and order (primordially felt at the separation during birth from the mother). Confrontation with the abject summons the Imaginary Order. Here the abject becomes a threat to our very existence. The abject is very much connected with Lacan's *objet petit a* and the idea of *jouis-sance*. As Kristeva (1982, 3) tells us, "one thus understands why so many victims of the abject are its fascinated victims—if not its submissive and willing ones."

In penology, a good example of the play of abjection is found in Martha Duncan's book *Romantic Outlaws, Beloved Prisons* (1996). Although not informed by Kristeva, Duncan points out how our conceptualization of the lawbreaker as "slime"[13] both distances us non-lawbreakers from the criminal, but yet, at a deeper level is repudiated with our attractions for those who go against the orderly world and law. Similarly, Duncan points out some prisoners' attraction to prison, seeing it as a womb, a haven where one is freed from responsibilities and requirements of the "free" world. The idea of abjection is brought out when we note the language of the feminine by the kept is often derogatory about feminine body parts, while at the same time, is the basis of attraction.

The fourth area in which Kristeva sheds some light is on an alternative methodology termed "semanalysis." This is the study of the production of meaning and its disruptions, subversions, and dislocations of subjectivity in discourse. She (1984) recognizes two kinds of writers: the "realist writer" and the "poetic writer." The former produces the "phenotext" which, based on the primacy of the symbolic, represses polyvocality and the heterogeneous (more akin to Barthe's "readerly text"); the latter, produces the "genotext" which comes under the influence of the disruptions of the semiotic (more akin to Barthe's "writerly text"). The latter is subversive, transgressive and eruptive—the breaking down of unities—identified with "madness, holiness and poetry" (Kristeva 1976). She offers examples of avant-garde texts; including, the writings of James Joyce, Stéphane Mallarme, Antonin Artaud, and Le Contedi Lautreamont. According to Sellers's (1994: 101) understanding, the poet "writes on the borderline between nature and culture: the motivating force of the instinctual drives and their (necessary) social-symbolic repression . . . the poet is brought to confront these tensions, transgressing and reformulating these boundaries in their work."

Kristeva argues that motherhood offers love based on the development of growth and of the greatest realization of potential. It is traced to the semiotic, the pre-oedipal and the *jouissance* of the body (JO), not phallic *jouissance* of the patriarchal order. Patriarchal forms are possessive or destructive of the other.

Kristeva (1984) further suggests three kinds of oppositions: (1) the "rebel" who must still remain in the master-slave dialectic; (2) the "psychoanalyst" who searches for an alternative language to challenge patriarchal order; and (3) the "writer" who attempts further disruptions in language itself setting up alternative forms (see also, 1996). So, too, the *avant-garde* (e.g., poets, artists), for Kristeva, provoke, disrupt, dislocate, and call forth the repressed, the excesses, the semiotic, the desire that is unspeakable. The poetic text provides an alternative construction of meaning, subjectivity, and pleasure than those constructions based in the patriarchal order.

Several examples of Kristeva's influence[14] are discernible in law; however, more limited applications are found in criminology and social justice. The domain of law includes: Cornell (examining the repressed maternal as a basis of theorizing an ethical feminism, 1991; gender hierarchy being reproduced in law and how a critical reading of Kristeva provides alternative transformative vistas, 1993); Mona Lynch (using abjection to explain sex offender legislation, 2002); Kate Sutherland (using abjection to explain the criminal regulation of consensual sex, 2000); and Marie Ashe (introducing a psychoanalytic theory of subjectivity into feminist legal theory, 1987, 1990). In criminology we note: Arrigo (integrating feminist jurisprudence and criminology as the basis for a critical pedagogy, 1995a); and Toril Moi (exploring the criminalized boundaries of sexual/textual politics, 1985). In social justice we find Butler (subversive practices which offer form to the feminine, 1990); Moi (canvassing Kristeva's semiotical, psychoanalytical, and political excursions on the feminine, 1988, 1990); and Nancy Fraser (exploring the boundaries of feminist-inspired versions of justice, 1997).

CHAPTER 3

The Second Wave: Interpreting the Past, Building the Present, and Looking Toward the Future

INTRODUCTION

In this chapter, we draw attention to how postmodern lines of inquiry can be interpreted. While we recognize that several skeptical versions of the perspective have received considerable attention in the literature, we suggest how affirmative renderings of postmodernism are not only possible but are already in operation. Indeed, on this latter point, we specifically identify the contributions of several second wave scholars who have appropriated the interpretive tools of the postmodern sciences and have fashioned integrative and affirmative strategies for engaging in law, crime, and social justice research. Several of these studies were cited in the first two chapters. However, in chapter 3 we specifically emphasize how the cross-fertilization of affirmative postmodern ideas and strains of analyses represent the birth of synthetic inroads awaiting refinement through future application studies.

In order to accomplish our conceptual and integrative enterprise, this chapter is divided into three sections. First, we revisit the pessimistic, fatalistic, and nihilistic forms of postmodern inquiry that underscore much of what is taken to represent this domain of scholarship in the academy today. Canvassing this material is useful as it summarizes the origins of the linguistic turn in postmodern analysis. Moreover, this section helps us understand why researchers in law, crime, and social justice have been reluctant to embrace the more relativistic and anti-foundational agenda skeptical postmodernists advance. Second, we identify and explain several noteworthy facets of affirmative postmodern inquiry. Examining these constituents is not an exhaustive enterprise. Indeed, such an undertaking would be anathema to the philosophical underpinnings of this heterodox form of criticism. Instead, our intent is to tease out some of the more protean areas of conceptual analyses that, we believe, deepen and recast our understanding of crime, law, and justice, making prospects for structural and material change more likely.[1] Finally, we consider several discernible attempts at postmodern integration. These include lines of thought that can be linked between and among first wave theorists, as well as efforts to establish synthetic forms of postmodern inquiry more generally. Again, this exercise is suggestive rather than definitive. Indeed, we want to put forth the thesis that an integrative and affirmative postmodern project is not only possible in theory, but also identifiable in practice. To this end, we conclude the chapter by delineating several representative examples of second wave scholarship that have appropriated the insights of affirmative and integrative postmodern inquiry and have applied them to enduring questions in law, crime, and justice. In the subsequent application chapters, we suggestively apply much of our synthetic and affirmative commentary as developed here, to notable themes in the crime, law, and social justice literature.

THE SKEPTICAL FORMS OF POSTMODERN ANALYSIS

Early developments of postmodern analysis tended to be of the skeptical or nihilistic form. For example, Derrida's notion of "antifoundationalism," tended to be interpreted in support of a conservative agenda. Since, according to the deconstructionist argument, any collection of criteria established to evaluate something could in turn be evaluated by another set of criteria, and that, in turn, by another (i.e., an infinite regress), why then bother? All is relative. Struggles are futile. Similarly, Baudrillard's thesis of an endless hyperreality devoid of grounding tended toward a nihilism, a denial of historically contingent foundation. The absence of any grounded reality or agreed upon social contract implies that progress, change, and justice are merely a part of an illusory nonreality that signifies our fragile and fictionalized existences. Further, Michel Foucault's assessment of power and the panoptic gaze established a hermeneutics of suspicion in which seemingly productive regimes of knowledge/truth functioned as stifling technologies of discipline and surveillance. In their wake, identity is policed; knowledge is territorialized; difference is vanquished. State-endorsed utility dynamics prevail.

Lacan's work, too, was sometimes accused of being overly dependent on a more conservative notion of desire. Desire was said to arise from an inherent "lack" traced back to the inauguration of the child into the Symbolic Order. At this instant, the subject gains mastery and control by the use of discourse, but loses her/his primordial connectedness to the real. S/he is separated (castrated) from the real while gaining a place from which to speak in linguistic coordinate systems. Thereafter, it was said, that these "gaps-in-being" (*manqué d'etre*) return as a person confronts various situations where meaning is unclear. At these moments, desire is mobilized and the person seeks objects of desire that overcome this inherent lack. Overcoming one's gaps-in-being is manifested in a sense of fulfillment and a *jouissance*, albeit momentary and often illusory. Nonetheless, the plight of the subject is to continuously confront various gaps, search for objects of desire that promise fulfillment and, in their fulfillment, experience a particular form of *jouissance* allowable in an otherwise phallic Symbolic Order, a phallic *jouissance*.

Other first wave thinkers have redefined this notion of the origins of desire. Deleuze and Guattari (1987) have offered a more playful, searching, rhizomatic form of desire. Kristeva (1984) and Irigaray (1985a, b) have suggested looking at pre-oedipal, and even pre-mirror stages. As they argue, it is necessary to look at the mother's womb and the semiotic chora that offers an alternative basis of subsequent developments of desire and a speaking subject. Thus Cornell (1999), building on Irigaray, Cixous, and Kristeva, has advocated for the possible materialization of an alternative discourse, one more dependant on a poetic, maternal discourse, drawing from a "corporeal logic" (a language of the body).

These more skeptical strains of analysis resonate deeply within the topography of postmodern thought. Moreover, they are not without their ancestral origins. Indeed, Hegel's thesis on the master-slave dialectic also has been identified as inherently conservative along similar, non-liberating dimensions. Following Marxist terminology, the master signifies the "bourgeois" and the slave the "proletariat." The master states values affirmatively; the slave develops values by first reacting to and then negating the master (i.e., a reaction-negation dynamics) (Deleuze 1983; Bogue 1989; Butler 1999). In these instances, nothing intrinsically new is being offered. How, then, is the "subaltern" (Spivak 1991) to speak? How, then, are the "true words" (Freire 1972) of the slave to find more genuine expressive form? In short, the Hegelian thesis unwittingly functions to legitimize the power of the status quo through the act of reaction-negation. The slave responds to the voice and force of the master; the slave negates the words and the values of the master. However, the position and identity of the slave remains unchanged: dispossession and anonymity still pervade (and perniciously silence) the slave's reality.

Other negative implications can be derived from the Hegelian form. To illustrate, consider the "reversal of hierarchies" phenomenon often attributed to Derrida's philosophical work. Reversing or inverting hierarchies could mean just that: the subordinate group, after the revolution, now becomes dominant, and the previous dominant group is subjected to brutal repression. In this context, reversing hierarchies does not meaningfully alter the relations of power; rather, it affirms them: one group exercises its dominion over another group; and one group's will is subordinated by the group now in control. In this instance, form remains while only content changes.

Cornell (1991, 1999) has adopted this perspective and applied this reasoning to her critique of Catherine MacKinnon's (1987, 1989) feminist jurisprudence. Cornell accuses MacKinnon of perpetuating "hate politics" or "revenge politics." The voice and identity of women, through the law, represents nothing more than malestream logic. Therefore, this logic is by and about men who define women only for themselves. Repudiating this epistemology requires a reaffirmation of women's sensibilities and a rearticulation of feminine ways of knowing, freed from the misogynous trappings of phallocentric thinking. In the extreme, this model of reform thoroughly renounces men and masculine reasoning, substituting them with feminine approaches to the (jurisprudential) knowledge process believing that they intrinsically embody and more fully affirm the experiences of (all) women.

We also note that this same extremist tendency has been observed within over zealous activist groups, producing forms of "schmarxism" or types of "exorcism" (Milovanovic 1991). The former is a neologism combining Marxism and schmucky, indicating dogmatic, rigid forms of indoctrination; the latter is a process of reality construction in which the other is defined as evil and then attacked and defiled based on this imputed construction. Perhaps the most vivid and alienating expressions of schmarxism and exorcism found in popular culture today are the forces of political correctness.

Political correctness actively polices and fervently renounces all thoughts, behaviors, beliefs, attitudes, and values that fail to be inclusive of different identities and divergent viewpoints (i.e., schmarxism), and then vilifies those individuals or groups opposed to such thinking, repudiating their right to their nonpolitically correct perspective while, all along, calling for tolerance, difference, inclusiveness (i.e., exorcism). Political correctness is a provocative and contemporary reminder that the Hegelian reversal of hierarchies does not fundamentally change the relations of power in society. Regrettably, however, much of what is taken to represent postmodern thought in the academy today has been linked to the logic of political correctness, reversal of hierarchies, reaction-negation dynamics, and other skeptical, nihilistic, and fatalistic tendencies. In the next section, we briefly sketch some of the more positive dynamics intrinsic to the affirmative postmodern enterprise.

DOING AFFIRMATIVE POSTMODERN ANALYSIS

In order to stave off the tendencies of the Hegelian dialectic, nihilism, fatalism, schmarxism, and exorcism, an *affirmative* postmodern framework is needed. One response is the fluid and evolving intervention of a cultural politics of difference (Young 1990). In this more liberating vision, law, crime, and justice are rooted in *contingent universalities* (Butler 1992; McLaren 1994: 211). Provisional truths, positional knowledges, and relational meanings abound. New social relations, practices, and institutions materialize, producing a different, more inclusive context within which divergent and discordant sensibilities interact (Mouffe 1992, 380). In other words, the multiplicity of political, economic, and cultural identities that constitute our collective society interactively and mutually contribute to discourse on law, crime, and social change.

A significant contribution reorienting postmodern analysis to its more affirmative form is the work of Laclau and Mouffe (1985; see also Laclau 1990, 1996a, 1996b). For example, in *Hegemony and Socialist Strategy* (1985), they explained how signifiers were being decoupled from signifieds, how increasingly they assumed the "floating" form, and how various political economies were behind these couplings motivated by their corresponding (marginalizing) effects. Moreover, their work suggests the inherent instability of any coupled signifier to signified. As such, meaning is understood to be in-process and to always be recreated.

More recently, Ernesto Laclau (1996a, 1996b) has argued for the notion of "structural dislocations." This concept indicates that positing a monolithic structure is passé, especially as we turn to postmodernity. In its place, social structure is inherently unstable, dynamic, conflictual, and in the process of rearticulation. Indeed, signifiers have multiple forms of connectedness and forms of expression, defying closure, boundedness, and finality.

One dimension to affirmative postmodern analysis is contained in the Nietzschean affirmative version of the master-slave dialectic (Deleuze 1983). At issue here is the establishment of an ethico-political context in which repressed voices (Spivak 1991) might flourish. In the Nietzschean paradigm, the slave states values actively and affirmatively; s/he is not inherently caught up in the Hegelian master-slave dialectic. The slave's affirmative action contains within it a beyond, a vision of the possible, a transpraxis. Transpraxis is the basis of the affirmative forms of postmodern analysis. It finds a nexus with interpreting Lacan's (1977) notion of desire not as inherently homeostatic, an overcoming of lack; but, rather, more in terms of a creative search with no clear end: a rhizomatic journey discovering other spaces, the in-betweens, the fractal spaces (see Deleuze and Guattari 1987).

Judith Butler's (1999) statement on the nature of desire is similarly depicted. After reviewing Lacan's notion of how desire finds and, at the same time, escapes expression in signifiers, and how his descriptive analysis specifies desire as constituted in relation to the law-of-the-father marking its limits,[2] she then critiques Georg Hegel. Butler takes issue with Hegel's overly rational construction of desire, the notion of the self-transparent subject, the reactive-negative basis of desire for the subaltern, and the ultimate development of *ressentiment* and envy by the slave. She suggests that it is Gilles Deleuze to whom we must turn for guidance, particularly in his notion of a desire defined as productive and generative activity. This is expressed in the Nietzschean notion of a "will to power" ("will" not to be read as a conscious agency; "power" not to be read as domination).

Butler's reading of Deleuze is that desire is a "productive response to life in which the force . . . of it multiplies and intensifies in the course of an exchange with alterity" (1999, 213; see also Deleuze 1983, 49–72; Bogue 1989, 20–34). The notion of "will" is "responsive and malleable, assuming new and more complicated forms of organization through the exchange of force constitutive of desire. . . . [D]esire is less a struggle to monopolize power than an exchange that intensifies and proliferates energy and power into a state of excess" (Butler 1999, 213). Her use of the word "power" intends, therefore, multiple loci of affirmative and active forces.

According to Butler, productive forms of desire can also be found in Foucault's (1980a) late work. For Foucault, desire finds itself captured in various historically contingent power relations crystallized in discursive practices. In Foucault's radicalized conception of the Hegelian dialectic, Butler maintains that law reflects both rigidity and plasticity; the former creating desire as lack, but law's inherent plasticity creates "desire as a creative act, a locus of innovation, the production of new cultural meanings" (Butler 1999, 231). In addition, Butler looks to Kristeva's (1984) work on the "semiotic" and "poetic language" as deterritorialized spaces abundant with possibilities and disruptive forces (see also Foucault's notion of the "heterotopic," 1986b).

Our own affirmative postmodern approach finds a nexus with Butler's critique and understanding of desire as productive and life-affirming. We add, however, that chaos theory is implicit in Nietzsche's and Deleuze's work, and that desire, once mobilized, is much like the rhizome activating, putting into resonance, COREL[3] sets (Henry and Milovanovic 1996) that ultimately defy closure, linear expression, and predictability while providing only momentary stabilized forms and "structures" (e.g., "dissipative structures"). The notion of "dissipative structures" reflects how temporary "structures" may emerge in what chaos theory defines as "far-from-equilibrium" conditions. In these conditions—contrasted with "equilibrium conditions" (homeostasis) assumed in more positive, functional approaches in the social sciences particularly in modernist forms of analysis—"structures" emerge providing relative stability but are always amenable to the slightest perturbation. In short, they are extremely sensitive to their environment, unlike the rigid bureaucratic forms we find in equilibrium conditions. In postmodern society characterized by "structural dislocations" (Laclau 1996a), emerging or potentially emerging dissipative structures are more reflective of social conditions providing insight as to alternative ways of being. As such, signifiers, as forms of dissipative structures, are not situated in an essentialist ontology; rather, they are more consistent with Butler's notion of "contingent universalities" and with a qualified notion of "intersectional foundations."

Returning to the notion of transpraxis (i.e., the ambulant and conditional vision of what could be), we note that it resides in discourse. The production of alternative expressions of desire, of "true words," requires that the voice(s) of alterity and multiplicity be embodied in civic life and human social behavior. Transpraxis involves the undecidability of interaction as a revelatory moment for potential and greater inclusiveness. As Derrida (1997, 107) notes, "the undecidable in discourse signifies "unstable identities . . . that . . . do not close over and form a seamless web of the selfsame." In short, the undecidability in discourse makes possible the articulation of new and different vocabularies of meaning embodying the voices of and ways of knowing for excluded or marginalized citizens and/or collectives. (For their potential origination, see especially the work of Kristeva, Irigaray, and Cixous; more recently, critical race theory offers an alternative view on disenfranchised voices and how to give them material form, see, chapter 5; see also chapter 6 on how alternative media representations allow for the materialization of alternative images and the development of replacement narratives).

Consistent with this emancipatory agenda of transpraxis, an affirmative postmodern approach involves *border crossings* (Giroux 1992, 19–36, 133–41, 170–176; see also JanMohamed 1994; Lippens 1997). Border crossings signify the deliberate displacement of established parameters of meaning, forms of consciousness, sites of knowledge, and loci of truth. Conventional boundaries are transgressed, resisted, debunked, and de-centered. Border crossings require one to embrace the confluence of multiple languages, experiences, and desires as folded into the polyvocal, multilayered, and transhistorical narratives reflective of a society of difference (Giroux 1992, 29; Irigaray 1993a; Butler 1999). Thus, the desiring voice of marginalized subjects and of those others seeking recognition and legitimacy, would be imbued with pluri-significant, contradictory, incomplete, effusive, fragmented, and multiaccentuated expressions of identity. These borderlands, as languages of possibility rather than as technologies of discipline (Henry and Milovanovic 1996, 214–243), would be seen as "sites for both critical analysis and . . . a[s] potential source[s] of experimentation [and] creativity" (Giroux 1992, 34).

Affirmative postmodern analysis therefore views the emerging postmodern society with its dislocations, logic of differences, undecidabilities, and boundary transgressions (Laclau 1996a; see also Lash and Urry 1994) as an opportunity for new articulations of the Imaginary and Symbolic Orders, the occasions for new visions of the possible. In law, for example, Cornell (1991) indicates that within the constraints imposed by dominant discourse, metaphoric and metonymic slippages are at play, always suggestive of the new. In addition, Arrigo and Williams (1999b) contend that democratic justice and equality for minorities depend on the deconstructive and reconstructive activity of defining, on their own terms, identity freed from the trappings of majoritarian sensibilities. Similarly, critical race theory actively searches for new opportunities in "naming" injuries (Matsuda et al., 1993). In criminology, Adrian Howe (1994) offers a comparable analysis for the plight of incarcerated women. Drawing from Foucault, she argues for: (1) the development of various strategies for "naming" wrongs (1994, 169) that would (2) ". . . help create the conditions which permit prisoners to speak for themselves" (Howe citing Foucault 1994, 170). Greeg Barak (1988, 1994), too, has described the approach of "newsmaking criminology." He argues that criminal justicians need to be active, rather than passive, producers of knowledge when engaged with the media. In social justice literature, R. Schehr (1997) outlines a "fourth" social movement approach, "intentional communities," informed by the orderly disorder perspective of chaos theory.

As the next section of this chapter reports, considerable research in the area of crime, law, and social justice has been undertaken as of late, building on the insights of an affirmative postmodern line of inquiry. Although this final portion of the chapter is merely suggestive, what is clear is that efforts at cross-fertilization consistent with a transformative and emancipating postmodern agenda are already taking place in the academy. Thus, the comments that follow draw attention to this conceptually animated and thoroughly provocative integrative work.

AFFIRMATIVE POSTMODERN INTEGRATIONS

Postmodernist thought is witnessing considerable integration in the contemporary scene, both between the physical and social sciences and within the social sciences. For example, by demonstrating the compatibility between chaos theory and the literary theory of post-structuralism, Katherine Hayles (1990) suggests the formation of an "ecology of ideas." Stanislaw Lem (1981) even describes a topological space within which certain forms of integration are more likely (see Hayles 1990, 185–86).[4] Consider as well the notion of iteration. It is found in chaos theory, in literary analysis, and in legal textual analysis (see Derrida and Balkin in chapter 2). Others argue for cross-fertilization and point out that the disciplinary boundaries have always been transgressed (Giroux 1992).

Within the social sciences, the integrative work of Barak (1998) and the "hyperintegrated" approach of Barak and Henry (1999) are exemplary (see also, Henry and Lanier 1998; Farnsworth 1989; Gibbons 1994; Einstadter and Henry 1996 chapter 12). These syntheses, however, as anarchists tell us, must be posited in nonstatic forms; hence, chaos's suggestion of "dissipative structures" is appropriate to all synthetic enterprises. In other words, global conceptualizing must ultimately proceed on a level of relative stability but, at the local level, instability and indeterminacy must prevail. Indeed, micro knowledge can never be completely subsumable within any "hyperintegrated" model. This notion perhaps is best expressed in K. Godel's (1962) argument about the inherent impossibility of closure within any formal theory. As he observed, when searching for potential closure, finality, and all-encompassing maxims, totalizing theory is an illusory exercise. This view was to form the basis of Jean-François Lyotard's (1984) notion of "paralogism." Paralogism privileges the existence of instabilities—nonlinear developments, chance, spontaneity, flux, intensity, indeterminacy, and irony.

Barak is particularly sensitive to this issue. He warns us that the modernist preoccupation is "aimed at the questionable objective of delivering some kind of positivist prediction of 'what causes criminal behavior'" (1998, 188). As Barak (1998) contends, in postmodernist integrations "everything, at both the micro and macro levels, affects everything else, and "these effects are continuously changing over time." Barak and Henry (1999, 191–92) also suggest that future integrationist theories should be sensitive to at least five problematics: "[1] [the matter of] integrat[ing] theoretical concepts or propositions; [2] [the question of] how propositions are logically related; [3] [the issue of] the nature of causality; [4] [the issue of] the *level* of concepts and theories that are integrated; [5] [and the question of] what is to be explained, or the *scope of integration*." In addition, efforts at theoretical synthesis must also consider the crucial role of social justice in any critical analysis. On this point, Barak and Henry (1999, 171) recommend the development of social justice ideas that both "deconstruct inequalities based on differences while celebrating differences."

Additional affirmative forms of postmodern integrative analyses are discernible. In law, for example, Cornell (1991, 1999) has developed an integrated approach drawing from Lacan, Irigaray, Derrida, Kristeva and Cixous, and indicates how an "ethical feminism" may begin to emerge. Butler's (1990) description of "contingent universalities" as a way of transcending the dichotomy of either relativism or essentialism, and her call for practices "subverting repetition," are similarly suggestive. These are lines of inquiry that integrate the works of Foucault, Kristeva, Irigaray, and Lacan. In addition, the idea of "contingent universalities" possesses a commonality with chaos theory's notion of "dissipative structures." Both allow relatively stable political agendas to reach a tentative stability that becomes the basis of mobilization and opposition; however, these "universalities" are subject to refinement, qualification, deletion, and substitution as a function of historical contingency.

In criminology, additional affirmative postmodern integrative efforts can be identified. Henry and Milovanovic's (1996, 2001) notion of COREL sets [see note 3] represents a synthesis of ideas from several critical lines of thought, culminating in a theory of constitutive dialectics. Constitutive criminology argues for the interconnectedness of phenomena.[5] The parts already include the whole, and the whole cannot be separated from the parts. Attempts to distinguish the parts from the whole produce a shortsighted view of the nature of human being, sociability, and prevalent institutions. In this view, causal priority shifts from any prioritizing of the singular effect to prioritizing the interconnected nature of phenomena. This notion of codetermination has it that "directionality and causality must always be questions of specific historical and contextual investigations" (Hunt 1993, 294).

For example, let us consider law practices. Duncan Kennedy (1997, 152) has been quite clear: "although legal discourse is in one sense driven by the underlying opposition of ideologized interests, it may also react back on the ideologies and the interests and transform them." And further, "the modern legal discourse of civil rights is as much a cause as an effect of civil rights thinking . . ." This appears as circular, as a tautology, but that is the precise point: the effect can in turn feedback and become the "cause." Thus, the relation between law and social practices is not only two-way, but "neither term is reducible to or explainable entirely in terms of the other" (Hunt 1993, 179). It is repetition that provides the sense of stability.

In this view, COREL sets are only relatively stable, and subject to rearticulations (see Milovanovic 2002, 255–258). Thus, essentialist types of analyses miss the mark regarding the inherently dynamic, unstable, and continuously reconfiguring states that constitute existence. These are with effects. Subjects engage in their coproduction, and with the structures produced, are then situated within moments of variously restrictive as well as enhancing conditions. Indeed, as Susan Silbey (1996, 243) tells us, "even the most personal story relies on and invokes collective narratives—symbols, linguistic formations, structures, and vocabularies of motive—without which the personal would remain unintelligible and uninterpretable."

Arrigo (1997b, 2001b), too, demonstrates how this constitutive process operates in his investigation of stable discourses evolving between and among various control institutions (jails, prisons, mental hospitals, juvenile homes). His notion of "transcarceration" indicates that a relatively stable discourse emerges which cuts across the various specificities of control, subsequently coproduced by the keepers and the kept. Transcarceration becomes the basis for the development of identities, ways of resistance, as well as for naming and giving meaning to various structures.

Moreover, Bruce Arrigo and T. R. Young's (1998) integration of semiotics, chaos theory, and topology forms the basis of a psychoanalytic critique of modernist criminological thought. They argue that the construction of theoretical criminology fails to include race, gender, and class differences as embedded within criminology's own conceptual language. A more macro-level integration also is found within Arrigo's (2000) efforts to conceptually synthesize various strains of critical criminological thought (see also, Arrigo, 2001a). Relying upon the insights of Foucault, Derrida, Lacan, and other first wave luminaries, Arrigo (2000) argues that various critical perspectives (e.g., peacemaking, Marxism, anarchism, socialist feminism) differently express their shared commitment to existential themes (e.g., the struggle to be human, the struggle to be free, being/becoming). In this fashion, criminological *verstehen* is reconfigured in ways that are more compatible with positional, provisional, and relational claims to truth or knowledge.

Integrations of various first wave French scholars have taken place when trying to explain the wherewithal of "edgework." A number of groundbreaking works[6] argue that positivist oriented theorizing in criminology has downplayed the significance of nonmaterialistic factors in motivations for behavior causing crime, as well as in the explanation of people being drawn to extreme sports or other activities. These activities can often bring humans subjects within moments of catastrophe, serious injury, and death. First and second wave postmodern social theorists can help facilitate our understanding of these phenomena. Indeed, as Milovanovic (2002, 2003) notes, "understanding the edgeworker is the 'royal road' to a more comprehensive understanding of what it means to be human." Edgework literature (Matza 1969; Lyng 1990; Katz 1988; O'Mally and Mugford 1994; Ferrell et al. 2001) suggests that people are attracted and seduced by the adrenalin-rush of experiences. In what follows, we briefly conceptualize various forms of edgework in terms of five intersecting dimensions.

The five dimensions include: (1) socioeconomic structures and historical contingencies that provide background relevancies (the real); (2) the legal/illegal dimension which incorporates the various discussions on "what is crime?" (i.e., the political economy behind particular sutures of the imaginary and symbolic); (3) the degree of intensity involved; (4) being in- or out-of-control during the experience; and (5) the form of *jouissance* implicated. In examining the form of

In examining the form of *jouissance* (phallic *jouissance* versus *jouissance* of the body), we also directly implicate Kristeva's work on the "abject" (see chapter 5). In other words, in the *jouissance* of the body, the person who is in the moment of becoming; that is, a full body without organs, is also in the maximal position for witnessing a more complete form of *jouissance*. The literature on edgework takes exception with much of the limited analysis found in modernist thought as the latter privileges the rational mind in the dualism of mind-body. We also now turn briefly to Grosz (1994) and Deleuze and Guattari (1987) to find a way for reconceptualizing this alternative monistic subject; one constituted by both mind and body.

Background space: structural (socioeconomic, historical contingencies)

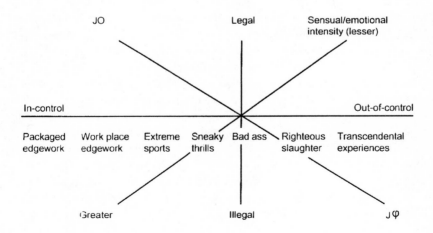

(Adapted from, Milovanovic 2002, 248; Milovanovic 2003, forthcoming)

In *Volatile Bodies* (1994), Grosz, reconciles the mind-body duality by relying on the topological structure of the Moebius strip.[7] She argues that the subject can be seen in terms of its journey along this strip, constituted, again, by both domains (corporeal logic, conceptual logic). She draws from Nietzsche, Lacan, Kristeva, Deleuze and Guattari in developing her integration. Edgework literature has yet to develop a bona fide conceptualization of the subject in the relevant research. We note, though, that David Matza's (1969) work still remains the most suggestive on this point. However, we turn to Deleuze and Guattari's insights (1987) on the body without organs (BwO) for some cursory guidance. From our perspective, this line of analysis could significantly enhance the explanation of the dynamics of edgework.

As we explained in chapter 1, Deleuze and Guattari build on Nietzsche's and Spinoza's notion of the body with various intersecting forces; that is, with different speeds, intensities, and directions. Recent theorizing (see Milovanovic 2002, 2003) suggests that those who confront various boundaries, edges, and limits find themselves often released from "molar organizations" (Deleuze and Guattari 1987) in their contestations. As such, they undergo a deterritorialization of the various stabilized forces and revisit "molecular organizations" where things are in flux, where desire is rooted in production and undergoes rhizomatic journeys. This is where various "becomings" take place. The full BwO is that person who escapes from repetition, undergoes deterritorizalization, and mobilizes a greater range of potentialities that are often confined by the oedipalization of desire and by its nexus with capitalist logic (Deleuze and Guattari 1983) on the one hand, and the "disciplinary mechanisms" (Foucault 1977) on the other. The edgeworker engages in becoming. The full BwO is the more productive form. The empty BwO is one in which a person is imprisoned in repetition. This individual is caught in stasis, in an emptying of flows, forces, flux, intensities, and alternative configurations in terms of dissipative structures. The empty BwO can also be likened to the "excessive investor" where domination of the other is pursued (Henry and Milovanovic 1996).

Grosz's (1994) work is quite suggestive when integrated with Deleuze and Guattari's notion of the BwO. The integrated model sees the possibility of the resurrections of the monistic subject as depicted by the Moebius strip. By interpreting the edgeworker in terms of becoming, in terms of a BwO, one is in the position to develop a more comprehensive understanding of the full range of human potentials.

Moreover, Henry and Milovanovic (1996, 2001) have offered an alternative definition of crime as either "harms of reduction" or "harms of repression." The former occurs "when an offended party experiences a loss of some quality relative to their present standing." The latter occurs "when an offended party experiences a limit or restriction preventing them from achieving a desired position or standing" (Henry and Milovanovic 1996, 103).

Henry and Milovanovic (2001, 167–168) further indicate that distinguishing between "harm" and mere change depends on four factors. First, whether the entity suffering the change perceives it as a loss; second, whether the person or entity is fully free to object to the exercise of power responsible for imposing the reduction; third, whether the individual is free to resist it; and fourth, whether the person resisting is able to prevent the reduction from occurring. In short, "crimes of reduction and crimes of repression are harms because they diminish a person's or group's position, or they deny them the opportunity to attain a position they desire, a position that does not deny another from attaining her or his or their own position" (2001). In this view, the "criminal" could be perceived as an "excessive investor," and harm as "the expression of some agency's energy to make a difference to others and it is the exclusion of those others who in the instant are rendered powerless to maintain or express their humanity" (2002, 170; Henry and Milovanovic 1996, 116). In this instance, "agency" could include a person, but also institutions, social relations, social systems, the legal apparatus, law, the state, and so forth.[8]

Several additional second-wave attempts at affirmative and integrative postmodern analysis are apparent in the crime, law, and social justice literature. Some of these include: Arrigo and Schehr (integrating chaos and semiotics as applied to an assessment of victim offender mediation programs for juveniles, 1998); Schehr and Milovanovic (synthesizing semiotics, chaos, and catastrophe theory as linked to a critique of (inter)national mediation programs, 1999); Arrigo and Williams (integrating semiotics, restorative justice, and chaos theory as applied to victim impact statements in capital trials, 2003); Milovanovic (offering some suggestions for an emerging orderly (dis)order, for an alternative social structure, agency, law, community, and criminology, 1997); Schehr (describing the development of a "third " and even "fourth" approach in social movement literature based on a synthesis of chaos theory and semiotic analysis, 1996, 1997); Arrigo (integrating various critical and postmodern approaches in the law-psychology sub-specialization as a basis by which to establish a theory of social justice, 2002b, 2003a); Henry and Milovanovic (suggesting "social judo" as a metaphor for dealing with excessive investors in doing harm, 1996); and Williams and Arrigo (synthesizing chaos theory and anarchism in an assessment of citizen justice and collective well-being, 2001).

CONCLUSION

As this chapter argued, affirmative and integrative postmodern analysis offers the researcher novel lines of inquiry when investigating legal, criminological, and social justice phenomena. To demonstrate the significance of our proposed approach for future theoretical, applied, and policy investigations, the next five chapters specifically explore some of the more controversial sociolegal topics confronting the academy today. In particular: chapter 4 examines confinement and prison resistance; chapter 5 reviews critical race theory and a jurisprudence of color; chapter 6 investigates media/literary studies and feminism; chapter 7 explores restorative justice and victim offender mediation; and chapter 8 considers social movements. To substantiate our analyses, we rely heavily on the insights of French postmodern social theorists as articulated in chapters 1 and 2. In addition, though, we synthesize these observations suggestively demonstrating how each topic could be examined consistent with affirmative and transformative postmodern inquiry. Thus, we contend that the examples chosen in the subsequent chapters represent alternative directions for engaging in sophisticated sociolegal research and praxis.

CHAPTER 4

Confinement Law and Prison Resistance:

Applications in Critical Penology

INTRODUCTION

In this chapter, we examine two facets of critical penology: capital punishment in relation to persons identified as competent but mentally ill; and various approaches, interpretations, and strategies for promoting prison resistance. In the first section, the precedent case law giving rise to death row executions for psychiatrically disordered convicts is summarily reviewed. We follow with an assessment as to how an affirmative and integrative postmodern reading of confinement, competency, mental illness, and treatment would yield alternative (and more liberating) interpretations for the meaning of capital punishment as applied to psychiatrically disordered offenders.

In the second portion of the chapter, four areas of prison resistance are examined.[1] These include: (1) Adrian Howe's (1994) poststructuralist feminist critique; (2) Mary Bosworth's (1999a, 1999b) analysis of agency and resistance in women's prisons; (3) Jim Thomas and Dragan Milovanovic's (1989, 1999) jailhouse lawyers; and (4) Dragan Milovanovic and Stuart Henry's (1991, 2002) constitutive penology. In each case we briefly state some central ideas in these respective areas, and then suggest further lines of analysis informed by first- and second-wave French postmodern scholars.

Our investigation of confinement law and prison resistance is not exhaustive. Indeed, we do not claim to provide definitive solutions; rather, we seek to provide the interested reader with further tools for critical penological inquiry. Accordingly, we conclude the chapter with some provisional thoughts on the emergence of political resistance and replacement discourses.

CONFINEMENT LAW AND EXECUTING THE MENTALLY ILL

A Review of the Precedent Case Law

The United State Supreme Court has determined that, under specific conditions, persons with psychiatric disorders can be subject to capital punishment. Execution of the mentally ill is problematic when questions are raised concerning the death row prisoner's right to refuse treatment, especially where competency restoration is the objective (Winick 1997). In other words, to what extent is it allowable or acceptable to "rehabilitate" a condemned inmate only to then execute him/her?[2] There are a number of appellate cases that chart the development of the mental health law in this area; however, in recent years, three cases are particularly noteworthy: *Ford v. Wainwright*, (1986); *Washington v. Harper*, (1990); and *State v. Perry* (1992) (e.g., Winick 1992; Arrigo and Tasca 1999). These cases are briefly summarized below.

The *Ford* case examined whether the Eighth Amendment's prohibition against cruel and unusual punishment prevented the state from executing an incompetent death row prisoner. The Court concluded that a prisoner must understand the death penalty and the reasons for the sentence before a state can carry out the execution (*Ford v. Wainwright* 1986, 420–422). The *Harper* case assessed whether it was permissible to forcibly medicate a prisoner for eventual execution if the coercive treatment furthered the goal of prison safety and promoted the prisoner's medical needs. The Court determined that an incompetent death row inmate is subject to forced treatment if (1) the prisoner suffers from a mental disorder and/or is gravely disabled such that, (2) the person poses a likelihood of serious harm to oneself, to others, and/or to another's property (*Washington v. Harper* 1990, 214). The *Perry* case considered whether the Eighth and Fourteenth Amendments prevented the state from forcibly injecting mind altering drugs into a condemned prisoner who was incompetent, when the medical intervention was administered *solely* for competency restoration resulting in execution. The Court found that when psychotropic drugs are used simply as a way to medicate and then execute, the medical intervention is unconstitutional: it neither improves prison safety nor is in the prisoner's best medical interest (*State v. Perry* 1992, 751–752).

Capital Punishment and the Mentally Ill: An Affirmative and Integrative Postmodern Analysis

We note that while a conventional reading of the three cases and the Court's respective rulings yield useful sociolegal information, an affirmative and integrative postmodern analysis offers additional and alternative insight substantially advancing our knowledge of mental health confinement law, policy, and practice. For example, key words and phrases form the basis of the Supreme Court's decisions above. Collectively, these expressions communicate something more about the law's unconscious intent, hidden assumptions, and implicit values for psychiatrically ill prisoners and the process of executing them (Arrigo and Williams, 1999a).[3] The words and phrases themselves signify an assembled "text" or narrative that can be evaluated or disassembled as such. All this takes place so that the condemned person appreciates the pending final act and the free citizen appreciates the impending end. After all, if this appreciation did not occur, how, then, would atonement be satisfied?

To elaborate, consistent with Roland Barthes' (1973b) textual analysis, standard sociolegal interpretations emphasize the "readerly approach" to sense making: truth is a certain destination, a clear endpoint where meaning is exhaustible. Conversely, affirmative postmodern assessments emphasize the "writerly approach" to interpretation: truth is a departure where an array of knowledges and perspectives are valued signifying no definitive reading of the text. Thus, we would argue, the "truth" of being must be situated in historical and political economic analysis of borders and their patrol. In our present case, the borders suggest acceptable notions of responsibility, competency, and the boundary between order and disorder.

Both Lyotard (1984) and Deleuze and Guattari (1986) offer similar analysis to Barthes. The former's use of *petit recit* (i.e., small narratives) rather than grand narratives, and the latter's comments on "minor literatures" are affirmative postmodern strategies that shatter and increase our understanding by disrupting and displacing conventional readings of a text. In short, they produce opportunities for locating instability rather than consensus in discourse (Lyotard 1988a), and make possible the deterritorialization of that which is written (Deleuze and Guattari 1987). Mental competency law offers a unique vista as to the degree to which deterritorialization may tend before "Leviathan" intervenes, proclaiming the boundaries to understood order.

In mental health confinement law, key expressions such as "mental illness," "treatment," "competency," "dangerous," and "execution," are *signs*; that is, they are words and phrases that convey multiple, fluid, and evolving meanings in the law.[4] Barthes (1974, 35–41) observes that a "galaxy of signifiers" makes up any text and that such signifiers (i.e., words and phrases) can be decoded as sense-making explodes and scatters. Jacques Derrida's (1977, 1978) position on the "undecidability" of meaning resonates with this logic. The play of *différance* (e.g., "competency vs. incompetency," "mental health vs. mental illness") reveals how each term in the binary opposition relates to the other. In other words, notwithstanding the logocentrism of the first value position in the two hierarchies, each term in binary opposition: (1) is differentiated from the other (i.e., they are distinct); (2) defers the other term (i.e., makes it "wait"); and (3) defers to the other term (i.e., is dependent upon the other for meaning). These relationships reflect the undecidable in discourse; that is, the "foundationless, provisional . . , or reversibl[e]" context within which sense-making takes place (Balkin 1987, 752). In the extreme, following Jean Baudrillard (1983a), *différance* and the writerly approach embody a "hypertext:" they signify a "hyper-reality" about our understanding of psychiatrically disordered prisoners on death row absent clear epistemological foundations or anchored sociolegal truths.[5] At the same time, they offer a resistance to the deteritorialization and possible reteritorialization of the body and its forms of expression.

Equally suggestive for purposes of an affirmative and integrative postmodern understanding of mental health confinement law is Foucault's (1972, 1977) power//knowledge construct, Lacan's (1977) notion of desire, and Lyotard's (1984) paralogy. Foucault insists that power, as knowledge-truth, assumes the form of a language in which thought and behavior are regulated through productive mechanisms of disciplinary control. The sign of mental illness must be "policed," (Foucault 1965), and persons identified as such must be normalized, depathologized, and corrected (Arrigo and Williams, 1999c). Capital punishment is *the* symbolic gesture, *the* ultimate act in which the prisoner's body, mind, and soul are territorialized. The trilogy of Supreme Court cases, representing the current state of mental health confinement law, legitimize the correctional system's use of execution as a productive mechanism for such territorialization. According to Foucault (1988), however, decentering this manifestation of power-knowledge through multiple sites of contestation and diverse expressions of identity is crucial to liberating the alienating subject from disciplinary control.

Where Foucault calls for active resistance to the territorialization of desire (Deleuze and Guattari 1987), Lacan (1991) psycho-semiotically explains how the subject is dismissed or silenced through discourse but can, nonetheless, be retrieved. The jargon of confinement law does not embody the experiences (i.e., the desire) of the mentally ill. Confinement law is a specialized system of communication (i.e., psycholegal discourse) privileging a (clinicolegal) narrative "producing a circumscribed knowledge understood [to be] psychiatric justice" (Arrigo 1997b, 32). Lacan's (1991) notion of the *master* discourse conveys the alienating and repressive effects of certain coordinated language systems, including psycholegal discourse.[6] In addition, however, Lacan (1991) argues that alienated subjects (i.e., mentally disordered offenders) have access to an alternative system of communication that embodies the subject's sense of identity and way of knowing. This replacement *desir* (desire) is captured in Lacan's (1991) discourse of the *hysteric*[7] coupled with his discourse of the *analyst*.[8] The joint effects of these two discourses suggest a way in which psychiatrically disordered offenders can overcome their lack, their *pas toute*, in repressive psycholegal discourse.

Let us consider a hunger striker. In a recent Illinois Appeals Court decision (The People of the State of Illinois ex rel. The Illinois Department of Corrections, January 2003), the court was faced with an order by the Illinois Department of Corrections to force-feed a prisoner on a hunger strike. The Court (two-person majority), after balancing the interests of corrections and those of the convict, found in favor of the prison officials and said that the only purpose for the offender's behavior "was to attempt to manipulate the system."

The dissenting view argued that the government's case did not establish possible disruptions to prison routine and, hence, the right of the person to refuse treatment should be binding in the case. However, both sides speculated as to the convict's "true" wishes and possible outcomes. And that is the problem. Both find themselves in the ongoing prison discourse; a language that has attained the dimensions of the hyperreal, impeding movement beyond it. On the other hand, the hunger strike prisoner remains in the discourse of the *hysteric*, susceptible to all sorts of impositions of discourses as to the "true" meaning of his act.[9] This brings out the issue of how in fact can the convict express his desires otherwise? Regrettably, since the late 1970s, the extent of outsiders coming to prison to do activist work has dwindled,[10] thereby removing possible advocates who may have entered a relationship reflective of the discourse of the *analyst* combined with the dialogical pedagogy of Paulo Freire in better producing "true" words.

This theme of overcoming one's lack in discourse resonates with Lyotard (1984, 1988a), particularly in his concept of paralogy. In paralogy the search for instabilities and resistance to totalities is emphasized. The goal of dialogue is sensitivity to various truths, forms of identity, and expressions of knowledge. Relatedly, Lyotard's (1984) use of chaos theory's notion of far-from-equilibrium conditions suggests that the law's desire to arrive at a fixed, equilibrium resolution (i.e., a point attractor) regarding the execution of psychiatrically ill prisoners, dismisses the more natural and fluid behavior of the law. The law is a system of signs (Kevelson 1988) and, as such, is more dynamic than static, more indeterminate than determinate, more unpredictable than predictable. Acknowledging the orderly disorder (i.e., chaos) of law opens up possibilities for exploring new vistas of sociolegal meaning and alternative interpretations for the signs of mental health confinement law, policy, and practice. Both are consistent with an affirmative and integrative postmodern textual analysis of execution for the mentally ill.

PRISON RESISTANCE

Towards a Feminist Analysis of Penality

In her groundbreaking book, *Punish and Critique*, Adrian Howe (1994), offers a poststructuralist critique of penality.[11] After reviewing the literature on the relation of the economy to incarceration, she reviews the question of penality informed by the insights of Foucault and postmodern feminism. Her disagreement with Foucault's (1977) work is with the male lens as the principal basis on which prisons are investigated. However, her agreement with Foucault is with how bodies are disciplined. Howe notes, though, that Foucault neglected the question concerning the disciplining of women's bodies (souls). Nonetheless, his various conceptions (e.g., micro physics of power, production of bodies of docility and utility, the movement from discipline of the body to the discipline of the soul, disciplinary mechanisms, panopticism, the political technology of the body, micro-power, power-knowledge, and a genealogy of the modern soul, etc.), all are appropriated to think about the feminine in penality.

Howe draws from a number of feminist writers (e.g., Carlen, Rafter, Dobash, Gutteridge, Zedner), and then applies the insights of other feminist scholars (Bartky, Bordo, Young, Spivak, Carlen) to fashion a poststructuralist account of female penality. She begins with T. de Lauretis's paradox of being a woman (Howe 1994, 166; de Lauretis 1990, 115) and acknowledges that the "starting point of feminist theory . . . depends on the nexus of language, subjectivity and consciousness" (1994). Thus, Howe seeks to identify how women are imprisoned, both discursively and materially, in penal settings. Drawing from Foucault, Howe explains that "all we can do apparently, is to help create the conditions which permit prisoners to speak for themselves and 'appreciate the fact that only those directly concerned can speak in a practical way on their own behalf'" (1994: Howe citing Foucault, 170, 209, and see also Foucault 1977, 206–09).

To this end, Howe (1994, 171) proposes two strategies: naming social injury and a "reductionist-abolitonist" strategy for female prisoners. In regard to the first proposal, she argues that tactics must be devised in naming injuries from a feminist perspective. For Howe, this is the only basis on which a sense of entitlement can be provided. In regard to the second proposal, a reductionist-abolitionist view would "measure the injuriousness of imprisonment against the social injuries of women's daily lives by drawing attention to the specific, concrete circumstances of women's criminalized actions and of their imprisonment" (1994, 172, see also Howe 1990). Her observations can be augmented by the contributions of first and second wave French thought.

First, postmodern thought could be productively brought to bear on the question of ways of speaking and naming by looking at Lacan's (1991) four discourses, perhaps integrated with Paulo Freire's (1972) dialogical pedagogy and the insights of chaos theory. Following Lacan (1977), women, in male conceived and dominated prisons, "do not exist," in so much as their voices are denied. In other words, their voices are more often located in the discourse of the *hysteric*. Moreover, we argue that in an activist agenda, a composite of Lacan's discourse of the *analyst* and *hysteric* would provide a point of departure in which to search for ways to make the feminine voice materialize in signifiers and discourse. Freire's (1972, 1985) work would be useful for indicating how the emergence of the feminine register would need to be situated in concrete contexts.[12] Chaos theory would specify how these developments would likely follow dialectical, rhizomatic, and nonlinear paths as the dialectics of struggle ran its course. In other words, the ends are not predictable in advance. There always exists the unexpected, the unintended consequences, and the effects of iteration that produce disproportional outcomes. All of these integrations suggestively (and provocatively) answer Spivak's question about how it is possible for the subaltern to speak, but neither in the form or content that could be predicted at the outset, nor which could be spelled out in a totalized image of the possible within ongoing struggle. Indeed, the proposed syntheses address the issue of how an alternative space could be created from which the feminine subject could speak (Howe 1994, 211); a space that offers extensive possibilities of being and becoming.

Second, Howe's work could be enhanced by an alternative definition of injury along the lines developed by constitutive criminology, especially in its notion of harms of reduction and harms of repression. This approach would transcend male oriented, and formally institutionalized discursive frameworks that narrowly define all harms in time and space, thereby excluding disenfranchised peoples. Additionally, seeing the offender as an "excessive investor;" that is, as one who imposes his/her will over the other, provides an alternative view linked to COREL sets and how the coproduction of structures is an ongoing, dialectical process.[13] For example, drawing from Butler (1990, 1993), we must devise strategies for "subverting repetition." In other words, rigidly constituted COREL sets tending toward repetition can be undermined by creative subversive practices: even the smallest of which, consistent with chaos theory, could produce disproportional effects in the social formation.

Third, following Foucault, Howe's view of the body and soul also could be augmented by the work of Grosz (1994) who reunites the body-mind duality. Modernist thought privileges only the "mind" in this binary relationship. For Grosz, the monistic subject—one constituted by both the emotional/sensual as well as the rational/logical—must be reestablished. It is the body that experiences the sensual perturbations as well as the mind. Thus, to exclude one and to privilege the other is to render half the story, at best, of repression and struggle. Following Howe's critique, all too often "disciplinary mechanisms" and panopticism (Foucault 1977) in prisons render women's bodies and souls from a male-centered framework. Moreover, they exclusively rely on the "mind" in the mind/body dualism in various scholarly explanations of effects.

Fourth, Howe's work is suggestive for other possible integrations, informed by additional first and second wave French thinkers. Deleuze and Guattari's (1987) notion of the full body without organs, becomings, and deterritorialization are useful. For example, imprisonment experiences and the voices of those in struggle offer insights as to alternative becomings in confined locations, and offer a fuller understanding of possible being and becoming. In addition, Kristeva's (1984) work suggesting sources of identity construction that precede the oedipal and the mirror stage also could shed some light on how to respond to the question of penality and alternatively based identity formations.

In sum, Howe's commentary resituates the discussion of the feminine within a non-phallic Symbolic Order. Here observations provide a fertile direction for coming to terms with the notion that "woman does not exist" or exists as lack. This penological direction is suggestive for other possible responses to institutional harms inflicted upon women.

Women's Resistance in Prison

Mary Bosworth (1999a, 1999b) has examined ethnographically how agency and power are connected in prison and how resistance can be engendered. She focuses on how the incarcerated woman's identity (e.g., identity politics) is constantly renegotiated. Bosworth argues that identity is always situated within the dialectics of agency and structure. In the context of penal regimes,

"regimes of femininity" materialize "within the employment and education typically offered in women's prisons—namely, sewing, cooking, cleaning and 'mothercraft'—which are meant to shape the women's identity and their presentation of self" (Bosworth 1999b, 103). In other words, within women's prisons work and education revolve around traditional notions of femininity (1999b, 104).

For Bosworth, identity politics becomes central: it is a way of responding to the "pains of imprisonment" (1999b, 108). Identity politics offers potential spaces for resistance and conflict inside the prison. Bosworth focuses on "the ways in which women assert their agency in prison through identifying with, and transforming, aspects of that idealized femininity which is encouraged at the institution" (1999b, 125). Some of these strategies entail wearing masks ("putting on a face"), engaging in narratives of their roles on the outside, and verbalizing what changes they underwent while incarcerated. These tactics challenge notions of the passive woman prisoner even as the correctional facility attempts to instill identities on her. As Bosworth (1999b, 120) tells us, "women resist the restrictions of imprisonment through enacting diverse images of femininity which, in their variety, subvert the dominant image of white, middle-class heterosexuality which is advocated by the prison and idealized in the community."

Drawing particularly from Carol Smart, Pat Carlen, Allison Young, and Judith Butler's work, Bosworth shows how resistance revolves around developing multiple identities outside of the dominant notion of "woman" on which prison authorities insist. This often entails privileging intersectional identities involving race, class, sexual orientation, nationality, and so forth, that confront the monolithic image of "hegemonic (white, heterosexual, passive) femininity" (1999a, 150).

Let us suggest how first and second wave French postmodern theorists could augment the insights developed in Bosworth's ethnographic study. First, her application of Butler's work on identity is exemplary. It establishes a new perspective on how identity develops in constrained places. Following Foucault, power is never monolithic: it leaves spaces and contradictions that open up possible struggles and alternative resistance narratives. Second, her notion that identity is dualistic (i.e., it is both the locus for resistance and the locus for various conflicts within the prison population) (1999a, 111) suggests how the dialectics of struggle occurs for women in prison. Here "intersectional standpoints" indicate how the fluidity of identity and meaning constructions,[14] when captured or imprisoned within static signifiers or discourses, results in the potential loss of alternative master signifiers that better embody the uniqueness of being human, and the potential loss of narrative constructions that build on them. This insight draws attention to a significant dilemma in feminist (penological) research. On the one hand, are women to follow Hélène Cixous (arguing for an *écriture féminine*) in devising a resistance discourse; an opportunistic discourse dealing with the various contingencies of being confined and suffering the pains of imprisonment to endure their incarceration? Or, on the other hand, can a catalyst be found by which the subaltern both constructs a revolutionary discourse without, at the same time, merely reversing hierarchies or inadvertently engaging in harms of reduction and repression towards others?

Third, and related to the second point, is the issue of wearing masks while incarcerated (Bosworth 1999a, 112–113) to offset the pains of imprisonment. Bosworth's work suggests how this activity further disempowers and alienates the subject ("It is, in short, difficult just to 'be yourself' in prison," 1999a, 113). In the Lacanian (1977) schema, this is akin to the construction of an "I" that inserts itself in an alien discourse, simultaneously attempting to distance and identify with it. In this instance, the (penal) institution is assured the continuance of a hyper-reality (Baudrillard 1983a), sustained by the coproduction of the subaltern. Drawing from the constitutive work of Anthony Giddens (1984, 1991), Bosworth suggests the importance of the woman finding a new basis for her identity (1999a, 115) relying somewhat from extra-prison normative views (1999a, 116), as well as from institutional contingencies. This notwithstanding, it is in the intersectional standpoints that identity finds support (1999a, 117–119). Thus, according to Bosworth, the constant identification with factors outside of the immediate penal environment is what allows for resistance to the pains of imprisonment. This observation gets to the heart of resistance and its very limitations (1999a, 128–32) as something that does not go beyond mere reaction without a vision of an alternative, a transpraxis.

In an integrated Lacanian-Freirian position, we do see how the possibility for the subaltern to speak "true words" does exist in the coproductive discursive constructions of people in struggle. Codification of repressive structures, their critique, and disidentification set the path for alternative signifiers to develop that more genuinely embody the desire of the subject in struggle. This activity indicates a movement from the discourse of the *hysteric* to the discourse of the *analyst* aided by the integration of a dialogical pedagogical dimension. Indeed, as we have argued in several passages of this book, this more transformative and emancipating approach cannot be seen as a linear production as chaos theory tells us; rather, it follows rhizomatic pathways to more authentic forms of self-expression. And it is here that the challenge for activists presents itself: to spell out the necessary and sufficient the emergence of replacement discourses that do not contain the components (the contaminants) of harms of reduction and repression while also providing enough suggestive qualities for the invocation of alternative visions of a better world.

Jailhouse Lawyers as Rebels or Revolutionaries?

Resistance in prison has appeared recently with jailhouse lawyers. Jailhouse lawyers are convicts who have taught themselves law while incarcerated and practice it while confined.[15] The question is whether their actions are indeed consistent with "political" revolutionaries. Thomas and Milovanovic (1989, 1999) liken jailhouse lawyers to "primitive rebels"; that is, more doers than subjects with full-blown political agendas. In this instance, the use of law remains one of the few weapons available to overcome the absurdity of incarceration and the existential vacuum of place.

Outwardly, it seems as if jailhouse lawyers could be conceived of as revolutionaries, in so much as they appear to represent the disenfranchised, the subaltern, especially in their various litigation efforts directed toward the keepers. However, this interpretation represents a narrow way to envision their actual resistance. Indeed, it is often the prisoner who witnesses daily the "pains of imprisonment," who recognizes that there are few avenues to maintain an identity with which to survive the conditions that otherwise lead to the "mortification of self" (Goffman 1961). Prison litigation provides an immediate challenge to conditions of confinement and allows for the development of an alternative identity; one in which the subject assumes an active agenda in his self-definition and in his ability to challenge institutional power (Thomas and Milovanovic 1989; see also, Thomas 1988).

Given this understanding of the jailhouse lawyer, a more postmodern perspective could provide further insight about the subject-in-process (Kristeva 1984). Then, too, this understanding of the jailhouse lawyer deepens our regard for the dialectics of struggle. Let us see how. Arguably, jailhouse lawyers, by acquiring their new status, could be seen as attaining the stage of "becoming" consistent with Deleuze and Guattari (1987): becoming-lawyer and, hence, becoming a body without organs. To further this line of inquiry, we draw from Lacan's (1991) formulations on discourse.

At the outset, we note that the jailhouse lawyer is more likely to position himself in the discourse of the *master*, whereby the other convict in seeking his help is relegated to the discourse of the *hysteric*. As such, the other prisoner is offered only dominant legal signifiers with which to construct narratives for his plight or grievance. Jailhouse lawyers are pragmatic: they argue that they do not have the luxury to engage in highly abstract analysis[16]; they are concerned with the immediate concrete conditions of disenfranchisement. Accordingly, however, narratives constructed are likely either to be more sterile, legalistic versions of "what happened," or of the grievance at hand. To this extent, jailhouse lawyers "help" other prisoners by providing them with the possibility of establishing some legal "standing" and, consequently, the possibility of redressing their grievance in law. However, they also unintentionally or inadvertently legitimize the rule of law ideology.

Let us propose another line of analysis.[17] Consistent with everyone else, jailhouse lawyers develop various forms of identification. Identities could be located within a three-dimensional space with each dimension representing a critical identification. Our three-dimensional configuration would include a y-axis, representing identification with language, an x-axis, representing identification with master signifiers, and a z-axis, representing identification with discursive subject positions. In what follows, we briefly propose how this three-dimensional phase space would function.[18]

The y-axis (representing identification with language) would include the abstract language of law on one end of the continuum and the body rooted more in the unsaid, the nonverbal, and the poetic at the other end of the continuum. Thus, in Lacanian (1977) terms, the Symbolic and Real Orders are respectively represented. The x-axis (representing identification with master signifiers) would include strong identification with the signifiers of law on one end of the spectrum, and strong disidentification at the other end of the continuum. This is the realm of the Lacanian (1977) Symbolic Order. The z-axis represents identification with discursive subject positions. These offer a location from which an "I" can take up momentary residence to speak. At one end, we would have identification with the juridic subject (e.g., the so-called reasonable man in law). Farther away we would have the identification of the individual as a skeptical subject; still farther away we would find the oppositional subject; and at the other end of the continuum, we would have the revolutionary subject. This is the realm of Lacan's Imaginary Order. We could then say that a person's identification was located within the various intersections on this three-dimensional phase space.

This proposed line of inquiry can be applied to the jailhouse lawyer. The evidence indicates that he is more likely to be located at the intersection of various identifications: with abstract language (legal discourse), with dominant legal (master) signifiers, and with the juridic subject. As such, he is more likely to construct the readerly text in law, tending toward linear logic. After all, in his pragmatic stance, it is only from within this position that he can find a door to address grievances in law. This is where the dialectics of struggle emerge. The jailhouse lawyer does contribute to facilitating the disenfranchised, the subaltern, to speak or to "have access to the courts;" however, in doing so, he upholds the legitimacy of the law, and renders the grievant partially *pas-toute*, not all, incomplete. The grievant becomes an alienated subject in the very willingly constructed story in law.

Given this realization, we note that important future research for activists remain. For example, how does a "subaltern" find a voice in law without, at the same time, legitimizing the rule of law ideology and without altering narratives to fit the sterile legal discourse, rendering the grievant a not-all in law? In other words, what are the necessary and sufficient conditions by which the jailhouse lawyer becomes a more politically oriented figure of social change? Milovanovic (1996a), for example, in applying Lacan and chaos theory to Gerald Lopez's (1994) work showed how Paulo Freire's "dialogical pedagogical" approach integrated with Lopez's "dialogical problem solving" genre, could result in *conscientization*. In this context, both the lawyer and client coproduced narratives that were more genuinely reflective of the grievance, such that they were both empowered and attained a more critical consciousness. In our proposed schema above, this was represented by a rhizomatic movement away from identifications that were aligned with abstract language, the juridic subject, and the master signifiers of law, toward identifications that were aligned with the language of the body, the revolutionary subject, and a disidentification with dominant master signifiers in law.

Thus, consistent with Deleuze and Guattari (1987), we could argue that the jailhouse lawyer once co-opted indeed becomes a body without organs but of the empty form.[19] In other words, he is engaged in the repetition of legalistic forms. However, our hypothetical revolutionary subject becomes a full body without organs, undermining formal law in alternative signifying practices while, at the same time, using law as a weapon for social change. Further research in this direction would examine how this balance can take place.[20]

Constitutive Penology

Our final example in confinement law and the application of postmodern analysis deals with the emerging field of constitutive penology.[21] In this view,

> Penology, in so far as it provides the discursive reference for actions that create, develop and sustain prison, provides some of the constitutive work that gives form, sustenance, and permanence to the subordination of human agency to its product. . . . Debates over being in and out of prison, over building more or less prisons, about prison overcrowding and prison overspending, about alternatives to prison and challenges to those

defending prison, all essentialize prison and neglect the continuous and reconstituting nature of the historically structured disciplinary discourse whose building blocks we construct around our selves. (Milovanovic and Henry 2002, 2).

Given this perspective, theorists, policy makers, and practitioners "coproduce a discourse that gives form and permanence to the very entity that they and we, collectively despise. Therein we are all imprisoned" (2002).[22] Prisons are not separated from society within which they are located; rather, there is more continuity between the two than public discourse recognizes.[23] In penal discourse we construct categories of the other separated from the conditions within which they and we find ourselves. In this language system, distinctions are made which become reified. Bosworth (1999b) explores this notion in her ethnography of three women prisons in England. She shows how identities are constructed within the ongoing conflict of various discourses. Some of these constructions materialize supportive of the passive woman prisoner; however, others undermine the otherwise monolithic meaning structure imposed by a phallocentrically-organized prison. Thus, even though prevalent practices witness coproduction of the identity of passive femininity, Bosworth indicates that opportunities do exist for resistance and for developing an alternative oppositional discourse. Similarly, Thomas and Milovanovic (1999) demonstrate how constitutive penology could be brought to bear on the study of jailhouse lawyers. As we explained in the previous section, because jailhouse lawyers accept as given legal discourse and legal signifiers and work within their constraints, they are, as a result, coproducers of the ideology and institutions we call law and the legal.

We see this constitutive theme of coproduction in Martha Duncan's (1996) work, *Romantic Outlaws, Beloved Prisons: The Unconscious Meaning of Punishment*. In her analysis she sees "criminals and noncriminals . . . [who] live together in a symbiotic as well as an adversarial relationship, needing each other, serving each other, living *for* as well as *off* each other, enriching each other's lives in profound and surprising ways" (1996, ix). Echoing Kristeva's (1982) analysis of the "abject," she concludes that we both admire the criminal and resist this admiration; the criminal represents a break from order, but it is our very commitment to this order that buttresses our identity and meaning. Hence, this dialectic remains unresolved in our ongoing relation with those who break the law. She then argues how the metaphor of "slime" comes to represent the criminal which finds its origination in "unconscious and forbidden allure" (1996, 4). Throughout her inquiry, Duncan relies on Freudian dynamics to explain these various aversions and attractions.

A Lacanian analysis would begin with Kristeva's notion of the abject, then indicate how metaphoric displacements produce new signifiers that come to stand for previous signifiers which now become repressed in the unconscious.[24] However, what keeps the new signifiers resonating with an old (seemingly forgotten) sensibility, are the repressed original signifiers that always seek to "speak," that always "insist." In Duncan's dependence on Freud, she can only conclude that "the prisoner's exalted conception of the prison and the noncriminal's glamorous vision of lawbreakers are both manifestations of a romantic yearning . . . a desire to escape from the mundane world-as-it-is into a nobler and more meaningful time and place. Such romanticism serves to defend against the narcissistic wound or our relative puniness and mortality" (1996, 5).

An affirmative postmodern analysis does not endorse this reading. This is the manifestation of the skeptical form. Rather, we situate ourselves in the optimistic spirit of Deleuze and Guattri, Kristeva, Irigaray and second wave thinkers such as Cornell (1999) and Butler (1990, 1993, 1999). Their respective contributions take up the challenge of establishing being and meaning in postmodern society. In this view, new sources of becomings can be initiated, new full bodies without organs can materialize, new transpraxis discourses, contingently based, can emerge, and a new sense of identification and of identities can find expression. For constitutive penologists, imprisonment experiences indicate the vast variability, the will to meaning, the possibilities of transcending the limitations of space,[25] the incredible vitality of a subject-in-process under the most compelling of circumstances.

Arrigo (2001b) also has developed constitutive penology, especially in his notion of "transcarceration." This concept stands for the ongoing routing of criminal and mentally ill offenders from one type of institution to another, with a common discourse emerging that provides a hyper-reality within which identities and meanings are constructed. In Arrigo's (2001b, 183) words: "What we discovered is how language and the agency-structure duality implicated in the coproduction of reality limited the role performances of the participants investigated, leaving little room to renegotiate their identities." Even the kept employ clinical language and other languages of control in their everyday constructions of reality and identity. Although Irving Goffman (1961) suggested that this could indeed be a strategic use of language for purposes of empowerment, we argue that in this situation the kept are coproducers of the very language that controls them. What is reified, then, is a sedimented discourse and master signifiers that limit what could be said. In this sense, repetition assures domination. However, revolutionaries must seek to create practices that subvert repetition. Postmodern analysis, informed by first and second wave French scholars, offer some possible directions for developing these strategies.

Discussion: Emergence of Political Resistance and Replacement Discourses

What does the material on confinement law and prison resistance, aided by first and second wave French scholars and activists, suggest to us about the possibility of social change? We posit that resistance is a necessary, but not a sufficient, condition, for the transformation to the better society.[26] As Wendy Brown (1995, 49; cited in Bosworth, 129) has said:

> Sharing with identity politics an excessively local viewpoint and tendency toward positioning without mapping, the contemporary vogue of resistance is more a symptom of postmodernism's crisis of political space than a coherent response to it . . . Resistance goes nowhere in particular, has no inherent attachments, and hails no particular vision; as Foucault makes clear, resistance is an effect of and reaction to power, not an abrogation of it.

Thus, in Foucault's view, as endorsed by Howe, when the revolutionary or activist functions to merely provide the grounds for the subaltern to speak, this misses the point.[27] First, this line of analysis echoes a rather conservative reaction-negation dynamics. Second, the subaltern always and already speaks in a coproduced discourse that limits the embodiment of desire, militates against speaking "true words" (Freire 1972), and is thwarted with aspirations of saying more. This is not an argument suggesting "false consciousness," the nails already have been hammered on this coffin. Rather, it is to note that existing discourses always limit the embodiment of desire. Thus, when the activist (for the mentally ill on death row; for persons incarcerated) simply privileges speakers from their positions (standpoints) of disenfranchisement without offering something more, then the rebel fails to address the concerns expressed by Freire (1972, 1985; see also JanMohammed 1994) identifying the coproduction of "reality" codifications, impacting the dispossessed.

For Freire (1972), dialogical pedagogical practices enable one's true words to find expression. Similarly, Lacan's (1991) work on the four discourses indicates how the discourse of the *master* and *hysteric* often deny the subaltern a place from which a legitimate "I" can take up residence to speak. Thus, resistance is a necessary condition.[28] However, standpoint epistemology does not go far enough. It is at this point that Paulo Freire's dialogical pedagogy and its implications for border crossings, along with Judith Butler's call for "contingent universalities" blend with Jacques Lacan's discourse of the *analysis*.

In addition, though, for a dialogical and transparent cultural intervention, cultural revolutionaries (activists) must also be receptive to becoming student, in the position of the *hysteric*, and to being informed by the flow of novel information in coming to terms with her or his own incompleteness. In other words, there remains an oscillation in standpoints out of which student becomes teacher, teacher becomes student, as the Lacanian "a," *le plus de jouir*, is sought expression and embodiment in new, more reflective, but yet resistive to closure, forms of master signifiers. This integration suggests a direction in establishing the sufficient conditions for the emergence of alternative master signifiers that better embody desire, that provide more open-ended conceptualizations in a constantly changing society, and that can be the basis for producing more critical understandings of being and social structure.[29]

Moreover, these master signifiers should also materialize in ways that do not engender further harms of reduction or repression. The final challenge would be to specify how these alternative master signifiers would be of such form as to imply replacement suggestions for establishing new positional, provisional, and relational vocabularies of meaning. Cornell (1998b) explores this notion. Not only does she advocate for "utopian thinking," but also for the safeguarding and expansion of the "imaginary domain."[30] Thus, new master signifiers would not only emerge, but also would be sutured to alternative images of the possible.

CONCLUSION

This chapter focused on confinement law and forms of prison resistance, drawing on the insights of first and second wave French postmodernist thought. In both instances, we indicated several alternative lines of critical inquiry that could lead to a more fully informed rearticulation of mental illness, confinement, execution, prison practices, penal identity, and resistance. Each of these phenomena was significant for better comprehending institutional control in psychiatric or penal settings and for envisioning new hypotheses for further research. Accordingly, we invite readers to devise more refined analyses that specify the "sufficient" conditions in which more genuine social justice practices can (and must) emerge.

CHAPTER 5

Critical Race Theory and Postmodern Analysis: Strength in Dialectical Unity

INTRODUCTION

Critical race theory finds itself in an uneasy alliance with both law and post-modern analysis.[1] Many CRT proponents argue that they do not have the luxury to remain in theoretical, abstract discussions or in more esoteric discourse, especially since the reality of repressive practices in law are ubiquitous and are a daily occurrence.[2] Thus, their analysis privileges pragmatism. As Mari Matsuda (1996, 6, 24, 48) asserts, "legalism is a tool of necessity . . . our critique is goal oriented." Law is one of the few weapons available to correct wrongs, "a tool of progressive social change" (1996, 48). However, other CRT scholars have acknowledged the usefulness of postmodern analysis in law (Crenshaw 1993, 114; Matsuda et al. 1993, 5–6). In addition, consider Matsuda's (1996, 47) observations, reflecting on the first formal annual meeting (1989) of CRT: "it was critical because we criticized and because we respected and drew on the tradition of postmodern critical thought then popular with left intellectuals." On yet other occasions, some key concepts—such as the notion of the effect of the unconscious—have been given much weight in theorizing. For example, Charles Lawrence's notion of "unconscious racism" in law (1987) and Richard Delgado and Jean Stefancic's (2001, 44) cursory integration of Lyotard's (1984) notion of "differand" have been important conceptualizations for the CRT agenda.

In this chapter, we suggest some possible integrations of first and second wave French postmodern social theory with critical race theory. As such, we argue for the development of additional insights relevant to the forms, bases and effects of racism, impeding progressive social change practices. Accordingly, we concentrate on three areas: storytelling and narrative construction; the wherewithal of subjectivity, particularly its intersectional forms; and an alternative, nontraditional methodology for understanding and for transpraxis. However, before we proceed, some provisional background material on CRT and what it signifies are in order.

CRITICAL RACE THEORY: AN OVERVIEW

The core critical race theory concepts have been articulated[3] by Delgado and Stefancic (2001, 6–9):

1. that racism is ordinary, not aberrational . . . the usual way society does its business . . .

2. our system of white-over-color . . . serves important purposes [functions], both psychical and material . . .

3. race and races are products of social thought and relations . . . races are categories that society invents, manipulates, or retires when convenient.

Given the progressive orientation delineated above, we note that CRT goes well beyond more traditional civil rights analysis. Indeed, it critiques such things as formal equality before the law, neutral principles in law, and legal reasoning and rationalism (2001, 3). Moreover, CRT focuses on understanding forms of oppression as well as actively seeking to change them. One dimension of this is the emergence of new CRT theories. Indeed, just as the formal beginnings of CRT could be traced to a differentiation within critical legal studies and the criticisms developed by feminist jurisprudence, we also note further differentiation with the development of LatCrit (latino/a), theory, queer-crit theory, and Asian-American studies. These conceptualizations represent additional lines of radical inquiry expanding or transforming the evolving CRT agenda (2001, 6).

MOMENTS OF INTEGRATION AND SYNTHESIS

Narrative, Storytelling, and Postmodern Thought

One camp[4] within CRT argues that oppression is found in discursive activities, wholesale categories, and nominal practices (Delgado and Stefancic 2001, 17). Storytelling based on every day experiences (i.e., slave narratives) in the form of autobiographies, parables, novels, and "counterstories" hold the potential for raising the repressed or denied voices of African Americans and other disenfranchised peoples (Bell 1987). Narrative theory argues that some stories have greater weight (e.g., in courtroom testimony) than others. "Language can construct understanding, language can assault, and language can exclude. Words have power . . . words are part of the struggle" (Matsuda 1996, xiii). In law, stories often disguise hidden forms of racism (i.e., unconscious racism, see Lawrence 1987).

We contend that critical race theory can find a scholarly ally in the work of postmodern analysis. We begin with Lacan and the usefulness of his discussion of the "four discourses." As recounted in chapter 1, Lacan (1991) developed the discourse of the *master* and *hysteric*. The discourse of the *master* prioritizes the speaker, driven by more unconscious axioms of truth. The receiver enacts these "truths" in producing knowledge and a circumscribed form of understanding. However, borrowing from CRT, speakers come from the position of differential power in hierarchical relations. In the discourse of the *hysteric* (interpreted here not in the strict clinical sense, but in the oppositional, defiant, or rebellious sense), the disenfranchised often succumb to using dominant signifiers and forms of reality construction when expressing their plight. Thus, when recipients enact knowledge and develop an understanding of reality, they remain *pas-toute*, incomplete. In effect, they are denied a more authentic connectedness to their inner beings in relation to others (see, for example aboriginal women before the law in Australia, Stacey 1996). However, precisely because this situation manifests itself, another form of *jouissance* remains available to subjects. This is the *jouissance* of the body, inexpressible in dominant discourse.

Interestingly, the oppressed, or the disenfranchised more generally, hold a disproportionate amount of capital, especially in terms of potentially developing alternative visions of human relations and social interaction. Contrastingly, the dominant order finds itself in feedback loops privileging its own hierarchies where they remain decidedly foremost. In this context, replacement visions of being human are repressed, dismissed, or, in the extreme, quashed. Thus, we see that some signifying practices are located in the dominant position, while others are in the minority position. Consequently, CRT scholars advocate for "perspectivism" and "standpoint" focused discourse.

These dualities have been well studied by Jacques Derrida (1977, 1978, 1981). One term of the duality remains privileged, but depends on its being, its existence, through its tension with the other term. In speaking the dominant discourse, the trace of the disenfranchised other remains in continuous relation. Lyotard's (1984) notion of "differand," suggests how concepts (such as "justice," "rights," "responsibility," etc.) often develop conflicting meanings (Delgado and Stefancic 2001, 44). Further, power differentials often determine whose meaning is legitimate. From this analysis, some postmodernist implications follow. For example, given Cixous's (1986) notion of *l'écriture féminine* (woman's writing), a new discourse for the dispossessed might seem not only possible but also warranted. In addition, following Derrida's analysis, some CRT scholars might argue for a "reversal of hierarchies" to correct the privileging of the binary term of the dualities, especially since it produces marginalizing (legal) system effects.

However, affirmative postmodern analysis contends that "reversal of hierarchies" serves only to reestablish dominant standpoints. Thus, Drucilla Cornell's (1999, 147) integration of Luce Irigaray's (1985b) perspective on "mimesis"—a position in which subordination is continuously disrupted and transformed into an affirmation of difference and respectability—and her integration of Cixous's (1976) notion of "retelling of the myth" (see also, Klages 1997), are offered in support of "utopian thinking" and the protection of the "imaginary domain" (Cornell 1999, 159). This is a place in which differences, identities, being, and relations are endlessly reconstituted. It is within the imaginary domain that the play of metaphor and metonymy provide for the slippage of meaning. This is where the excess, the *plus-de-jouir*, the *pas-toute*, are allowed new articulations that are the basis for alternative signifying practices.

Similarly, Judith Butler (1990, 1993) has advocated the idea of practices that subvert repetition. Repetition can be understood as a feedback loop in signifying relations, simply reaffirming what already is. This is consistent with Jean Baudrillard's (1983b) conception of the "hyperreal;" a condition in which we find the establishment of a discursive construction followed by copies of this construction, followed by copies of copies, and so forth. In this arrangement, the replicas or copies *ad infinitum* become the basis of social action and human identities.

To displace this sedimented (and alienating) line of thinking and way of being, Butler (1999, 179) advocates for the development of "a language between languages . . . it will be the labour of transaction and translation which belongs to no single site, but is the movement between languages, and has its final destination in this movement itself." Thus, in this view, the debate between essentialism versus nonessentialism resolves itself in the direction of the latter. Things are forever in-process, akin to what Kristeva (1984) refers to as a "subject-in-position." It is not possible to "capture" these relations in static discourses, categories, identities, or conceptualizations. Things are always contingent.

Based on the insights of first and second wave postmodern social theory, we understand that the prevalence of power inequalities have been responsible for the stabilization of some stories at the expense of several others. Moreover, we note how dominant narratives, with their exclusionary effects, establish the artificial categories of race, gender, and class. Indeed, these categories are simulated and contrived, consistent with the dominant discourse in use, because of their discursive makeup and because, as a consequence, their meanings are multiple and fluid, signifying that they could be other than, more than, what they are or have become.

A particular analysis bringing out the differences in stories is Gilles Deleuze and Felix Guattari's (1986) discussion of "minor literature." It is "that which a minority constructs within a major language," and which: (1) "has a high coefficient of deterritorialization" (1986, 16); (2) includes a high political content ("the individual concern . . . becomes all the more necessary, indispensable, magnified, because a whole other story is vibrating within it"); and (3) "takes on collective value" ("there are no possibilities for an individuated enunciation that would belong to this or that 'master' and that could be separated from a collective enunciation") (1986, 16–17). In short, minor literature is revolutionary. It debunks dominant myths and stories, and resurrects, ground up alternative readings. This notion, then, has very particular relevance to those developing a replacement narrative. It suggests how these forms may develop and how they could be the loci from which spring alternative constructions of reality, subjectivity, and possible ways of being and becoming.

Subjectivity and Postmodern Thought

The Lacanian (1977) informed conception of the subject is one that indicates a being intimately and inseparably connected to discourse. CRT is uniquely situated to further and deepen this analysis, especially in its assessment of the subject as an "intersectional" being; that is, one finding her/himself at the intersections of various structural locations (race, gender, and class in particular). As previously described, these categories are discursively constructed.

The notion of "intersectionality" has been a key conception within the more recent work of CRT scholars (Crenshaw 1993, 111–32; Delgado and Stefancic 2001, 51–63). For example, intersectionality suggests that women of color find themselves "subject to multiple systems of subordination" (Crenshaw 1993, 113). Elsewhere, Kimberle Crenshaw suggests a connectedness between intersectionality and the contributions of postmodern analysis (1993, 114). Whereas Lacan makes use of a monolithic discourse (e.g., the phallic Symbolic Order), CRT indicates the plurality of discourses in existence. This distinction notwithstanding, Lacan's (1977) logic regarding the intimacy of the subject to her/his discourse(s) remains. Thus, integrating these two perspectives provides a richer, more robust understanding of pragmatically oriented beings in structures of domination.

Crenshaw (1993, 114) argues that structural practices and class disadvantage ("structural intersectionality"), discursive practices ("political intersectionality"), and imaginary practices ("representational intersectionality") "erase" women of color. These women are denied full standing in the social formation. Of course, this is the notion of *pas-toute*, not all, or incompleteness that several first-wave postmodern thinkers offer. Middle class women have a different worldview ("perspectivism") than lower-class, African-American women, who, in turn, have a different view of the world than upper middle-class African-American women. In short, given these various standpoints, CRT proponents argue for multiple expressions of consciousness.

According to CRT, intersectionality can also lead to various, opposing positions on lawbreakers in their community. For example, in the "politics of distinction" the Black community dis-identifies with the lawbreaker in its community and advocates the full use of state power to control the offender (see Delgado and Stefancic 2001, 55). However, in the "politics of identification," the Black community identifies with its "race rebels" and dissuades the state from policing them (i.e., youth are seen as changeable and the Black community tries to instill change rather than having the criminal justice system attempt to deal with the lawbreaker).

These CRT observations also can be conceptualized as identification and disidentification with the "other" in the Lacanian (1977) schema. The other becomes an object of desire in so much as it reflects or mirrors one's own being. This disidentification process resonates with Katheryn Russell's (1998) notion of "black protectionism." This occurs when publicly fallen heroes witness African-American communities rising in support. However, as Russell argues, black protectionism does not necessarily extend to African-American women. This notion of contradictory identifications also can be fruitfully connected to Kristeva's (1982) notion of "abjection." The lawbreaker is both seen as an object of desire, a person who visibly challenges or resists the oppressive system, but yet is also the target of hostility and repulsion for the harms inflicted within the African-American community or for the lack of support of the Black community after attaining success (i.e., respectively, Rodney King, O. J. Simpson).

Postmodern analysis, in suggesting the three interacting orders (Real, Symbolic, Imaginary), would be useful here in providing the various psychological and sociopsychological mechanisms by which various identifications unfold with their corresponding impact. For example, in Lacan's (1977) Schema L the four cornered subject (I, other, moi, Other) and the two main constitutive diagonals (imaginary, between the moi or self and the other; unconscious, between the Other and the I) show how the "other" or (*autre*) is being constructed, how the self sees itself through these others, how the unconscious provides signifiers for discursive construction, and how an "I," as a representative of the subject, emerges in particular discourses where it may speak. This conceptualization of the decentered subject provides a useful way of understanding the multiple determinants of consciousness, some of which indeed may be contradictory.

In Lacan's (1977) topography on the unconscious, we see emerging only relatively stable crystallizations revolving around the two main diagonals, and we see how the subject may indeed take many relatively stabilized forms. In the case of Delgado and Stefancic's (2001) example regarding the politics of identification and distinction, we witness the subject in some cases identifying with the lawbreaker, and in others disidentifying with the lawbreaker. Moreover, in each instance, the speaking subject momentarily finds stability in its self-conception as it relates to the other. Given one of the two identifications, an already established discourse awaits usage in discursively constructing social reality. Further, given the selection of one identification over the other, two perhaps equally compelling narratives can emerge explaining the same instance of lawbreaking behavior. Thus, the further expansion of one discourse over the other can indeed culminate in what Baudrillard (1983b) has referred to as hyper-reality. Within hyper-reality one logical, rational rendition can be established which also becomes a coherent point for the subject's own stability: it provides a basis for the emergence of an "I" which can take up discursive subject-positions within which to speak.

Therefore, given a plurality of psychical "standpoints," various conflicting definitions of reality and of self will be produced. On the one hand, this produces an unstable basis for the development of a coherent "I" which can speak; on the other hand, it is the precondition for the development of subjects-in-process (Kristeva 1984). Based on the foregoing analysis, we note that critical race theory finds itself strategically linked to a central theme of postmodern analysis; namely, the inseparability of the subject and discourse. Accordingly, both postmodern scholars as well as CRT proponents could find future integrations quite fruitful.

Methodology: Jurisprudence of Color and Postmodern Thought

The third area to explore in which the insights of French postmodern inquiry can be integrated with the theoretical formulations of critical race theory is the potential for articulating a radical methodology. In particular, we draw attention to what others have defined as the "jurisprudence of color," or "outsider jurisprudence" (Crenshaw 1993, 18–19). In this methodology, CRT "attempts to know history from the bottom. . . ." This is an approach which has "forced these scholars to sources often ignored: journals, poems, oral histories, and stories from their own experiences of life in a hierarchically arranged world" (1993). This orientation is "realist," not "nihilist," and embraces "the pragmatic use of law as a tool for social change . . . it is jurisprudence recognizing, struggling within, and utilizing contradiction, dualism, and ambiguity" (Matsuda et al. 1993, 19). In this section, we explore one particular approach within this tradition dealing with consciousness raising and "learning to talk."

Matsuda (1996, 124–29) advocates one pedagogical form in "learning to talk" (in a classroom setting). In her pedagogy, she attempts to create a space in which students become teachers and teachers became students by asking classroom learners/educators to tell funny but troublesome stories where identities were mistaken (1996, 125). Following Matsuda (1996), consider this scenario: recall a time when you heard a discussion about a colleague who is a white woman, a woman of color, or a man of color implicitly or explicitly questioning their ability. How did you respond? Matsuda's focus in creating this space is manifold. She explodes stereotypes, sensitizes each person to the condition of the other, unearths disenfranchised voices, and raises consciousness.[5]

By employing Lacan's (1991) four discourses (see Bracher 1993; Arrigo 1998; Milovanovic 1996, see also 2002, chapter 8), postmodern analysis can be seen as furthering this project. For Mark Bracher, the classroom experience should be informed by a discourse of the *analyst* whereby literature is analyzed and unconscious desires, identifications, and anxieties are unearthed. As Bracher explains, this is where "ego-alien impulses will be undermined" (1993, 191). In Lacan's discourse of the *analyst*, the analyst (read teacher) reflects back to the student the left-out, the *past-toute*. The student enacts this information in producing knowledge. In the discourse of the *analyst*, the student undergoes consciousness-raising when s/he begins to confront the master signifiers that constitute her/his ego, and begins to dis-identify with and separate from those signifiers tending toward closure and intolerance. In the space created in the classroom, students begin to replace master signifiers with alternatives ones that are "less exclusive, restrictive, and conflictual" (1993, 72). These new master signifiers are "less absolute, exclusive, and rigid in [their] establishment of the subject's identity, and more open, fluid, and processual: constituted, in a word, by relativity and textuality" (1993, 73). These new master signifiers remain engaged "in a continuous flight from meaning and closure, in a displacement that never ceases" (1993).

Arrigo (1998) has suggested the use of Lacan's (1991) discourse of the *analyst* in law classes to introduce students in an alternative form of reality construction. The law professor could create an alternative space to the one marked by the Socratic style and a "banking" logic of education. Rather, this replacement space would allow students to confront their embedded master signifiers that support the ego, and to gradually coproduce alternative master signifiers that could be the basis of narrative constructions benefiting disenfranchised peoples.

Milovanovic (1996a; see also, 2002: chapter 8) has offered an integration of Lacan's (1991) discourse of the *analyst* in combination with the discourse of the *hysteric*,[6] Freire's dialogical pedagogy (1972), and chaos theory in suggesting how alternative master signifiers may take form and how conscientization (Freire 1972) develops. Milovanovic argues that the "cultural revolutionary" (i.e., teacher, practitioner, activist, social change agent, etc.) is both teacher and student. As teacher, s/he finds her/himself in the position of the analyst (upper left-hand corner in the schema) in the discourse of the *analyst*; as student (or "hysteric"), s/he finds her/himself in the position of opposing, challenging, questioning, defying. The subject alternates between the two, never fully stabilized in either. Freire's work on consciousness-raising assumes that both the cultural revolutionary and the "hysteric" can work together in deconstructing systems of oppression, coproducing new signifiers which become the basis for more authentic narrative constructions. His insights ground theoretical discourse in concrete struggles of disenfranchised people. Hence, his contributions are an important component for establishing a more genuine transpraxis.

Chaos theory also is useful here. It suggests how rigid point attractors give way to strange attractors where ambivalence, differences, contradictions, ambiguity, and the novel are encountered. The strange attractor traces the nonlinear flow of desire.

In applying this integration, Milovanovic looked to Gerald Lopez's (1994) work on "rebellious laywering." Lopez suggested how everyday lawyers, particularly public defenders, could develop an alternative "dialogical problem-solving" approach to law whereby the client and lawyer together produced narratives, underwent "conscientization," and were both empowered in the process. Milovanovic argued that by integrating the components (chaos theory, Lacan's four discourses, Freire's dialogical pedagogy, Lopez's pragmatism), more liberating legal practices could take form that subsequently could be mapped to and applied in other relevant sociolegal contexts.

By utilizing the pedagogy of "learning to talk," critical race theory, in combination with the theoretical explications above, could be in an even better position to devise additional strategies relevant to a jurisprudence of color in legal pedagogy.[7] Stories could be coproduced, histories could be rewritten, voices and perspectives could be resurrected, and a developing center of new master signifiers could start taking form. These replacement narratives would be the basis of counterstorytelling, critical discursive constructions of what is, and visions of what could be.[8]

Another contribution of postmodern analysis to CRT comes from the phenomenon of racial profiling (Cole 1999). In this instance, we can conceptualize how the "other" is being constituted in an imaginary and symbolic manner, such that the construction is functional for the dominant group(s). As Delgado and Stefancic (2001, 7) argue, "races are categories that society invents, manipulates, or retires when convenient." Indeed, given the dominant order, race is more responsive to "interest convergence" (Bell 1987; Delgado and Stefancic 2001, 41). Interest convergence means that change takes place only when it is seen as beneficial to dominant groups,[9] or when contradictions between our practices and ideals become so excessive that a "contradiction-closing case" emerges (Delgado and Stefancic 2001, 31). Examples of this are found in novel rulings tendered by the United States Supreme Court, including the case of *Brown v. Board of Education* (1954). As Derrick Bell (1980) notes, this was a decision where concessions indeed were made. This notwithstanding, the driving force was less "humanistic" and more a factor of maintaining legitimation in the social formation. In short, what were being mobilized were the ideological and repressive functions of law.

Postmodern analysis can be integrated with racial profiling to show how the "other" takes on historical forms geared more to political economic conditions. In undermining racial profiling practices, postmodern thought indicates how the Symbolic Order can be reconstituted to accommodate contradictions in the development of new signifiers that reflect "understanding," "compassion," and "support" for the disenfranchised. Further, postmodern inquiry shows how the Imaginary Order can be expanded to accommodate for differences in identity, being, and self-hood.

Another example of how postmodern analysis can be usefully synthesized with critical race theory is in the area of jury nullification. This phenomenon occurs when jurors vote not to acquit following wide police misconduct or actions believed to be predominantly discriminatory against a particular group (Conrad 1998). In this instance, jury members do not situate themselves in the privileged (legal) discursive structures in rendering decisions; rather, they situate themselves in an alternative, more oppositional linguistic coordinate system within which to construct the "what happened" in the case. Thus, they decide the matter at hand guided by a concern for social rather than criminal justice. In the Lacanian schema, the jurors dis-identify with the dominant legal discourse and take up a residence as an "I" in an alternative, grounds-up discourse of lived experience. Momentarily, then, "minor literature" (Deleuze and Guattari 1986) has predominated over "major literature."

Relatedly, we note the issue of prosecutorial misconduct, especially when invoking, implicitly or otherwise, racial stereotypes in "closing arguments" to the jurors (see Johnson 2001). In this situation, racial imagery and metaphors are strategically, or, at least, unconsciously used (Lawrence 1987) to suggest to jurors how a Black defendant is connected with uninhibited lawbreaking behavior. Sheri Johnson (2001, 79) offers the following compelling example:

> Bennett, who is African American, was sentenced [to death] by an all white jury . . . The prosecutors told jurors that [the victim's encounter with Bennet] was "like running into King Kong on a bad day." (Closing argument by South Carolina prosecutor in 2000)

We contend that postmodern analysis could be integrated with CRT to show how the Lacanian (1977) notion of the play of metaphor and metonymy suggest certain reality constructions by jurors, which then materialize in presumptions of guilt.[10]

A Question of Validity (authority/legitimacy): A Postmodern Intervention

Given critical race theory's focus on stories, narratives, and counterstories, a number of commentators have profoundly and forcefully questioned its validity (Tushnet 1992; Farber and Sherry 1993; Kennedy 1989).[11] For example, as critics assert, by what standard can we judge the validity of these stories? Moreover, how are CRT claims to be evaluated or judged? What about the truthfulness of narratives based on a jurisprudence of color? What measure can be employed to assess their veracity? And finally, and most pointedly, is the challenge to narrative jurisprudence proper. As opponents question, doesn't this endeavor represent an endless storytelling enterprise where anything goes?

In perhaps one of the more well-developed critiques in the literature on the issue of validity, Daniel Farber and Suzanna Sherry (1993) found objectionable the reliance of the emotive dimension of CRT without reasoned analysis. Richard Delgado's (1993, 666) response to Farber and Sherry (who do not totally dismiss narrative jurisprudence but accept a weaker version of it), was that "majoritarians tell stories too. But the ones they tell—about merit, causation, blame, responsibility, and racial justice—do not seem to them like stories at all, but the truth." He also argued that CRT does acknowledge the importance of case authority, statistics, and doctrinal analysis (1993, 668; see also, Delgado 1989, 1997).

One early attempt at establishing some criteria in validity measures is "in terms of its ability to advance the interests of the *outsider* community" (Coombs 1992, 713, emphasis added). Delgado's (1993, 668) suggests that the counterstory itself moves to foster this end when it seeks to "jar, mock, or displace a tenet of the majoritarian faith." Moreover, for Delgado, since racism is so embedded in the dominant discourse, our very attempts to provide counterstories that are strongly confrontational will be seen as nothing short of incoherent (1993, 669). Delgado concludes by suggesting that CRT is in its adolescent stage, still developing, and that validity standards await further refinement.

Other critiques from the Left (Tushnet 1992) contend that the work of Derrick Bell (1987) and Patricia Williams (1987) fail in terms of "narrative integrity." Gary Peller's (1992) response has been that Tushnet misses the point by developing a standard of validity rooted in the positivistic sciences. To this observation we add that Tushnet's critique is steeped in modernist thought and logic.

Postmodern analysis can contribute to this discussion in providing alternative standards of validity. For example, Norman Denzin's (1997) groundbreaking book exploring the basis for a postmodern ethnography argues for an alternate set of criteria to the modernist orientation, anchored more in emotionality, feeling, subjectivity, and so forth. As Denzin (1997, 9) states in his work at the outset, validity should be replaced with "legitimation" and "authority." He then suggests three sources in the development of validity. First, a "good text" is one that "exposes how race, class, and gender work their ways into the concrete lives of interacting individuals" (1997, 10). This is what P. Lather (1986) describes as "catalytic validity" or the degree to which a particular research project empowers and emancipates a research community (Denzin 1997, 10).

The second source of validity concerns "verisimilitude," or the degree to which a text maps the real. It is not absolute, but only approached. Another way to convey this notion is in the phenomenon of approximation or representation.

The third source of validity draws from the work of Lather (1993). This source entails the grouping of four conceptualizations: the ironic, the paralogic, rhizomatics, and the voluptuous.[12] We focus on the middle two notions.

Paralogic validity can be linked to Lyotard's (1984) work in *The Postmodern Condition*. Traced to and drawn from quantum mechanics and Thom's catastrophe theory, what is celebrated here is instability existing in otherwise stable dynamics. Relying on chaos theory, fractals, dissipative structures, and far-from-equilibrium conditions are validated. Turning to Ludwig Wittgenstein (1953), what is posited are the proliferation of "language games" wherein each represents the basis of logic, rationality and meaning. In short, parologic validity is akin to the ideals articulated by Lyotard (1984), as opposed to Habermas (1975, 1984) in his "ideal speech situation." For Lyotard, the attainment of consensus signifies the exception.

Along with paralogic validity is the "rhizomatic." This notion is borrowed from the commentaries authored by Deleuze and Guattari (1987). Denzin's (1997, 14, 23, 26) read of the rhizomatic is that it "represents attempts to present nonlinear texts with multiple centers in which multiple voices speak and articulate their definitions of the situation." The writings of James Joyce are exemplary on this point. The rhizomatic portrays how epiphanies may emerge that call out their own language that relate sound, words, and visions in some temporary stable forms. Denzin (1997, 26) succinctly explains how rhizomatic validity operates. As he observes,

> this will be a language that refuses the old categories, that reflexively and parasitically, in a rhizomatic manner . . . charts its own course against . . . repressive structures of history, economy, religion, race, class and gender . . . It will allow ordinary people to speak out and to articulate the interpretive theories that they use to make sense of their lives.

In short, the postmodern text is at best a "messy story." It defies closure. It defies finality. It works to rhizomatically create meaning anew. Hence, notions of validity in texts, whether legal or otherwise, must begin and unfold with this realization in mind.

CONCLUSION

As we have argued, critical race theory and postmodern analysis possess a great deal of compatibility. Each perspective can profoundly invigorate the other. Each perspective recognizes the inescapability of dialectical (nonlinear) historical development. The dialectics of struggle assumes no definable end, only subjects in process. The task ahead is to expand our imaginary and symbolic domains to entertain new modes of being, new interpersonal relations, and new forms of "structures" that encourage, rather than diminish, self- and social actualization.

CHAPTER 6

Cinema and Literary Texts, *Différance,*

and Social Justice Studies

INTRODUCTION

French postmodernist thought has contributed substantially to cultural studies and media analysis, and, in particular, to cinema studies. The Lacanian cinema model was developed in the 1970s to early 1980s in the work of C. Metz (1981) and Kaja Silverman (1983). At about the same time, the Birmingham cultural studies group actively engaged Louis Althusser's (1971) notion of "interpellation," offering a critique of capitalist economy. Subsequent to a number of second wave commentaries (e.g., Jameson 1981), feminists in particular, offered an alternative analysis of Lacan's work as applied to cinema. Their investigations provide valuable insight on the denial of voices for other disenfranchised peoples. Alternative Lacanian-based models can be developed from Kristeva's (1982) analysis of "abjection," Grosz's (1994) reconceptualization of the mind/body dualisms, Richard Dienst's (1994) Derridean and revisionist Marxist analysis, Patricia Clough's (2000) "autoaffection," and queer theory's assessment on the politics of sexuality (e.g., Clough 2000; Butler 1993, Grosz 1994).[1]

The beginning point for each of the above periodizations has been the notion of inexpressible voices and *différance* (e.g., for Lacan, "woman does not exist" in the phallocentric Symbolic Order). In this chapter, we develop each of them by indicating the various contributions made on behalf of first wave French postmodern social theorists (Barthes, Baudrillard, Lyotard, Derrida), as well as others (Benveniste, Jackobson). Along the way, we also suggest their contributions to law, criminology, and social justice.

LACANIAN MODEL (MIRROR, MIRROR ON THE WALL . . .)

The Lacanian model applied to cinema and literary analysis needs to be complimented by the notion of the spoken subject; that is, the viewer/reader of texts, and her acceptance of and identification with the discursive subject positions offered. By so doing, subjects begin to see the world as the director/writer suggests (Metz 1981; Silverman 1983).

This analysis draws from Émile Benveniste's (1971) position on the nature of the personal pronouns, "I" and "you." By themselves, neither pronoun has meaning outside of context. They are "shifters." Cinema and literary texts offer discursive subject positions with which to identify: the "I" is provided content in this context. The director makes use of lighting equipment, tape recordings, mixing of recording and sound, camera shots, editing, composition, the script employed, and the use of lap dissolves, fades, pans, zooms, and close-ups. All of these are connected with the notion of metaphor and metonymy; that is, the play of desire and its momentary materialization in images and signifiers. The director (much like a lawyer in a trial court) attempts to suggest certain readings of otherwise unexplainable and puzzling presentations.

The activities of the director resonate at a much deeper level with Lacan's notion of *manqué d'être*; a lack of being experienced primordially with the entrance of the infant into the Symbolic Order. This is unsettling to the subject. It is the notion of suture in which momentary connections between the imaginary and the symbolic produce meaning and *jouissance*.

Cinema employs a series of shots, reverse shots, and angles. In this production, certain shots are selected (paradigm) over others and placed in linear orderings (syntagm). Much like the unfolding of a dream so insightfully developed by Freud (1965) in *The Interpretations of Dreams*, the play of condensation and displacement gives form to unconscious desires. Indeed, the viewer/reader is often in a more passive state, approaching the sleep mode and, as such, is more receptive to some forms of suture over others. Desire is mobilized as lack is confronted. Fantasy, symbolized by Lacan as $ <> a$ (the S with a slash through it), finds the appropriate objects of desire that overcome this lack. Thus, during suture, gaps-in-being are temporarily overcome by the viewer/reader appropriating signifiers, endowing them with her/his desire. These signifiers then provide a degree of plausibility or meaning to the unfolding events. This activity is akin to what Roland Barthes (1974) defined as a "readerly text." This is a text that tends toward closure and finality. Of course, Barthes also made reference to the "writerly text." This is a text in which nonlinear readings are encouraged, where closure is impossible, where only temporary understanding can be attained, where, at best, momentary epiphanies arise.

The Lacanian filmic model prioritizes the mirror stage (pre-oedipal) in the imaginary development of the subject. It privileges traditional identifications (male, female) such that the male's role is that of voyeur (identification with the gaze) and the female's role is that of subject of the gaze (identification with the spectacle) (Mulvey 1990). In Laura Mulvey's (1990, originally 1975) early analysis, film plays on sexual differences already established at the mirror and the oedipal stage. In her account, the male subject is given the privileged power position as the viewing subject, and the female is given the subordinate position as the passive subject of the gaze.

The Lacanian cinema/literary text model, as developed by C. Metz (1981) and Kaja Silverman (1983), also suggests that at the deeper level of semiotic production, the primary process (condensation and displacement) accounts for meaning production. However, at the more conscious level, the secondary process of metaphor and metonymy accounts for the unique embodiment of desire. We note, though, that the play of the two in the context of existing forms (paradigm, syntagm) or particular genre (i.e., legal discourse), for example, ultimately generates specialized meaning.

Application of the Lacanian Cinema Model

Applications of this model to the advertisement industry (Williamson 1987), as well as to trial court proceedings are particularly instructive. The ad-industry often provides scenes in which the viewer finds her/himself lacking, and then provides objects of desire that can overcome this lack. When the subject recognizes the capability of the object of desire to overcome lack, the ad is successful ("things go better with coke").

Trial court proceedings can be likened to cinema. The lawyer (director), whether defense counsel or prosecutor, attempts to present a script to the jurors with suggestions as to the defendant's innocence (or guilt). The juror is much like the viewing subject who is provided suggestions as to how to overcome *manqué d' être*. Each makes use of metaphor and metonymy. Each is also bound by the constraints of the juridic linguistic coordinate system (e.g., deductive logic, rules of evidence, nonnarrative responses, courtroom procedures, as well as the use of allowable legal signifiers with which to create narratives). Thus, the lawyer (director) strives toward the establishment of a readerly text. The clash of the two litigants provides the grounds for a particular verdict by the juror.

In sum, the Lacanian cinema/literary model is established on the assumed inherent lack in the subject. Mobilized desire attempts to overcome this lack-in-being. It also plays on oedipal constructions whereby male and female subjects identify with particular master discursive subject positions within which they may take up residence as an "I" which can speak (*l' être parlant*). Thus, the male is often portrayed as the voyeur; the female is often depicted as the object of the gaze.

The director also can undo the conventional images he or she constructs in film. For instance, consider the film, *House of Games,* where reversals are presented. Initially, the female psychiatrist is the subject of a con game; however, she eventually turns the tables and cons the conner. In addition, consider the film *Thelma and Louis.* In this motion picture, conventional female roles are reversed. The female protagonists are not victims or vilified; they are not objects of the gaze.

Other examples come from trial court proceedings. To illustrate, consider the O. J. Simpson double murder case. The trial indicates how the jurors undermined the apparently overwhelming case against O. J. Simpson. Indeed, they reverted to a writerly text whereby an alternative reality was constructed based on the historic context of racism and brutality directed toward the African-American population by the Los Angeles police.

M. Doane's (1987, 1988) application of the "masquerade" is equally illustrative of the Lacanian cinema/literary text model. It is Doane's (1987) contention that women adopt a masquerade of femininity to compensate for their interpellation (Althusser 1971) as masculine subjects through the spectatorial process. In this way, Doane draws on Lacan's (1985), "The Meaning of the Phallas," to specify the conditions under which and the reasons why women flaunt their femininity (Holmund 1993). Since femininity is a masquerade, it creates a discursive gap between the woman and the image (1993, 213). This discursive opening is what enables women to generate alternative renderings of symbolic imagery, thereby promoting a more liberating feminist discourse. Most interesting is the fact that Doan's application of the masquerade can be applied to numerous and distinct forms of gendered identity, particularly as it relates to filmic imagery (e.g., lesbian butch, drag queen).

Relatedly, in his article, "Martial Arts Films and the Action-Cop Genre: Ideology, Violence and Spectatorshp," R. Schehr (2000a) closely relies on Doan's "masquerade" concept by emphasizing D. McKinney's (1984) view that violence in film forces spectators to consider their moral foundations.

According to this view, acts consisting of strong violence encourage engagement with filmic discourses, thereby opening up the possibility for greater spectatorial participation in the construction of meaning. Finally, L. Williams (1990) applies the idea of the masquerade to her analysis of pornographic film. Rather than becoming victims of a sadistic male gaze, women produce their own interpretations and meanings with regard to the images presented in pornography. To argue otherwise would promote an essentialism antithetical to the way spectators actually interpret images. Moreover, this kind of essentialism would generate even greater criticism of those relationships falling outside the bounds of the dominant heterosexual master narrative. In short, women are active consumers of filmic imagery. Through application of the masquerade, they construct a space that enables them to seek pleasure through a process that often contradicts surface appearances of discursive presentations.

Additional examples applying a more Lacanian-based cinema model are discernible. Two illustrations come readily to mind. The first focuses on "reality TV" police programming; the second focuses on detective fiction. The remainder of this section examines both phenomena.

Since the late 1980s a number of "reality TV" programs have emerged particularly with criminal justice themes. One version is exemplified in *Cops* where no narrator appears and short 7–8 minute vignettes are presented of police in patrol cars engaged in their work practices (Cavender 1998; Shon 1999). In the second version, exemplified by *America's Most Wanted*, we have a narrator authoritatively commenting on actors playing out a crime, and the criminal justice system bringing them to justice. Thus, we have visual and literary material that can correlate with Lacan's (1977) Imaginary and Symbolic Orders.

In these shows, the editor carefully crafts a complete story—from the beginning disorder and chaos fashioned by the criminal to the reestablishment of order (discourse of the *master*). This is a story constructed along the lines of Barthe's "readerly text." The viewer is encouraged to take up a discursive subject position in which s/he identifies with the police and with law and order. This is accomplished by contextualizing the police; that is, providing them with an identity and a legitimate function, while doing little to portray the plight of the citizen/suspect. In the reality television show *Cops*, the police often provide their own narrative (i.e., "what we have here is . . ."). This storytelling helps to overcome the gaps-in-being (see Doyle 1998). The viewer sutures over these gaps in a conventional manner, thereby supporting the ongoing centrality of "law and order." Moreover, by dis-identifying with the plight of the disenfranchised, the viewer is carefully encouraged to establish an "us" versus "them" mindset. In addition, *Cops*, presents a narrow range of crimes, minimizes the complexities of conflicts, focuses on certain groups, and has little to say about alternative resolutions outside of the ones devised by the police.

Hence, crime and the criminal can be likened to floating signifiers in circulation much like in Lacan's (1988) examination of Poe's *Purloined Letter*. The meaning (signified) is always structurally determined as the criminal and her/his imagery circulates within the media (Milovanovic 2002, 165). Indeed, the momentary meanings established in radio, print, and television outlets discursively help to constitute the "true" (i.e., circumscribed) meaning in subsequent street encounters in ways suggested by constitutive criminology (Henry and Milovanovic 1996). This attests to the primacy of the signifier, or as Lacan emphatically says, "the signifier represents the subject for another signifier." However, A. Doyle's (1998, 108) view, consistent with ours, is that this is not a linear development; rather, media has a "cultivation" effect on street encounters and constructed meanings.[2] Police and police recruits/cadets also are provided a contextualization and signifiers by which to construct events. Thus, a nonlinear feedback mechanism exists by which a hyper-reality (Baudrillard 1983a) is continuously reconstructed[3]; what is real and what is fictional becomes blurred, reality and appearance collapse and collide (Cavender 1998; Dolye 1998).

A second application of Lacanian cinema analysis can be linked to the literary genre of detective fiction. Two rather different versions can be presented. The first comes from Allison Young's (1996) chapter, "The Scene of the Crime" in her book, *Imagining Crime*. The second comes from Norman Denzin's (1997) chapter, "The Private Eye," in his work, *Interpretive Ethnography*.

In Young's version, the seduction for reading detective fiction stems from the self-administered arousal of fear, suspense, voyeurism, and the ability (albeit vicarious) to bring order to an otherwise chaotic world. In these genres, the hero or the detective is a positivist criminologist making use of semiotics and providing order to an otherwise disordered world.[4] The protagonist suggests ways to overcome the gaps-in-being numerously confronted in the big city. The hero helps restore meaning, identity, order and stability (Young 1996, 86). In other words, the reader is encouraged to identify with the detective in seeing the world as s/he suggests. To the degree that this linear development takes place, the initial suspense and fear is overcome with a feeling of *jouissance* (Lacan's punning: *j'oui sense*, I hear sense).

The detective/hero also is portrayed with faults (e.g., Sherlock Holmes uses cocaine, Philip Marlowe is an excessive drinker, and James Burke's Dave

Robicheaux and John Straley's Sam Spade both have soiled personalities). This fact helps the reader recognize that the detective is not some mythical superhero beyond personal identification. Indeed, given the hero's faults, the reader can find some consulation knowing that even s/he can possess some of the powers being portrayed by the detective.

Moreover, when we are presented with the hero as a woman, she is often portrayed in the context of being liberated from the male-dominated home. However, Young (1996) tells us that often, in solving the crime, the conventional phallocentric Symbolic Order is reconstituted. Indeed, postmodern feminist detective fiction, according to Young—which abandons much of the conventional devices and plots—leaves her personally "very bored" (1996, 103). Thus, the readerly text is often continuously reaffirmed, and with it unquestioned assumptions of law, order, and consensus prevail.

Norman Denzin's (1997) analysis of the postmodern detective offers an alternative. His exemplifications are in the characters of James Burke and John Straley. In his view (1997, 174), "these writers attempt a form of discourse that captures a mobile, unstable consciousness recording its relationship to an ever-changing external world. This complex world, with its multiple perspectives, is then connected to a constantly changing external world, in which nothing is firm or certain. Consequently, there can be no single truth; the only truth is that of self-discovery—the moral rebirth of the detective." Thus, a Lacanian spin here is that an affirmative form of desire is aroused, one not based on lack, one more rooted in Deleuze and Guattari's (1987) notion of desire as production. The postmodern detective needs to be read in the context of a writerly text. Things are uncertain, meaning is fleeting and more open, identities are often unclear, stabilities are effervescent, the boundary between law and order is often crossed, the solutions to disorder are often complex.

REVISIONIST AND INTEGRATIVE LACANIAN CINEMA/LITERARY MODELS ("SHATTERED MIRRORS") AND INTERSECTIONAL STANDPOINTS

A number of Lacanian informed models have emerged questioning Lacan's apparently more conservative formulations. Although to a substantial degree they remain indebted to the work of Lacan, these models attempt to provide alternative notions to lack and to the strictures of the oedipal configurations.[5] In both film and literature these models provide new insight into how otherwise denied voices and "realities" can be given expression. In this portion of the chapter, we first offer an analysis of Kristeva's (1982) notion of abjection and its potential relevance in cinema and in literary texts, especially for suggesting alternative constructions in gender, race, class, and sexual preferences.

Kristeva, Shattered Mirrors, Abject and Abjection

Kristeva's Lacanian informed model traces the development of the subject to a prior point (pre-specular); that is, to the mirror stage and oedipal configurations. In other words, the fetus in the womb is already subjected to maternal rhythms, sounds, fluids—this is part of the "semiotic." The decisive break from the mother at the point of the infant's separation from her is with consequence. During the oedipal stage, while the more primordial factors related to the connectedness and separation from the mother are repressed, they constantly seek expression. To the extent that they do, these primoridial factors disrupt the masculine order, calling forth alternative codifications. Tina Chanter's (2002) reading of Kristeva's notion of "abjection" provides a possible reconceptualization in film theory, allowing for a better understanding of the emergence of the feminine as well as other disenfranchised voices (race, class, gender, and sexual preferences).

In penological research, the application of "abjection" based on a more Freudian account is supplied by Duncan (1996) in her text, *Romantic Outlaws, Beloved Prisons*. Her notion of "slime" simultaneously indicates revulsion and hostility toward the lawbreaker, as well as attraction toward this offender (who offers an imaginary liberation from order). In legal research, we find the concept of "abjection" employed in explaining sex offender legislation (Lynch 2002) and the criminal regulation of consensual sex (Sutherland 2000).

In this section, we want to briefly review some applications to filmic texts concerning sexual preference (Neil Jordan's *The Crying Game*), and to literary texts concerning: (1) postcolonial writings and Maori identity (Keri Hulme's *The Bone People*); (2) parodies in revisionist fairy tales providing insight into gender relations (Angela Carter's *Bloody Chamber* and *The Tiger's Bride*); and (3) other novels concerning gender constructions (Jane Gardam's *The Queen of the Tambourine)*.

Although criticized for its apparent demonization and racial stereotypes (Edge 1995; hooks 1994), Neil Jordan's *The Crying Game* explores the transvestite identity. The film is about Fergus (Stephen Rea), hiding his identity from the Irish Republican Army (IRA), and his shock about learning that his loved one, Dil (Jaye Davidson), a black man, is anatomically a man. Dil works as a hairdresser. The third key figure is Jody (Forest Whitaker) who is portrayed as articulate, liberated, and "straight." Jody is from Antigua, West Indies, a former British colony. The fourth key figure, Jude, helps capture Jody. In the situation of being a hostage of the IRA, we see a complex interplay of ethnicity, race, and postcolonial factors. The film revolves around various identities being hidden.

The scene of abjection is where Dil reveals her "true" identity as a man by exposing "her" penis. Fergus, upon realizing that his loved one is really a transvestite, vomits in disgust. It is at this point that the abject materializes. According to Chanter's (2002) interpretation based on Kristeva's (1982) work, this moment is the replay of the infant separating itself from the mother ("Fergus vomits the mother"), wherein Fergus aligns himself in a heterosexual identification that is fundamentally challenged when confronted with an unacceptable other. On the one hand, this is a moment of fear and aggression; on the other hand, there remains lingering love and attraction for the other (Dil). In this instance, boundaries are in disarray (2002, 11). As Chanter observes, "the moment of abjection is a moment when all his [Fergus'] prior assumptions come tumbling down, and he is faced with an abyss. He must renegotiate his identity, come to terms with who he is, what he has done, who he loves, and what he will become" (2002).

In the film, Dil murders Jude, and Fergus, in turmoil over his continuous love for Dil given her true anatomical identity, takes the fall for the murder. While in prison, Fergus is separated from Dil by a glass panel. Each in their confined space plays out their independent identities. In Chanter's (2002) interpretation, the law ultimately asserts itself: Fergus is allowed to distance himself from an alternative symbolic construction of his relation to an anatomically defined man; Dil is allowed to play out her feminine role with her paramour (2002, 9). "He [Fergus] would rather serve time for something he did not do, than do something that his idea of himself cannot serve. He enters into prison, under the watchful eyes of the law, as a haven, which preserves his love for Dil, and hers for his, in an idealized, but unrealizable form" (2002, 10).

Chanter also argues that it is not just sexual preference at play in the movie, but also gender, race, and class and their intersections along side sexual preference (lesbian, bisexual desires). This is where the value of Kristeva's notion of the abject and abjection materialize. The abject provides a profound concept for understanding how the pre-oedipal, the premirror, may emerge to subvert identities and encourage alternative constructions very much in line with Kristeva's (1984) call for understanding the person as a "subject-in-process."

We also wish to review briefly some applications of the abject to literary texts. Keri Hulme's, *The Bone People,* can be interpreted as a statement about postcolonial identities (Maori). The abject appears in the form of Simon who is washed ashore and is unable to provide a verbalization for his own identity.

He cannot speak and must communicate by the written word. He has numerous scars reflecting abuse but is unable to explain them; his psychic health is questionable and he is constantly hearing voices and having nightmares. His age is unknown, he is thought to be Irish, and he exists between the Maori and Western culture. In short, as abject, he represents misery (Pentony 1996). He is seen as feral and is associated with the devil. The novel progresses in showing various relations with Simon (Joe's underlying homosexual impulses and rage directed toward Simon; Binny pays Simon for kisses; Kerewin is drawn to the violence inflicted on Simon by Joe, secretly in delight) (1996, 3).

In chapter 8 of the novel, Simon is thrashed by Joe, is removed from school, and suffers a final beating inflicted by Joe. In Pentony's read (1996, 4), the author (Hulme) "successfully creates a state of a living death or death in life." In chapter 8 of this book, Simon's beating is presented with poetic language. This language is amplified when Simon's unspoken thoughts are verbalized for us, despite his inability to speak (1996). For Pentony, the prevalence of violence throughout the novel helps deconstruct any unity of the text (1996). Where unity does occur, it is at the expense of Simon who undergoes continuous violence, pain, and suffering (1996). In short, Simon is abject, portraying the dark side of humanity (1996).

Another example applying the abject to literary texts is found in Angela Carter's parody and revisionist fairy tales, *The Bloody Chamber* (parody of *Bluebeard*), and *The Tiger's Bride* (parody of *Beauty and the Beast*).[6] These works underscore gender role identifications. The fairy tale genre has rather rigid rules and conventions based on dualisms and polarities (Pentony 1996, 2): "the handsome prince and passive heroine, good and evil, and light and dark." The fairy tale also reinforces the patriarchical Symbolic Order (1996). When the heroine enters the bloody chamber, her traditional role as a woman is confronted. This is a world of blood, horror, death, and mutilation. By crossing the boundary, both meaning and her identity are challenged, undermined, undone (1996). According to Pentony (1996), abjection is used "as a conscious strategy to disrupt the conventions of the fairy tale. [Abjection] also introduces features of pornography and horror which undermine the traditional conventions of the fairy tale genre by incorporating, and sustaining, elements of subconscious desire" (1996, 2).

In *The Tiger's Bride*, the abject appears in the form of the beast. The heroine is attracted to the beast in terms of pity and curiosity. In the parody, they both present their naked bodies to each other. Beauty joins the beast in his own domain, subject to an alternative meaning structure. She crosses the imaginary boundary. "She is what Kristeva describes as a 'willing victim'"

(1996, 3). In this work, Carter's "heroine is strong, in control, and actively orchestrating events on her own terms. Beauty's transformation takes the genre into the realm of fantasy and surrealism. This is underpinned by a feminist message that advocates taking control of one's life" (1996).

In short, we note that the use of Kristeva's (1982) abject is strategic in undermining the opposing binaries in traditional fairy tales (Pentony 1996.). It is disruptive, suggestive, and transformative. It is a form of the "writerly text."

Our final example on the use of the abject deals with gender relations in Jane Gardam's, *The Queen of the Tambourine*. The abject appears in the character of Eliza. Eliza suffers from traumas that follow from a miscarriage, a hysterectomy, and an affair by her partner and their child. These traumas cause her to go mad. Eliza attempts to deal with them in writing the unwritable (Sorenson 1996, 2). The abject "cannot be named and . . . has to be evaded and controlled through being 'sublimated,' labeled, and named as something else" (1996). Eliza writes to herself much like James Joyce in *Finnegan's Wake*. In this instance, the semiotic order is avoided. This is a place where her being would be otherwise shaken, undermined, fragmented, and, ultimately, destroyed. According to Sorenson, "Eliza's madness places her in a liminal space between madness and sanity, and between fiction and reality." She "exists between the noncoherence between signifiers and signifieds of the semiotic chaos that madness represents." Her "madness confronts her with the semiotic order, the archaic state of the presymbolic order, and makes her notion of identity dissolve" (1996, 2–3).

However, Sorenson's literary criticism does see a positive play here. The abject cannot be verbalized, cannot be neatly placed within the confines of discourse or the dominant Symbolic Order. The abject is continuously active in undermining traditional meanings. Consequently, this allows for a revisiting of the semiotic and a new confrontation with a mirror that may help constitute alternative identities and meanings through reentrance into the Symbolic Order. "Now, Eliza can diagnose herself as being mad, she can name and discuss the reasons for her traumas, communicate with Harry and indeed write real letters to a real Joan" (1996, 3).

Recent Re-Conceptualizations: Intersectional Standpoints, Body without Organs, Queer Theory

In this final section of chapter 6, we move away from a review of the abject to other provocative analyses regarding literary and cinematic texts, emphasizing possible integrations of the (modified) Lacanian perspective. For purposes of exposition, we have selected T. Minh-Ha Trinh's films and literary works. We begin with Norman Denzin's (1997) postmodern evaluation of her work and then integrate Lacanian and post-Lacanian orientations as a way of demonstrating the contributions these syntheses offer.

Denzin places Trinh's work in a revisionist standpoint epistemology genre of critical analysis. As a postcolonial woman she stands in three vulnerable positions: woman, woman of color, and writer (Trinh 1989, 28). She is a border crosser, defying the fixity of boundaries in identity makeup. She takes up residence in the liminal zone, the space that defies precise verbalization. As Trinh (1991, 163–64) tells it, "it is not sufficient to know the personal but to know—to speak in a different way." In her films[7] she questions the "stable, unbiased, middle-class gaze" (Denzin 1997, 78; Trinh 1991, 97–98). Her focus is on the "pensive image;" one that "unsettles the male apparatus of the gaze, in which men own, articulate, and create the look of woman as either being looked at . . . [or as one who] holds the [male] look to signify the master's desire" (Denzin 1997, 78 citing Trinh 1991, 115). In short, the camera's gaze is made transparent.

Trinh's film, *Surname Viet Given Name Nam* (1989), traces the lives of Vietnamese women who marry foreigners or Vietnamese men, indicating five locations from which they speak (lineage, age, gender, leadership role, historical moment). She also looks at the method of interviewing. Thus, her stories are about various truths, how film can create a space within which stories are retold, reflecting otherwise denied voices. Following Barthes (1974), she resists the manifestation of the realist (readerly) text; she endeavors to produce texts that encourage the "plural, sliding relationship between ear and eye and to leave room for the spectators to decide what they want to make out of a statement or a sequence of images" (Trinh 1991, 206). In Denzin's (1997, 82) words, "truth and certainty are constantly displaced, deferred, and postponed." In short, it is a writerly text.

Although making reference to Barthes, Trinh's work does not draw heavily from Lacan or revisionist Lacanian thought. We believe this could add substantially to the illuminating insights already developed by Trinh. First, the notion of an intersectional standpoint, if we may term it so, could be further augmented by the notion of varieties of abjects that could possibly surface at these intersections, boundaries, and liminal zones. Each of these would then become the basis of deconstructive and reconstructive practices.

Second, the Lacanian notion of identification is critical in understanding how an "I" emerges in particular discourses; a location from which speech production is possible. Trinh's work suggests various identifications, various sutures of the imaginary and symbolic, which momentarily can only be a relatively stabilized basis for meaning and identity construction. These identifications and sutures are consistent with what chaos theorists call "dissipative structures."

Third, in the unsettled liminal zones, we certainly can see the work of Elizabeth Grosz (1994) on mind/body dualism and Deleuze and Guattari's (1987) insights on the body without organs as being integratable. Grosz showed how the dualisms found in Western modernist thought could be overcome by reference to the Moebius strip whereby the inside (mind) and outside (body) could be reconciled in a monistic subject. In their notion of "schizoanalysis," Deleuze and Guattari (1983) showed how dominant structures, thoughts, meanings, and identities could be undermined wherein new ones emerge; that is, how more rigid "molar structures" could be supplanted by "molecular structures" whereby desire was allowed more creative expression and was not connected to lack. In molecular structures, desire takes on a rhizomatic journey to fuller embodiment in language. In this state, we have various becomings: becoming-other, becoming-woman, becoming-child, becoming-imperceptible. This is the state of "bodies without organs" (BwO) where productive desire allows for an infinite possible variation of energies that otherwise are bounded by oedipal and post-oedipal restraints.

Fourth, Lacan's (1991) notion of the four discourses is instructive. When tempered by a synthesis of Freire's (1972) dialogical pedagogy and critical race theory's notion of "intersectionality" (Delgado and Stefancic 2001), a liminal zone emerges in which a modified discourse of the *analyst* generates alternative master signifiers more reflective of being and the existent social formation. In addition, following the proposed integration, the cinematic gaze is more consistent with the discourse of the *hysteric* whereby the transparency of the gaze makes the ethnographer or film critic reflective of her/his own meaning and identity structure as linked to her/his choice of shots, scenes, scripts, and so forth.

Fifth, we find informative a body of recent knowledge, sometimes referred to as queer theory (Stockdill 1999). Queer theory goes beyond the binary oppositions (male/female) found in some forms of critical feminist analysis. In this view, sexual preference (lesbian, gay men, bisexual, and transgendered people) encourages us to looking beyond binary oppositions and to look at the variety of identity constructions that may take form (Butler 1993; Clough 2000). In this way, we transcend thinking in terms of binaries.

Sixth, Richard Dienst's (1994) appropriation of Deleuze's work on cinema (1986, 1989), indicates that television is the postmodern machinery that offers various metaphors of capitalist logic. However, when this line of reasoning is tempered with Derrida's (1973, 1977, 1978, 1981) insights, we note that no message is perfectly targeted and never attains its "conscious" intent. Indeed, at best we have "time-images"—"no representation, only images in conjunction at different angles and speeds, intersecting aspects of bodies in motion" (Dienst 1994, 151). On the one hand, Trinh's work is particularly well suited in this evolving critical cinema analysis for indicating the intersectional standpoints, the sundry spaces, the various discourses, and the multiple borders crossed in the constitution of subjectivity and meaning. On the other hand, it is quite informative for its possible depiction by the director.[8]

Seventh, the notion of the male gaze is undermined in Trinh's films and is consistent with the recent writings of Silverman (1992). Indeed, the gaze cannot be appropriated, nor can it be totally congruent with the eye (Clough 2000, 55). The gaze always goes beyond the male or female characters (2000). Aligning herself more with Foucault and Derrida, Clough seems to suggest that the gaze is connected to and exhibits force from historically specific technologies, the optic machines of the moment (2000, 57).

In summary, notwithstanding the insights already generated, Trinh's films on intersectional standpoints could be the starting point for further integration by emerging post first wave social theorists. Critical film and literary analysis in the direction of the writerly text is the basis of a new sensitivity. These domains offer the possible means toward the development of alternative master signifiers, of complex identifications, of meaning structures that see the other in "I-thou" forms, and new becomings.[9]

CONCLUSION

In this chapter, we have been concerned with evolving critical film and literary theory that draws from first and second wave French postmodern thought. To a great extent, we have focused on gender and sexual preference issues in suggesting a new awareness, an alternative direction in understanding identity and meaning constructions. We encourage future postmodern thinkers to be engaged in more intense integrations and syntheses of the various emergents discussed throughout this chapter, especially given their relevance to rediscovering crime, law, and social justice.

CHAPTER 7

Restorative Justice and Victim Offender Mediation: Towards a Transformative Praxis

INTRODUCTION

The issued posed in this chapter is whether restorative justice[1] and victim offender mediation[2] (VOM) can be developed as a form of transformative praxis.[3] Alternatively stated, we explore whether VOM, as a dialogical exchange that currently functions as a procedural arm of the restorative justice movement, can meaningfully work to facilitate social justice (Schehr 2000b). Realizing this goal is important because the expressed purpose of restorative justice is the promotion of healing among victims, offenders, and the community at large (Umbreit 2001). To explore these matters, we divide our remarks into four areas. First, we provide background on restorative and community justice. Second, we offer background on victim offender mediation. Third, we present several critical criminological challenges to restorative justice and VOM. Fourth, we delineate the postmodern challenges to victim offender mediation.

Preliminarily we note that VOM adheres to a kind of legal formalism characteristic of relations between lawyers, clients, and the courts. Since 1994, the American Bar Association has supported the application of VOM in both presentencing diversion matters and in cases involving postsentencing conditions of parole. Ostensibly, this support is based on the perception that VOM signifies a less combative application of legal principles to dispute resolution than more formal adjudicatory remedies.[4] Moreover, when examining the relevance of legal formalism in relation to VOM practices, the presence of an overt power imbalance, particularly impacting youthful offenders, is observable. The presence of these power differentials in victim offender mediation raises a number of concerns. Among these concerns are the following: (1) the privileging of hierarchical representations, (2) the supposition of order, (3) the celebration of ideal speech situations and consensus dynamics, (4) the continuous encroachment of legal discourse at the expense of alternative discourses, and (5) the lack of connected strategies between the macro and micro domains (Schehr and Milovanovic 1999, 209; Arrigo and Schehr 1998; Arrigo and Williams 2004).

To our knowledge, as of yet there is no recognition in the mainstream restorative justice literature of any of the key insights generated by first or second wave French postmodern social theorists.[5] This is surprising, especially since several instructive critiques exploring mediation practices, peace activism, and international conflict have been developed, relying upon the contributions of various postmodern luminaries (e.g., see, Pavlich 1996, 1999, utilizing the philosophy of Foucault; and Arrigo and Schehr 1998, incorporating the formulations of Lacan). Accordingly, in this chapter, we revisit the foundational assumptions characteristic of restorative justice and victim offender mediation. Along these lines, we describe and synthesize the various efforts to date that have turned to critical and postmodern thought for conceptual (and pragmatic) guidance. In addition, where useful and appropriate, we incorporate into our exposition additional insights generated by first and second wave authors, as a way of extending and deepening our assessment of conflict mediation and dispute resolution strategies. Given the thrust of chapter 7, we note that our goal is to establish a more radically inspired approach to restorative justice and VOM; one that endorses transformation through transpraxis rather than restoration. However, before we attend to these matters, some background information on what restorative justice is and how victim offender mediation functions is warranted.

BACKGROUND ON RESTORARTIVE
AND COMMUNITY JUSTICE

For thousands of years indigenous peoples throughout the world have practiced what is commonly referred to today as "restorative justice" (Umbreit 2001; Nielsen 1999; Banks 1999; Braithwaite 2002). Current manifestations of it in contemporary society are guided by the following assumptions: (1) violations are viewed as against persons and communities and not the state; (2) problem solving through dialogue and mediation is emphasized; (3) restitution for harm caused is pursued; (4) offender accountability is promoted; and (5) justice is equated with the "right" or "correct" relationships and outcomes (Zehr 1985). Interestingly, while there are periodic references to indigenous practitioners in the relevant literature, contemporary scholars identify the origins of the restorative justice paradigm as emerging with the articulation of its principles by Howard Zehr in 1985 (cf. Sullivan and Tifft 2001). International conferences held in Italy (1990), New Zealand (1995), the United States (1996), and Belgium (1997), as well as annual meetings each year since its North American inception, represent a demonstrable indicator that there is considerable and growing global interest in restorative justice theory and practice.[6]

In the United States, the American Bar Association's official support for restorative justice appeared in 1994. In 1996, the United States Department of Justice initiated what would become a series of conferences taking place between 1996 and 1998 to discuss the theoretical and applied aspects of this phenomenon (Umbreit 2001). While still controversial among its membership, in 1995 the National Organization for Victim Assistance officially endorsed the notion of "restorative community justice" as an alternative to the formal court system (M. Young 1995). Moreover, in addition to support for restorative justice promulgated by official state agencies and policy making bodies, a ground swell of public approval seems to be emerging as well (Pranis and Umbreit 1992; Bae 1992).

The Office of Juvenile Justice and Delinquency Prevention (OJJDP), through its Balanced And Restorative Justice (BARJ) project, launched a number of initiatives across the United States, principally emphasizing the victim offender mediation model.[7] Survey's conducted throughout the United States indicated that there was strong public support for victims and offenders (especially juveniles) to have an opportunity to meet and, if possible, make restitution for criminal transgressions. By involving community members to serve as volunteers in mediation sessions, local courts began diverting most cases involving violations up to simple assault to community mediation centers, thereby removing hundreds of cases that otherwise would have required adjudication.

To date, the most dramatic example of systemic adoption of restorative justice has taken place in the Vermont Department of Corrections where they created Reparative Probation Community Boards (Umbreit 2001). The Boards are staffed by citizen volunteers and are responsible for hearing violations of local, state, and federal statutes relating to nonviolent criminal activity. The Board can recommend victim offender mediation, determine restitution, and construct novel methods for offenders to demonstrate their sense of remorse.[8] Despite the innovation and creativity demonstrated by the Vermont Department of Corrections, victim offender mediation programs continue to proliferate as they represent the dominant approach to restorative justice practices.

The most recent addition to the concept of restorative justice is the phenomenon of "community justice." The most coherent articulation of community justice emerged in Deschutes County, Oregon, where longtime restorative justice advocate and practitioner, Dennis Maloney, and his colleague, Deevy Holcomb, described their approach. As they explained, community justice is a "new social contract between people and their governments to keep the public safe" (Maloney and Holcomb 2001, 297). More specifically, the community justice approach echoes the principles of restorative justice by establishing the following four assumptions as foundational: (1) everyone is responsible for and affected by community safety; (2) crime victims are the primary customers of our justice system; (3) restorative justice helps repair the victim and the community; and (4) government must be accountable to citizens (2001, 297–298).

Based on the assumption that a strong sense of neighborhood is both desirable and achievable,[9] the primary emphasis of community justice is to engage members so that they take responsibility for creating and maintaining safe living conditions in their environs. Finally, community justice, similar to the way restorative justice manifests itself in victim offender mediation, requires offenders to repay the community for harms caused through "restorative service requirements." To reach the point of restitution, community justice programs use VOM.

BACKGROUND ON VICTIM OFFENDER MEDIATION

VOM constitutes one procedural arm of balanced and restorative justice. Interestingly, however, seldom has the question been asked—"restored to what?" The answer to this question seems to be contextualized within the communitarian framework espoused by A. Etzioni (1995a, 1995b), and the reintegrative shaming philosophy first proposed by John Braithwaite (1989, 2002). Each emphasizes the need to heal victims, offenders, and communities (Zehr 1990; Umbreit 2001; Van Ness and Strong 2002).

Aside from its religious and medical overtones, the more sociologically grounded aspects of VOM emerge from a Durkheimian adherence to solidification of normative practices, consistent with dominant cultural interests.

Arguably, what this produces for victims is a sense of healing related to emotional and psychological damage caused by invasions of private space (both objective and subjective). Moreover, as supporters of VOM contend, this healing emerges when victims can physically (since most crimes are committed by teens without any adult present) and verbally confront those who have injured them. Procedural emphasis in VOM sessions is on verbally reconstructing the offense. In other words, much like the confessional (Foucault 1977), the situational effect of VOM is to provide a sanctuary setting for the narrative exposition of pain and suffering (Cobb 1997; Silbey and Sarat 1989; Greatbatch and Dingwall 1989; Chilton 1986).

Insofar as healing applies to offenders, it ostensibly occurs through the recognition of harms caused by one's victimizing actions and any subsequent overtures demonstrating a commitment to make recompense for one's deleterious behavior. Payment can manifest itself in many forms (e.g., money, services, apology). However, whether, and to what extent, healing pervades the community represents a more ambiguous and, consequently, ideological aspect of VOM, and it is this amorphous ideology that is consistent with its rhetorical commitment to system maintenance. The "neighborhood" signified in VOM discourse and practice parallels the communitarian vision of community. In other words, the assumption is that there exists a definable, self-referential, geographically situated, and relatively homogenous body of individuals, who adopt and embrace the same values and interests. Healing takes place when offenders are held accountable for harms caused and when they are led to understand—if necessary through shaming—their place in the broader political, economic, and cultural web of life. To the degree that offenders acknowledge their responsibility for harm and demonstrate a commitment to dominant cultural norms and institutional arrangements, they can be reintegrated into the community and, consequently, they can be healed.

Linked closely to juridical discourse, VOM serves to promote the status quo by narrowly channeling narrative constructions of meaning into the same requirements for legal mootness, standing, and relevance to the specific act committed as is common in most courtroom trials. Conducted as they are in a sanctuary-like setting, discursive interactions between victims, offenders, and mediators are constituted by the power invested in the "keeper of tales." In short, mediators serve as secular priests positioned to probe all aspects of one's secrets and fears (Cobb 1997; Pavlich 1996).[10] This is especially true during the information-gathering phase of mediation where, if the parties are agreeable, mediators conduct in-depth interviews. The most valuable setting for these interviews is the subject's home. In this setting, a wealth of interpretive data unfolds for the mediator. Interestingly, however, victims and offenders have approximately five and ten minutes each during the actual mediation session in which to speak to their concerns.[11] The premediation interview, though, is not performed in all cases but is strongly advised (Van Ness and Strong 2002). This strategy exists as a way to safeguard against the possibility that the victim or offender will change their respective stories. As such, it signifies a commitment to quality control.

The aspects of VOM procedure appropriate to our critical and postmodern excursion center around the actual mediation session itself. Indeed, while the premediation interviews are relevant to establishing the role of the mediator as one who "hears confessions," the more formal aspects of VOM procedure (those recognized by supporters as its strength) are precisely where attention to legal formalism is most evident. While some variations exist in the way VOM procedures unfold, there are recognizable patterns that have developed, in large part due to the standardization of training. The mediation session generally lasts one hour and typically involves the following components:

- Introductory statements by the mediator
- Storytelling by the offender and victim
- Clarification of facts and sharing of information
- Reviewing victim losses and options for compensation
- Developing written restitution agreement
- Closing statement by the mediator

While not specifically directed at VOM, the views expressed by S. Leviton and J. Greenstone (1997) illustrate the restricted and linear emphasis placed on getting to an agreement. They make it clear that any probing questions (or caucuses to meet with recalcitrant participants) must be directed solely to the issue at hand. Moreover, they are quite clear that the mediator must always remain neutral ("change the disputant's perspective; don't try to change his mind"). The perspective taken by Leviton and Greenstone (1997) is consistent with VOM training and expectations. To be a good mediator, one must be impartial.

Overall, the preponderance of the data seem to indicate that VOM is successful at promoting restitution and inhibiting recidivism. For example, in a recently published meta-analysis of four studies relating to the likelihood of recidivism following VOM sessions, W. R. Nugent, M. Umbreit, and L. Wiinamaki, and J. B. Paddock (2001) suggest that among the 1,298 juveniles studied, their rate of reoffense was 32 percent, lower than those who had not been exposed to participation in VOM.[12]

CRITICAL CRIMINOLOGICAL CHALLENGES TO
RESTORATIVE JUSTICE AND VOM

Notwithstanding the well-intended theory and practice of restorative justice and victim offender mediation, clear voices of criticism have emerged since the mid-1980s questioning their efficacy, especially in regard to promoting justice for victims (Harris 1989; Cobb 1997). For example, relying on the insights of critical criminology, M. Kay Harris (1989) leveled the first assault and proposed three significant areas of contestation: (1) the individualization of criminal activity in rhetoric and remedy; (2) failure to acknowledge the constitutive affect of political, economic, and cultural factors interpellating subjects; and (3) the inattention of proponents of VOM to their own coercive discourse.

Harris's (1989) invective directly challenged the rationalist and cultural reproducing aspects of VOM. Her critique took exception to the explicit assumptions of individual responsibility for harms caused, particularly since this logic mostly neglected the political, economic, and cultural factors that influenced and coshaped human actors. In addition, Harris expressed serious doubt that VOM was any less coercive than conventional adjudication processes. Specifically, as she observed, "a far worse imbalance will emerge with the offender finding himself or herself not only lined up in defense against the state but also against the victim and perhaps some new entity or presence put there to represent the 'community'" (1989, 34).

In addition to her concern for the coercive dimensions of victim offender mediation practices, Harris leveled the first real challenge to the assumption that offenders would benefit, in any meaningful way, from VOM. In effect, her critique anticipated Braithwaite's (1989, 2002) emphasis on reintegrative shaming. In particular, she regarded expectations of offender penitence with suspicion, especially when assessing the extent to which any real gain would accrue to either the offender or the community.

While Harris's carefully argued challenges to VOM (and restorative justice more generally) represented an important initial standpoint for critical criminology, a subsequent flurry of criticism emerged, directing attention toward the mediation process itself and to the discursive formulation of events (e.g., Chilton 1986; Greatbatch and Dingwall 1989; Harrington 1985; Lerman 1984; Cobb 1997; Pavlich 1996, 1998; Sarat and Kearns 1991). Among those who challenged VOM and the mediation process, the work of Sara Cobb (1997) and George Pavlich (1996, 1999) signify a theoretical transition between Harris's critical criminological assessment and the position we propose below, inspired by first and second wave French postmodern social theory.

Cobb's (1997) critique differs from Harris's in that her primary emphasis is on the revictimization of crime victims through the application of VOM rhetoric in mediation sessions. Drawing mostly from the work of Michel Foucault (1977), E. Scarry (1985), Martha Minow (1987), and Austin Sarat and Thomas Kearns (1991), Cobb contends that VOM discourse relies on Cartesian duality manifested in the distinction between those cases requiring adjudication in the courts (criminal cases), and those qualifying for mediation through VOM (relational cases). VOM removes (indeed, sanitizes) the presence of violence by replacing the rights-based discourse characteristic of adjudication processes with a needs-based discourse more appropriate to relational cases. As Cobb suggests, this process delegitimates the voice of the victim through a "domestication process." This phenomenon refers to the act of perpetuating the oppression of women by refusing to acknowledge the actual violence perpetrated against them. Cobb also notes that the mediation process assumes a veil of moral neutrality in which anything may be said by anyone in the session and it (ostensibly) will not be judged as possessing any greater or lesser degree of legitimacy. Thus, by avoiding the condemnation of violent acts committed against victims through the assumption of a laissez-faire morality, persons harmed are denied any meaningful acknowledgement for the pain they experienced. In this context, Cobb invokes Foucault's (1977) notion on the "micro politics of power" in which VOM discourse signifies the perpetuation of violence against, and the oppression of, women. Nor, in this response, are social structural conditions examined for their coproduction of the offense.

In a similar fashion, Pavlich's (1996) critique of VOM invokes a Foucauldian (1965, 1972, 1973, 1977) emphasis on discipline and control through the microphysics of power. Pavlich contends that VOM processes serve the interests of the state by disciplining subjects. His position finds contemporary expression in Schehr's (2000b) explication of VOM as a mode of legal formalism; a system-reproducing steering mechanism (Jessop 1991; Bertramensen, Thomsend, and Torfing 1991; Habermas 1984) employed by the state to assist unstable sectors of society (in this case, criminal justice) toward stasis. In this analysis, Schehr argues that mediators guide restitution agreements toward activities consistent with dominant cultural interests by cajoling offenders (especially youth) into participating in secondary-sector labor market activities.[13] Similar to Pavlich (1996), Schehr emphasizes how the rhetoric adopted by VOM practitioners emphasizes a commitment to dominant cultural norms and values (especially those relating to respect for authority, hard work, property, merit, and nationalism). While this process may result in lower recidivism rates, it comes at the expense of promoting system-stabilizing discourse and activity, thereby thwarting prospects for alternative, and more meaningful, forms of recompense and healing.

The insights of Harris (1989), Cobb (1997), Pavlich (1996), and Schehr (2000b) draw attention to the system-sustaining aspects of VOM discourse and processes, unconsciously and prethematically taken to be legitimate. However, missing from these investigations is a more fully integrated and affirmative postmodern assessment of restorative justice and victim offender mediation. As such, in the final section of the chapter, we turn to the contributions of first and second wave scholars for additional guidance. As we explain, the appeal to French postmodern social theory helps promote a transformative agenda in VOM practices in which transpraxis underpins the interests of victims, offenders, and the community to which both are intimately connected.

POSTMODERN CHALLENGES TO VOM

Drawing on Lacan's (1991) notion of the four discourses, Arrigo and Schehr (1998) contend that the rhetorical configuration of VOM language functions much like the discourse of the *master*. Building on the work of Pavlich (1996), Cobb (1997), and Delgado (1997), Arrigo and Schehr establish the ways in which VOM processes situate offenders and victims within system reproducing frames that promote stability and predictability. This is discursively accomplished through reference to master signifiers like "reconciliation," "healing," "restitution," "community," "responsibility," and so forth. For victims and offenders, VOM discursive practices only offer the opportunity to locate experiences of pain, hurt, confusion, regret, retribution, and the like, within a *master* discourse. Cobb's (1997) insight is important here because VOM processes limit the mode and content of communication (e.g., the unique embodiment of desire) to a terrain consistent with dominant signifiers. In Cobb's view, by separating the discourse appropriate to VOM into one emphasizing needs (master discourse) as opposed to one grounded in the preservation of rights, victims are revictimized by the overt omission of their experiences of physical and psychical violence. Indeed, they have no way to articulate the full extent of their experiences with harm, effectively denying them the possibility of a truly satisfactory restorative outcome.

Cobb's (1997) position echoes the Lacanian (1991) view that divided subjects, as *pas toute*, cannot realize *jouissance* (wholeness, satisfaction of desire), so long as their mode of communication is dictated by master signifiers which serve the interests of dominant culture and the preservation of power beyond the interlocutors. Indeed, in this dialogical exchange, the only knowledge that can be produced is one that endorses system-stabilizing meanings for pain, suffering, reconciliation, and restoration. Thus, the reality of the VOM session is circumscribed by the self-referential, limiting and, ultimately, alienating linguistic coordinates into which subjects are inserted or situate themselves.

Arrigo and Schehr (1998) further contend that not only do VOM practices deny victims a more complete opportunity to express their felt sense of harm, they limit the ability of offenders to articulate their sense of identity, being, and belonging. Consistent with Lacan's (1991) discourse of the *hysteric*, offenders confront the stifling limitations imposed upon them by the (advertent and inadvertent) acceptance of master signifiers that fail to embody their unique subjectivity. Moreover, given the limited range of available ways to communicate their feelings and emotions to victims, lawbreakers reconstitute their own way of communicating so that it is compatible with more culturally acceptable, though personally alienating, ways of speaking, interacting, knowing. Lost in this more scripted process is the opportunity for more genuine self-disclosure, more authentic healing; occasions that would otherwise facilitate the subject to speak his/her own "true" words (Freire 1972).

When reviewing how victims and offenders are interpellated (Althusser, 1971), Bulter's observations (1990, 1993) on repetition are instructive. Repetition refers to the process in which discursive practices occurring in various situational contexts (VOM session) or organizational settings (mediation center) reproduce and, therefore, reaffirm what is. This is consistent with Baudrillard's (1983b) notion of the hyperreal; a reality manufactured in discourse replicating what has already been spoken and lived wherein these replicas are imitated *ad infinitum* and are taken to be more real than the reality on which they are premised. The self-referential language of the VOM session serves only to reproduce a narratively coherent, though mostly bounded, story about actors and events endorsing institutional meanings of restorative justice. Both victims and offenders reenact and reaffirm this logic by invoking the discourse signifying VOM.

To this extent, Lacan's (1977) often expressed definition of a signifier is quite applicable: "a signifier represents the subject for another signifier." In short, spoken (acceptable) signifiers come to represent the speaking subject within a closed, self-referential linguistic coordinate system within which the subject remains excluded. These signifiers call out for their own linearly accepted narrative constructions. While this becomes legitimate discourse within VOM, minority language, on the other hand, is denied expression.

In order to liberate victims and offenders from the marginalizing constraints of VOM language, an affirmative and integrative postmodern inquiry is instructive. For example, we note that Lyotard's (1984) notion of "differand" indicates how concepts such as "reconciliation," "harm," "recompense," "healing," and "justice," and so forth are signs freighted with multiple meanings (see also, Volosinov 1986 on the multiaccentuation of the sign.[14] Moreover, unequal distributions of economic and political power often determine what meanings are defined as legitimate and illegitimate (Rossi-Landi 1977). Derrida's (1977, 1978) observations on the metaphysics of presence and absence are informative here as well. While manifold signifieds lodged within signifiers typically are reduced to system-stabilizing contents, privileged terms depend on their existence for the concealed, repressed, overt terms relegated in the binary opposition as an absence or as a lack in discourse. Thus, when the dominant discourse of VOM is spoken, the trace of the offender, as disenfranchised, lingers in continuous relation to it. S/he remains *pas-toute*, not all, denied the ability to express her/himself.

However, unlike the Derridean call for a reversal of hierarchies, we argue that the key to promoting transformative praxis in victim offender mediation does not merely entail the privileging of alternative standpoints thereby reconstituting the dominant discourse. Rather, positional, relational, and provisional truths (Arrigo 1995c) about harm and healing need to find expression in the dialogical exchange. This perspective resonates with Luce Irigaray's (1985b) notion of mimesis; an activity wherein subordination is continuously deconstructed and transformed into an affirmation of alterity. This is a discursive process in which the "retelling of myths" (Cixous 1976; Klages 1997), the revival of cultural images, and the rediscovery of ancestral legends are recounted where liquid identities (Bauman 2001) are continuously redis-covered and reconstituted (see also Norman Denzin's "sixth moment" in ethnographic research, 1997).[15]

Similarly, we note that Lacan's (1991) discourse of the *analyst* offers the potential for reinvigorating and emancipating VOM discourse such that par-ticipating subjects experience *jouissance*. Indeed, as Arrigo and Schehr (1998) note, the mediator, as *analyst*, conveys information to the alienated subjected (here, the victim and offender). The subject, as divided, as *pas toute*, once exposed to alternative signifiers more consistent with the subject's way of being, realizes that replacement signified meanings for his/her plight can be anchored in discourse. In other words, Lacan's notion that master signifiers—which are core signifiers internalized by people constituting a unitary ego—can be undone and replaced by alternative master signifiers that are more reflective of one's being. These replacement meanings represent a body of knowledge that heretofore was ignored, dismissed, or altogether quashed in the VOM process. However, once articulated, the possibility for novel ways of reconciling conflict or restoring justice emerge.[16]

In an effort to address both victim offender mediation and other modes of conflict resolution at the macro and micro levels, Schehr and Milovanovic (1999) further elucidate how an affirmative and integrative postmodern analysis would be fruitful to this enterprise. As they argue, international peace activism often represents Lacan's (1991) hierarchical discourse of the *master*, or what chaos theorists identify as a point or limit attractor, signifying circumscribed knowledge, values, and beliefs in which dominant culture is unreflectively perceived to be legitimate (*Ibid*. 1999, 212). However, there are two primary effects that flow from this form of consensus dynamics. First, participation in conflict mediation sessions is limited to those individuals or groups in possession of the cultural capital valued as a part of the discourse of the *master*. Second, by way of omission, subaltern discourse (Spivak 1991)—the voice of the dispossessed, silenced and/or excluded—is marginalized and repressed.

In addition, Schehr and Milovanovic (1999) assert that conventional dispute resolution literatures view conflict as an abnormal and negative cultural force that generates disequilibrium (1999, 215). However, by way of contrast and consistent with chaos theory's emphasis on far from equilibrium conditions, states of flux and disorganization are proposed as constitutive and natural dimensions of any complex system in which individuals or groups interact.[17] This position resonates with Lyotard's (1984) call for instability and parology. Following Lyotard (1984), forms of unity, expressions of totality, linearity, predictability, and routinization, cause and effect, and deductive reasoning are rejected. These are the emblems of the modern episteme. In their place, fractal spaces, bifurcations, discontinuities, nonlinearities, dissipative structures, and the notion of orderly (dis)order are offered.

Barthe's (1968b, 1974), too, makes a similar observation in his notion of the "writerly" text. The goal of dialogue, discourse, and narrativity is not closure or finality. Structure, form, and thesis are actively resisted and debunked. Multiple interpretations abound; voices otherwise silenced are embedded in words awaiting recognition. Judith Kristeva (1984) substantiates this theme in her notion of semanalysis. This is a meaning making process in which the disruptions, subversions, and dislocations of subjectivity lodged within discourse are articulated. For Kristeva, this activity recognizes how discourse as method transgresses semiotic codes and language systems (i.e., conventional VOM discourse) in which a grammar of poetics akin to Lacan's (1977) Real Order, is made articulable. Thus, in order to transform international and domestic efforts at peace activism and dispute resolution into occasions for transpraxis, integrative and affirmative postmodern social theory explains why and how the fit between justice and consensus must be disrupted. Indeed, consensus is nothing more than a temporary state in dialogical exchanges. As such, it must not be viewed as an end in and of itself.

French postmodern social theory also is instructive when assessing the temporal and spatial aspects of conflict mediation. Mainstream attempts to remedy disputes are bound by considerable time and space limitations (e.g., Sullivan and Tifft 2001). Agreements between interlocutors that take too long to produce or are too costly to implement are regarded as inefficient (Achilles 2001; see also Arrigo and Williams 2003). After all, the point is to get to "yes." However, application of nonlinearity through chaos theory challenges the conditions under which decisions are made. Space is conceived as being smooth rather than striated (Deleuze and Guattari 1987). Striated space is the background spatio-temporal framework that follows more Euclidean geometry and the modernist sciences. Smooth space engenders bountiful and boundaryless articulations of events, thereby enhancing opportunities for all voices to be expressed and in ways that may completely belie any attempt to channel communication consistent with the discourse of the *master*. Moreover, acceptance of the ambulant nature of human social interaction among diverse populations—especially when considering international dispute resolution—leads to the realization that the negotiation of difference never produces a final settlement (Walzer 1994). This is because we all live "thick" cultures that are uniquely our own (1994).

We note that considerable attention to matters of time and space emerges in those analyses of dispute resolution characteristic of indigenous people (Nielsen 1999; Joseph 2001). For example, in the Navajo Peacemaker tradition many days may pass and many themes may surface before anything approaching restitution is reached. There are few spatial limitations with this peacemaking process. Indeed, family members are called from all over the reservation, and there are no limitations placed on the amount of time a person can communicate his or her feelings (Nielsen 1999).

The insights of Deleuze and Guattari (1983, 1986, 1987) amplify how the spatial and temporal dynamics of VOM could be reconfigured. As they explain, the subject, in its most liberated state, is a full body without organs (BwO). As such, the subject knows only multiplicities, stories that forever unfold, and continuous becomings. Each of these phenomena experience varying degrees of intensity, frequency, and duration. This is the realm in which Lacanian (1977) desire is deterritorialized. Moreover, by adopting the political strategy of schizoanalysis (Deleuze and Guattari 1983), ossified beliefs and established representations are demystified and destroyed. Thus, temporal and spatial limits in VOM sessions signify nothing more than arti-facts of modernist reasoning and sensibility, undermining and undoing prospects for breakthroughs or epiphanies. Schizoanalysis is a return to the molecular level in which continuous variation, fuzzy logic, and heterogeneity abound. By employing this approach to VOM dialogical exchanges, radical transformations are increasingly made possible. This is a rhizomatic politics of desire in which the "root" or essentialist positions of restorative justice and of VOM practices are unearthed and displaced. This is a call for transpraxis in which lines of escape, of deterritorialization, are identified and languages of healing, of restoration, are spoken.

This does not underestimate material conditions and possible nexi between dominant discourses and the various dominant logics within a capitalist economy. Moreover, it does not mean that a transpraxis can result in fundamental changes *just* in discourse. Indeed, political economies that maintain hierarchy and privilege and related master discourses that are their supports need to be undermined and replaced. Thus, one of the overarching dominant discourses developed by way of the oedipalization of desire must be deterritorialized, replaced, whereby new subject identifications and discourses can emerge.

We believe that VOM sessions, as currently structured hierarchical relations and conditions, become little more than control mechanisms, undermining prospects for transformative justice. The "excessive investor"—agents (be it a person, institution, legal apparatus, agents of social control, the state, etc.), "who invest energy in denying others through harms of reduction or repression" (Henry and Milovanovic 2001, 170), who "deny others their ability to make a difference" (Henry and Milovanovic 1996, 116)—need to be first understood as situated in hierarchically based conditions where the other becomes merely an object, an "it," denied an identity, denied the ability to make a difference in the instant. Within COREL sets (see chapter 3) that have ossified, constitutive criminology would argue that repetition must be subverted and undermined (Butler 1993), releasing new forms of suturing practices (Lacan 1977; also see Laclau and Mouffe, 1985).[18] It is within these structural dislocative practices that alternative voices may begin to find embodiment.

It is in this sense, too, that responding to excessive investors provides an opportunity for understanding ossified COREL sets,[19] empty body without organs, the dynamics of repetition, and the prevalence of stabilized instrumental rhetorics and their effects (Schwendinger and Schwendinger 1985) that objectify the other as an "it." In addition, this is an occasion for understanding differences and the other, as well as an opportunity, through more genuine VOM programs, to turn negative energy into positive energy in the form of the metaphor of "social judo" (Henry and Milovanovic 1996). This metaphor creates bonds of solidarity, not separation, instituting the development of new master signifiers and narratives that better embody desire and practices that follow without occurring at the expense of the other. This goes beyond restoration to transformation.

Accordingly, rather than the more conservative "restorative justice" (restoration to what was?), we advocate a form of transformative justice (Roth 1994).[20] In this view, response is not just focused on those more immediately involved with the violation, even if it does include the "community," but also offers the occasion whereby structural and more immediate social problems could be brought within a more holistic purview in understanding and responding to harms. Rather than relegating relatively stabilized complexes of harmful conditions to side discussion or to irrelevancy in conflict disputes, these should be raised as co-equal in creative responses. It goes without saying that if the conditions that maximize negative energy flow and if the emergent of excessive investors in doing harm remain unexamined and in place—only to focus on dealing with the casualties—this is a rather conservative agenda. In fact, these procedures "cool out the mark," leaving political economic arrangements free of critique and possible change.[21]

Transformative justice provides the opportunity for those harmed, as well as the excessive investor, to have her/his story told. This is not to devalue stories at the outset, nor to place them in a necessary privileged hierarchy; rather it is to recognize the various desires of human beings and the complex relations within which they might emerge. Of course, this would provide the occasion for a plethora of neutralizations by the offender; but this is precisely the point: these are often lurking in the background, remaining unexamined in existing VOM programs.[22] We think that their voicing would provide additional understanding of the harm done, an opportunity to undermine neutralization rhetorics, and the occasion whereby a new discourse could emerge; a discourse which would open space for the subject of becoming, not being. If, for example, a critical mass of new narratives is reached that condemns some local political economic practice (in workplaces, schools, hospitals, etc.) then the basis of developing new social and economic policies may begin to be weighed more seriously. In other words, transformative justice practices could be one component of various others in engendering social change.

This is consistent with Schehr's (2000b) analysis. Reintegration and restoration sought through what is already an unjust, unequal, and politicized set of discursive relationships reproduces dominant cultural hegemony. However, a commitment to transformative justice requires recognition of the multiple sites of power, oppression, dehumanization, and inequity pervading each historical epoch. To promote transformative justice as a component of

VOM, especially as it pertains to participation by youth, Schehr recommends the implementation of critical literacy as a core component of any restitution/reconciliation process. In this formulation, Schehr applies the insights of critical pedagogy to the role of mediators. In this scenario, mediators assume the position of activists capable of navigating the "politics of marginality" (Kristeva 1986). Thus, the mediation session contains a discursive component that aids in the deconstruction of discrimination, alienation, violence and aggression, oppression, and inequity by uncoupling participants' articulations via political, economic, and cultural institutions. Education appears as a space, an outcome basin, in which meaning is made (Wexler 1992). Through exposure to a critical evaluation of identity construction in relation to dominant cultural institutions promoting the experience of a "body without organs," youth may experience what Paulo Freire (1972) referred to as *conscientization*—the process of attaining political consciousness.

The curricular content constituting critical literacy that would provide the basis for critical pedagogy in VOM includes the following (Schehr 2000b, 166):

- Accept and promote tolerance of cultural diversity
- Accept and promote tolerance of sex/gender diversity
- Pursue equity with regard to political and economic access
- Expose associations between political, economic, and cultural inequity, poor education, and nonnormative behavior (including violence)
- Promote the value of a politically intelligent and alert citizenry
- Deconstruct interests behind expressions of political, economic, and cultural power
- Teach community organizing and political strategy skills
- Draw on student experiences for pedagogical practices
- Promote self-sufficiency in food production, housing construction, child care, and the like
- Promote awareness of environment and our relation to it
- Promote peacemaking
- Promote fairness and equity in the administration of justice

We maintain that by exposing youth to critical literacy as a component of restitution, the seeds of a transformative transpraxis could be planted. A curriculum founded on the principles of critical pedagogy amounts to what J. Kozol (1985, 92) referred to as "civil disobedience in pedagogic clothes." This kind of pragmatic and affirmative application of discursive processes associated with VOM, allows us to envision how the transformation of various modes of political, economic, and cultural oppression could take place.

Thus, we note that the call for transformative justice, built around the notion of transpraxis, is an ongoing deconstruction and reconstruction of subject positions. In these moments, a critical engagement with economic, political, and cultural forces that shape and are shaped by human agency are examined. Language becomes the catalyst for reflexivity and action, enabling the articulation of true words. This is an affirmative struggle; one in which all participants in the dialogical process more completely rediscover identity, meaning, harm, community, and reconciliation.

CONCLUSION

Although the theory of restorative justice and the practice of victim offender mediation endeavor to promote a form of empowerment benefiting victims, offenders, and the community that binds both, their theoretical assumptions and programmatic effects are problematic. In order to develop an emancipating agenda in VOM sessions, conventional interpretations of discourse, subjectivity, knowledge, conflict, time, and space must be reconfigured. In this chapter, we have proposed how such efforts could be undertaken for both victims and offenders, drawing attention to the insights of first- and second-wave French postmodern social theory. The challenge that lies ahead is for advocates and practitioners to apply our observations to both local and global sites of contestation. From our perspective, this is the path toward a transformative praxis.

CHAPTER 8

Social Movements as Nonlinearity: On Innocence Projects and Intentional Communities

INTRODUCTION

In this chapter, we apply affirmative and integrative postmodern inquiry to the study of social movements. In particular, we examine the phenomena of innocence projects and intentional communities. We note that our analysis here is speculative and provisional. Our intent is merely to document how other facets of social life, impacted by criminological and legal thought, could benefit from a critical examination informed by French postmodern theory.

We begin by outlining the literature on new social movement theory (NSM),[1] emphasizing the general conceptual orientation of this model.[2] We then briefly describe a fourth approach to social movements as developed by Schehr (1997, 1999). Delineating this material is significant in that it "builds primarily upon the insights of the NSM literature but . . . endeavors to move beyond what is conceptualized . . . as a still limited articulation of movement potential" (1997, 158). More specifically, we utilize several insights found in chaos theory or nonlinear dynamical systems theory as a way of identifying forms of resistance, cultural capital, and identity construction not otherwise accessible through traditional discourse that theorizes social movements (Laclau and Mouffe 1985). From our perspective, articulating "the cultural milieu of oppressed peoples" (Schehr 1997, 158) and describing the imaginary domain of sense-making for indigenous groups (Cornell 1998b), necessitates a language absent an appeal to the conventional. We then present two recent manifestations of the fourth approach in social movement literature: innocence projects as a response to wrongful convictions[3] and intentional communities designed to house the homeless. In addition, where useful and appropriate, we apply the insights of first and second wave French postmodern social theory to our understanding of these phenomena.

NEW SOCIAL MOVEMENT THEORY

In this section, we draw on the work of D. McAdam, J. McCarthy, and M. Zald (1996) to emphasize three aspects of social movements that appear salient to our analysis: (1) political opportunity structures, (2) mobilizing structures, and (3) framing processes. In addition, we include the work of M. Diani (1992). His insights suggest the aggregation of key movement characteristics in the following way: (1) networks of informal interaction, (2) shared beliefs and solidarity, (3) collective action on conflictual issues, and (4) action that primarily occurs outside the institutional sphere and the routine procedures of social life.

Political Opportunity Structures, Mobilizing Structures, Framing Processes

McAdam, McCarthy, and Zald (1996) describe political opportunity structures as temporally bounded historical moments that provide opportunities and constraints within the political environment for making claims to power.[4] Shifting political alliances produce greater instability, thereby enhancing opportunities for social change. The extent to which these opportunities are acknowledged and taken advantage of influences the degree of success for claims-makers. Examples of political opportunity structures include the division among Southern Dixicrats and Northern Liberals in the United States Congress during the 1950s and 1960s. Given this political division, leaders of the Civil Rights movement had the opportunity they needed to leverage changes in discriminatory laws.

To be effective, movement actors must construct mobilizing structures capable of articulating a theme or set of themes to the broader public. At least initially, this is typically accomplished through frequent and intense interactions among a set of homogenous movement actors (McAdam, McCarthy, and Zald 1996, 19). Mobilizing structures can be formal and informal, and include the use of networks that allow people to mobilize around a set of movement activities.

Political opportunities and mobilizing structures must rely on careful framing processes to carry a social movement's message beyond its base of support. Here, McAdam, McCarthy, and Zald (1996) rely heavily on the work of D. Snow and R. Benford (1988). Perhaps most interesting in Snow et al.'s (1986) work, as it relates to the constitution of a social movement, is his insistence that it is essentially a cultural construct. In other words, social movements succeed or fail based on their ability to effectively position system attributes in disaffecting ways. Snow et al. (1986) suggest the framing process amounts to, "Conscious strategic efforts by a group of people to fashion shared understandings of the world and of themselves that legitimate and motivate collective action" (cited in McAdam, McCarthy, and Zald 1996, 6).

Framing serves to mediate between political opportunity structures and mobilizing structures through the process of signification and nomination. In other words, agents working within social movements actively construct meanings and definitions of situations consistent with observable events and subjective expectations. Framing observable events in ways consistent with movement interests delegitimates the system.

Diani's Contributions

M. Diani's (1992) contribution to social movement studies comes in the form of his aggregation of four key elements. First, Diani indicates how social movements can be recognized by their *networks of informal interaction*. Networks facilitate the "circulation of resources (information, expertise, material resources), as well as broader systems of meaning" (2001, 7–8). Diani argues that informal networks are a precondition to creating a social movement, as well as crucial to the promotion of social movement signification.

The second of Diani's social movement characteristics is *shared beliefs and solidarity*. Here, Diani cites the work of many theorists who have written in the New Social Movement tradition with their specific emphasis on identity (e.g., Melucci, Touraine). His emphasis closely parallel's Snow et al.'s (1986) view that the process of identity creation is an ever-changing one; one that requires mediation and "realignment." Establishing collective identity enables movement supporters to provide collective interpretations of system attributions, thus producing common expressions of ways to comprehend and to change them. What is important for our purpose is Diani's (1992) acknowledgment that identity construction and framing persist even when public expressions of movement interests are lacking or not at all present (e.g., protest demonstrations). Indeed, the less public but nonetheless ongoing identity construction maintained through informal movement networks provides movement actors with the shared sense of purpose they need to continue their work.

Diani's third criterion, *collective action on conflictual issues*, is a core component of much social movement theorizing in that it emphasizes the existence of conflict. For A. Melucci (1988, 1990, 1995), actions only become social movements when they engage in system-level conflict that in one way or another possess the capacity of destabilizing the system. However, for New Social Movement authors, including Melucci, challenges to cultural interpretations of reality are as significant a goal as those directed at changes in the political and economic sphere.

Finally, Diani acknowledges a fourth criterion: *action that primarily occurs outside the institutional sphere and the routine procedures of social life.* These are actions that attempt to distinguish social movements from routinized activities representing normative ways of interacting with political, economic, and cultural institutions. This criterion is the most controversial in that it presumes social movement actors must always seek remedies to political, economic, and cultural ills through nonnormative means. While acknowledging those traditions in sociology that have articulated this view, Diani argues for a more inclusive set of activities that may include many normative practices (e.g., lobbying, public protest, voting). Diani's view emphasizes the many choices made by movement activists as they consider the full array of strategic options available to them.

A FOURTH APPROACH TO SOCIAL MOVEMENT THEORY: CONTRIBUTIONS FROM CHAOS THEORY

In this section, we describe a fourth approach to social movement theory.[5] In particular, we rely on the observations of Schehr (1997). As we argue, his appropriation of chaos theory principles[6] establishes a new, provocative, and suggestive direction for conceiving movement potential and actors, including the activity of innocence projects and intentional communities.[7]

There are six concepts relevant to Schehr's (1997, 1999) analysis of social movements and chaos theory. These concepts include the following: (1) nonlinearity, (2) fractal space, (3) attractors, (4) self-similarity, (5) bifurcations, and (6) dissipative structures. Each of these notions is provisionally described. Along the way, we generally link these observations to concrete examples of crime and justice social movement activities.

Chaos theory's notion of nonlinearity signifies how certain minor increases in an input variable can have dramatic, even disproportional, effects on an outcome value. In short, seemingly insignificant events can be the impetus for wholesale change. Another way to convey this notion is expressed in the adage: "sometimes less is more."

Consider, for example, the mobilization of AIDS activism. Initially, and for several long years, the face of AIDS was equated with sexually promiscuous homosexuals or drug dependent and needle using prostitutes. Organization building, resource allocation, political lobbying, and intergroup networking to combat the disease were effectively halted. However, when an adolescent boy (Ryan White) from the heartland of America contracted AIDS, public and political attitudes toward this devastating disease shifted considerably (e.g., Stockdill 1999). The singular presence of this boy and his personal story of hope in the face of imminent death, catapulted civic consciousness to new heights beyond what activists had been able to muster.

Chaos theory's concept of fractal space agues that truth values are a matter of degree. Shades of meaning and levels of accountability more fully reflect the constitution of reality. To this extent, absolute categories of right or wrong, good or bad, health or illness, guilt or innocence are convenient fictions, socially conceived to promote certain ideological ends. Instead, nonlinear dynamical systems theory claims that much like multiple and mutable states of becoming, truth is always and already fluid, fragmented, partial, and incomplete.

To illustrate, consider the inordinate and excessive attention surrounding former President William Jefferson Clinton's alleged sexual involvement with Ms. Monica Lewinsky. Politicians, pundits, civic leaders, governmental officials, and religious crusaders rallied to either impeach or vindicate Clinton. After nearly two years of resource mobilization, political wrangling and strategic maneuvering, and after spending several million dollars of taxpayers' money to support these movement activities, the conclusion reached was that there was some culpability for Clinton *and* Lewinsky.

A similar fractal logic existed when the United States, on the brink of war, networked globally and feverishly to legitimize the "righteousness" of its position and the "inhumanity" of Iraq's. The position taken by the United States was that it knew best when investigating to nuclear build ups, sinister schemes to dominate the world, and mass destruction. Of course, the only nation to ever use such weapons against a foreign "enemy" was the United States; a decision fueled in part because its position as a world leader and would-be corporate giant was in serious jeopardy during World War II.

The notion of attractors as developed by chaos theory refers to the behavioral pattern a system settles into over time. Systems can be natural (the movement of the stars) or they can be social (the organization of activists). According to chaos theory, there are point, limit, torus, and strange attractors. The more complex and adaptive the system, the more likely it is that levels of disorder and unpredictability will be high in local, situational or micrological encounters. However, over time, with enough iterations of self-similar inputs, a global pattern will emerge that can be plotted in phase-space. Chaologists refer to this as the butterfly effect or the strange attractor.

An example of how attractors function in social movements comes from the anarchist countercultural scene of graffiti art (Ferrell 1996). As a loose assemblage of mobilization actors challenging and resisting traditional imagery, language, dress, and ideals, their attention to local networking, resource allocation, political lobbying, long-range planning, and strategic interventions are all dismissed in favor of the adrenaline rush, the unpredictable moment, the visceral experience, and the serendipitous event. These behaviors, all unstaged, unplanned, and unprogrammed, are reflective of the creative and the chaotic; meaning emerges in the wake of the unanticipated, truth unfolds in the ambiguity of it all, and identity is expressed through style. For the counterculture graffiti artist, the attraction is to high states of local disorganization. Over time, with enough opportunities for creative self-expression, this produces an orderly disorder consistent with the anarchist commitment to change, difference, uncertainty, and becoming.

In nonlinear dynamical systems theory behavior never repeats itself because it does not precisely follow the same path twice. This is the phenomenon of self-similarity. While there are certainly approximations or while replications of sorts can appear, these can never be identical, given initial conditions. At best there can be representations or simulations. Baudrillard's (1983a) work on hyper-reality and Derrida's observations on the undecidability of the text (1973, 1977) resonate with this logic. Associated with the notion of self-similarity is chaos theory's concept of iteration. Approximations are never exact fits because there is always a degree of sensitivity to the initial conditions that established the behavior in the first place. In other words, "sensitive dependence on such original circumstances can produce disproportionate outcomes after several attempts at repeating or replicating a given situation" (Arrigo 1997c, 187).

A social movement event that signifies the problem of self-similarity and iteration comes from the failed attempts to replicate the passion, politics, and culture of the 1960s through two Woodstock revivals. This was a period, personified in music, for peace, love, and understanding. Although organizers endeavored to establish conditions similar to the original event in 1969 (e.g., location, season, extracurricular activities), both revivals never captured the mood of the original extravaganza. In fact, the most recent Woodstock event ended violently when people went hungry, women were victimized, and fires erupted.

Related to self-similarity and iteration, is the notion of bifurcation.[8] This concept refers to the effect of increasing levels of system chaos such that the entity, unable to absorb such inputs, eventually splits into two. In other words, a new order emerges seemingly out of nothing. This self-organization tendency is a natural component of all healthy, adaptive systems. It is an order-out-of-chaos phenomenon.[9]

Some advocates for persons with psychiatric disorders adopt the position of nonlinear dynamical systems theory and bifurcation in their efforts to promote change in civil commitment statutes and clinical predictions of dangerous. For example, Williams and Arrigo (2002) have argued that states of being are fluid not fixed, and that tight, rigid control of mental "disorder" denies citizens their organic ability to self-heal, to self-organize (see also, Butz 1997). Moreover, S. Barton (1994) notes that when drug therapy is administered as the preferred method of intervention and is used to curtail or reduce disorganized speech, thought, and behavior patterns, much more is lost in the process. Indeed, as he cautions, "have we not also wiped out the seeds of a more adaptive psychological order—an order that may have taken days, weeks, months, or even years to develop in the complex electrochemical organization of the brain?" (1994, 695). Social movement efforts for persons with psychiatric disorders would do well to assess how the notion of bifurcation is consistent with their interests in establishing least restrictive and least invasive forms of medicolegal treatment.

The concept of dissipative structures suggests that far-from-equilibrium conditions are a more organic representation of social life and human activity than are equilibrium conditions. A blending of order and disorder (i.e., chaos) signifies the natural and healthy dimensions under which the behavior of any system can optimally function. Thus, structure and disorganization, predictability and impermanence, stability and change are the cornerstones of a social movement in touch with the cultural mapping of its individual and group members and their evolving, incomplete, and fluid identities.

Each of the previously cited examples illustrates the importance of dissipative structures. AIDS coalitions, sexual politics, military campaigns, graffiti activism, counterculture musical revivals, and mental health advocacy all symbolize how the mix of flux and stasis, spontaneity and predictability, deviance and conformity, absurdity and sensibility, *pathos* and *logos* inform and texture the social world we inhabit and make. Thus, a fourth way in social movement theory would reach beyond the confines of established lines of reasoning and routinized patterns of behavior to resurrect a "resounding mosaic of resistance" (Schehr 1997, 174). In this configuration, movement potential would include the emergence of new cultural forms where replacement expressions of identity, sexuality, truth, leadership, and neighborhood, were reconstructed and recovered (Arrigo 1997c, 189).

INNOCENCE PROJECTS AND INTENTIONAL COMMUNITIES AS NONLINEAR SOCIAL MOVEMENTS

Efforts to challenge dominant cultural institutions and practices often operate at subaltern levels and in ambulant, rather than linear, ways. However, by way of contrast, most contemporary theorizing about social movement activity privileges large-scale mass mobilizations of rational actors capable of resource mobilization, organization building, networking, and long-range planning (McAdam, McCarthy, and Zald 1996). Indeed, attention is directed typically at large-scale actions aimed at changes in political and/or economic policies and institutions. Moreover, interest groups, advocacy coalitions, and charismatic personalities unaffiliated with any specific organization tend, for purposes of theoretical clarity, to be viewed as something other than a social movement.[10] Indeed, the examples described in the previous section generally are not considered social movements. While we believe there is some justification for this—especially as an effort to avoid conceptual ubiquity to the point of uselessness—efforts to construct a meta-narrative of movement potential has, in our view, erred both theoretically and empirically. New social movement theory too narrowly restricts identification of movement actors, organizational configurations, resource generation, networking, lobbying, and issue advocacy. The result is a failure to acknowledge dynamic activism consonant with the more liberating narratives of postmodern inquiry.

The primary points to be developed in this portion of chapter 8 are twofold: (1) demonstrate how efforts to describe movement activities using linear, cause-effect conceptual tools fail to capture the dynamic nature of social movement actors and actions; and (2) resituate the debate on social movements within the discourse and logic of French postmodern social theory. To address the first point we rely on the contemporary emergence of "Innocence Projects" and wrongful convictions[11] in the United States and around the world.[12] We also describe intentional communities in the form of novel strategies to house the homeless. As instances of nonlinear social movement activity, we suggest how these initiatives acknowledge the contingent nature of subjectivity and institutional relations. To address the second point, we tentatively explore how admittedly selective, though key, insights from the first-wave theoreticians discussed in chapters 1 and 2 could further our regard for the applied literature on social movements in general and innocence projects and intentional communities in particular.

Innocence Projects as Nonlinear Social Movements

While innocence projects manifest themselves in many unique ways, four organizational patterns are discernible. These include the following: (1) law school affiliated; (2) law school affiliated and additional university-based school or department affiliation; (3) university-based school or department affiliation; and (4) nonprofit community-based affiliation. With the exception of nonprofit organizations, university-based (and law school) innocence projects are structured to allow *students* to investigate possible cases of wrongful conviction.[13] Each innocence project must determine the kinds of cases it will review. Some examples include cases addressing only factual innocence, sentencing violations and violations of due process, or cases where DNA evidence exists. Once pertinent information is uncovered, faculty affiliated with a law school or attorney volunteers associated with a community-based organization pursue the case.

Innocence projects have produced overwhelming successes as determined by exonerations.[14] But exonerations alone are not the standard by which to measure their efficacy.[15] That is to say, while exonerations are the goal of every innocence project, their singular existence may be sufficient to promote changes in local and state due process. Indeed, borrowing from chaos theory, the appearance of innocence projects signifies the emergence of a fixed point attractor adding an additional bifurcation point in the phase space commonly occupied by the otherwise narrowly conceived legal discourse in use. The presence of fractals, in this case innocence projects, generate the possibility of a new outcome basin wherein innovation, creativity, and change within dominant culture can flourish.[16] We take this nonlinear reconfiguration of innocence projects to be a new direction in understanding social movements, consistent with postmodern lines of inquiry. In what follows, we briefly justify our position.

Innocence Projects and Postmodernism

B. Moyer (2001, 10) describes social movements as ". . . collective actions in which the populace is alerted, educated, and mobilized, sometimes over years and decades, to challenge the power-holders and the whole society to redress social problems or grievances and restore critical social values" (see also, McAdam, McCarthy, and Zald 1996, for more on the conventional theoretical context of social movements). Two key elements emerge from this perspective: a social movement strategy and a grand strategy. The social movement strategy is to "alert, educate, and win over an ever-increasing majority of the public" (1996, 17). Convincing the public that a social problem exists and that policies need to be changed facilitates this support. Mobilization of the public follows. The grand strategy refers to, "a broad framework that describes the overall process of movement success. It provides movement activists with a model they can use to create goals, strategies, tactics, and programs that are consistent with the movement's long-term goals" (1996)[17]

However, by turning to the insights of French postmodern social theory, alternative interpretations for social movements are discernible, consistent with our discussion of innocence projects. For example, chaos theory promotes nonlinear articulations of organic activity. Through the use of "trouser diagrams" (Gregersen and Sailer 1993; see also Henry and Milovanovic 1996, 165; Milovanovic 2003, 74–77) theorists are able to consider a far greater number of intervening variables than is possible with linear path analysis, thus displaying a more comprehensive portrait of intersecting micro- and macro-level forces. Trouser diagrams also eschew the use of causal arrows, a conceptual and empirical representation of organic fluidity leading to system stability. While patterned relationships do emerge, their path is often not charted on straight lines. Deleuze and Guattari (1987) identify this distinction as between smooth and striated space. Lyotard (1984) endorses this notion through the concept of parology, especially the small narrative (*petit recit*) over the grand narrative (*les grand recits*).

A thoughtful and more complete depiction of systemic activity, then, is located at the juncture between smooth and striated space, a negotiated realm that incorporates both unpredictability and the pressure of preexisting social relationships. Since all relationships are fluid, capable of generating new point attractors and subsequently new branches of activity and meaning, theorists must avoid morphological accounts of social movement activity that adhere to clearly delineated beginning, middle, and end points. Indeed, it is our view that there is no end to social movements. Movement actors transmogrify as conditions and positionalties change over time.

In this context, postmodern social movements are akin to Kristeva's (1984) notion of subjects-in process, in which a *jouissance* of the body (Irigary 1985b; Grosz 1990) and an *écriture féminine* (Cixous 1976; Klages 1997) are validated. These are lines of thought in which language and meaning are polyvalent, fluid, heterogenous, discontinuous, and poetic. Barthes' (1968b, 1974) notion of the writerly approach to interpreting texts captures this position as well. In the writerly approach, multiplicities in interpretation are emphasized in which truth is not an arrival but a departure. Again, there is no end product. Thus, postmodern social movement actors and activities represent a becoming that is always and already in flux, evolving, and uncertain (see also, Derrida 1976, on the unde-cidability of the text, Baudrillard 1983a, on the "hyper-real" text, and Foucault 1980, on normalization, *dispositif*, and positive power).

Moreover, postmodern social movement actors function much like Lacan's (1991) discourse of the *analyst*. As reformists, the innocence project lawyer conveys new information to the alienated, though desiring, subject (a death row prisoner) about his/her suffering. This information produces replacement signifier to signified anchorings, consistent with the despairing subject's longing for recognition (wrongful conviction) and change (release from confinement). In this configuration, local, provisional, and relational truths are affirmed and legitimized in the discourse of social movements.[18]

Chaos theory also posits the possibility that minute changes occurring at the micro level will produce certain but unanticipated consequences at the macro level. Unlike contemporary social scientists, chaos theorists assume that nonlinearity and flux are as much a part of normal systems as states of equilibrium. This "fractal" activity hovers in what are known as "outcome basins," regions in systems (social and other organic entities) that tend toward order at the macro level (Prigogene and Stengers 1984). Among the number of possible outcomes in a given phase space, the one most representative of social movement activity, is the torus attractor.[19] Torus attractors signify systemic openings affording alternate or competing representations of dominant patterns. In other words, with social movement activity, torus attractors signify competing definitions of situations. This condition is comparable to what some postmodernists have termed languages of possibility (Henry and Milovanovic 1996). While the pressure from the torus attractor stimulates a systemic steering response through the regulation of constitutive sectors (see note 16), it does not induce crippling transformations in structural conditions.

With respect to the claims made by innocence projects, efforts to transform due process and criminal procedure are conducted within the discursively acceptable limits imposed by the phase space. The phase space most commonly configured for articulation of changes to due process and criminal procedure is the realm of legislative politics and the courts. Within each phase space, multiple degrees of freedom are generated to stimulate changes in cases of wrongful conviction, while attending to local, state, and federal legislation affecting changes in due process and criminal procedure.

Political Opportunity Structures (POSs), then, appear when located within the context of chaos theory as temporally and spatially bounded moments of truth, of reality.[20] These are ambulant, fleeting opportunities to take advantage of bounded conditions to promote systemic changes or what Butler (1992) describes as contingent universalties. Recognition of this aspect of organic systems enhances our ability to locate possible points of contestation within a narrow phase space, while also accepting the inevitability of continuous transformation of that space. Conceptual similarities also exist in the discussion of "framing" (McAdam, McCarthy, and Zald 1996). More genuinely framing movement activities requires attention to identity construction beyond what we have sketched above. However, we argue that ways to frame social movement issues that speak directly to interpersonal relations, as well as to associations with institutions, could benefit from additional applications of French postmodern "first wave" social theory.

Intentional Communities as Nonlinear Social Movements

R. Schehr (1997) contends that there are eight characteristics that distinguish contemporary intentional communities (ICs) from their predecessors (see also, Questenberry 1995; Kozeny 1995). These include the following: (1) ICs are enthusiastically committed to innovative and diverse expressions of cohabitation based on spiritual, psychological, sociological, and philosophical belief systems; (2) ICs are not linear or hierarchical (process-oriented and feminist-conceived models of decision making routinely are employed); (3) IC members are both producers and users of creative, nonviolent dispute resolution tactics, employed in the service of self-actualization; (4) where possible, ICs utilize ecologically sensitive technology (e.g., solar power; electric cars), mindful of their commitment to the environment; (5) ICs are dedicated to outreach work and neighborhood service efforts expressed through communal meetings and ongoing publications; (6) IC members strive for balance in their personal and professional lives, yielding richer and more meaningful experiences of work, play, love, identity, and relationships; (7) ICs value self-reliance and economic self-sufficiency, innovatively expressed through food cooperatives, alternative farming methods, and so forth; and (8) ICs strongly support peace, justice, racial and gender equality, and communal harmony. Utilizing several principles from chaos theory and applying them to one intentional community designed to house the homeless, we tentatively suggest how ICs can operate as a social movement consistent with the fourth way in movement activity; namely, the nonlinear paradigm.

Wood Street Commons, Intentional Communities, and Nonlinearity

One example of an intentional community is Wood Street Commons; a single room occupancy (SRO) facility in Pittsburgh, Pennsylvania developed to shelter the homeless (Arrigo 1997c).[21] Although the facility underwent two ecological stages of protracted development, its eventual organizational and interpersonal configuration was consistent with the philosophy of intentional communities, built around themes derived from chaos theory.

Each resident occupied his or her own room that included several basic amenities (e.g., wash basin, chest of drawers, desk and chair). However, social-psychological components emphasized the importance of communal spaces strategically and centrally located in the facility. Geographically positioned in close proximity were a shared cooking and dining space, and centers for conferencing, reading, recreating, and entertaining. This guaranteed that much of the cohabitation would be shared and consensual. Indeed, occasions for food, self-governance, communication, play, and contemplation unfolded nonhier- archically, nonlinearly, and fluidly, signifying how these primitive practices could be transformed into moments of celebration and connection, healing and redemption.

When disputes arose on individual floors among residents, "block leaders" worked to reconcile differences. When disagreements materialized in communal spaces, the tenant advocacy group intervened to resolve problems. Here, guided by principles of fractals, attractors, and bifurcations, the indi- vidual outcomes of these disputes stressed the fuzzy logic of situational ethics, degrees of accountability, local disorder, and self-organization. From the "outside" looking in, mapping cultural and individual identity appeared incon- sistent, in disarray, and unpredictable. However, at the situational and inter- personal level, these were moments of becoming for residents.

WSC developed formal and informal lines of communication designed to reach out to members of its vertical neighborhood. A tenant newsletter was disseminated monthly to residents. It was developed, written, produced, and funded by tenants (the latter was based on an economy of scale). The newsletter also included paid advertisements by local shopkeepers and busi- nesses owners in downtown Pittsburgh. The contents included housing infor- mation, local events, and creative self-expression (tenant poetry and cartoons were regular features). In addition, though, monthly resident meetings and floor meetings were held. These events addressed the social needs and indi- vidual accomplishments of occupants. Characteristically, tenant leadership disputes would erupt, creating periods of communication breakdown. Excessive levels of chaos would abound, compelling WSC, as a social system, into a bifurcation state. However, over time, a new order would emerge; the newsletter would resurrect itself, participation in floor or communal advocacy would come from different, untapped sources, self-organization would prevail.

WSC emphasized economic self-sufficiency and developed a number of fluid initiatives in support of this objective. Several residents were employed as para-professional staff, assisting with refining the cultural milieu (recre- ational specialists), making and serving the meals (food service specialists) cleaning and maintaining rooms and floors (housekeeping and janitorial spe- cialists), and interviewing and screening potential residents (housing spe- cialists). In addition, a steadfast commitment to racial and gender equality, participation, and accountability were seen as important components of living peacefully with others. To this extent, tenants sought to explore their evolving regard for love, play, relationships, and identity. Although several residents struggled in the face of their reflection (e.g., drug use for some was rampant, social deviance in the form of property damage occasionally occurred, several tenants experienced routine difficulty in paying rent), the internal ecology valorized far-from-equilibrium conditions and dissipative structures. Nonconventional social arrangements materialized: persons with psychiatric disorders were elected floor representatives; drug-use was situationally accepted and legitimized to the extent that one's routine interactions and ongoing responsibilities did not result in total disintegration; and a loose, evolving, and flexible confederation of rules and procedures informed resident decision making in the community.

Intentional Communities and Postmodernism

As an intentional community designed to assist the homeless, Wood Street Commons demonstrated how movement potential, activities, and actors were framed in nonlinear ways. Consistent with chaos theory, the organizational ecology and tenant behavior of this facility also reflected some affinities for postmodernism. In what follows, we apply several selected principles from first-wave postmodern social theory to explain where and how this occurred.

As an effusive script, the cultural mapping of the building's organization and the residents' identities were steeped in the evolving logic of meta-narratives absent totalizing foundation. Much like Lyotard's (1984) notions of the *differand* and parology, the ethical dimension of community encompassed continual renewal and discovery (Britt 1998), without universal truths. Indeed, pluralism, heterogeneity, multiplicity, and becoming were very much a part of the social life of tenant existences. To the degree that residents embraced the fragmented, unstable, positional, and contingent nature of their ongoing interactions and perceived that they were connected to a richer social fabric of communal life, multiple expressions of political events (governance structure), economic transactions (food purchases), and cultural activities (newsletter, sports league), creatively, spontaneously, and continually emerged.

For residents in this nonlinear intentional community, an aesthetic of immediacy and change devoid of judgment nurtured the desiring body without organs (Deleuze and Guattari 1987). Nomadic in their storytelling, free-floating in their imagery, rhizomatic in their movement, and proliferating in their becoming, tenant activism was akin to schizoanalysis (Deleuze and Guattari 1983). The deterritorializaiton of normative speech codes, modes of comportment, social configurations, and intergroup activities, enabled momentary breakthroughs. These de-oedipalizing occasions were reflexive junctures inducing substance abuse recovery, family reunification, literacy classes, and job training. However, these tendencies were rooted in disruptions, departures, and dislocations from conventional interpretations of civic life. Indeed, the communal ethos celebrated alterity, fluidity, and the subaltern (Spivak 1991), producing fractured and unpredictable segmentation and multiple lines of escape.

The absence of any "grand" scheme for tenant identity meant that knowledge about self and others was not homogenized and that difference was not vanquished. This theme resonates with Foucault's (1977) thesis on particularism, power, and discourse. "Power [spoken] produces; it produces reality; it produces domains of objects and rituals of truth (1977, 194). However, particularity hermeneutically instantiates individuality, displacing mechanisms of disciplinary control and destabilizing techniques of panoptic surveillance. Derrida's concept of the metaphysics of presence and absence (1976), Baudrillard's (1983a) rendering of the hyperreal, and Barthes' (1968b, 1974) articulation of the writerly approach also are suggestive here. Multiple and ambulant expressions of the possible—how communal events unfolded, how relationships were formed and severed, what resident actions were acceptable and problematic—implied that communal truth was a departure in meaning, never fully recognizable or retrievable, subject, at best, to simulations and to interpretative realities.

Perhaps most profound is how the discourse of homelessness and poverty got valorized while, at the same time, was transformed into a language of transpraxis. Rendered a lack, *pas toute*, in the dominant linguistic system of law, medicine, criminal justice, and social services, tenants typically invoked metaphors of "disease" "skill deficits, " "needs," "incapacities or infirmaries" "deviance," and "violence," to explain their humanity. These articulations are much like Kristeva's (1982) notion of abjection. As Barbara Creed (1993, 1) observes, ". . . the abject is where meaning collapses, the place where I am not." In other words, these images of the self, first mobilized for the residents of WSC in the Imaginary Order and then activated in the Symbolic Order, were both the source and product of the subject's lack. Tenants endeavored to resist these alienating descriptors but were repeatedly drawn to them because they gave meaning to their otherwise incomplete existences.

This notion of abjection, as remarkably pronounced in the lives of WSC residents, can also be explained through Lacan's (1991) insights on the discourses of the *master, hysteric,* and *analyst.* In the discourse of the *master,* key signifiers representing the identity of residents were invoked ("diseased," "deviant," "dangerous") by agents of social control (mental health, social service, and criminal justice personnel), producing a circumscribed knowledge about the tenants rendering them incomplete and divided. In the discourse of the *hysteric*, residents attempted to convey their felt oppression, alienation, and lack to others but inserted themselves or were situated within a grammar that valorized master signifiers that reconstituted their longing and desire into acceptable and conventional discourse on homelessness, mental illness, poverty, and so forth. Thus, as interpellated subjects (Althusser, 1971), WSC residents re-presented knowledge about their plight in traditional ways that, although familiar, left them divided and unfulfilled. However, over time, while building tenants explored their identity and while the building ecology was perceived as fluid, residents, along with community organizers, re-articulated the conditions of their existences and of their becomings.

In the discourse of the *analyst*, organizers as healers and reformers conveyed information to alienated tenants about their reality. Tenants were described as "artists," "sports enthusiasts," "writers," "politicians," "chefs," "dancers," and so forth. In short, they were defined not in terms of what they lacked but in terms of what they could be, based on their movement potential activities in the community. And while these definitions were positional, contingent, and relational, and while these descriptors were differentially interpreted, depending on the person to whom they were assigned, this alternative data established replacement meanings for resident identities. Indeed, identities were increasingly negotiated; transformed, based on affirmative signified anchorings, into possible new forms of self-expression (see also note 18). And while the linguistic baggage of homelessness, poverty, illiteracy, mental illness consigned some residents to a state of psychic disorganization and social disequilbrium, others channeled the marginalizing residue of these descriptors into more fully affirming and more fully liberating rearticulations of their capacity to transcend adversity.

In part, this transformation is what Luce Irigaray (1985b) intends when describing the phenomenon of mimesis. Rather than condoning or accepting passive imitations of symbolic and imaginary forms, mimesis implies the conversion of subordination into affirmation based on rhetorical and discursive ploys. By surrendering the self to the label of homelessness, poverty, drug addict, and the like, new meanings for these signifiers emerged, beyond those definitions lodged within the limits of dominant discourse. Thus, many residents transformed their otherwise stigmatizing labels into meanings that were more or other than what prevailing culture intended. On these occasions, lack became *jouissance* as fulfillment materialized through subversive linguistic tactics.

CONCLUSION

This chapter explored the phenomenon of social movements as nonlinear expressions of human potential and activities. To substantiate this claim, we reviewed the literature on new social movement theory, described a fourth way in conceiving the identity paradigm, and applied our analysis to innocence projects and intentional communities, mindful of those insights within French postmodern social theory that could further our understanding of these phenomena. We invite readers and activists, researchers and educators to utilize chaos theory as a basis to explore how additional examples of movement activities could be envisioned nonlinearly. From our perspective, these efforts will help promote greater prospects for citizen justice, collective well-being, and social change consistent with the postmodern era.

Back to the Future:

Rediscovering Crime, Law, and Social Change

INTRODUCTION

In this concluding chapter, we reflect on four important themes underpinning our collective call to write this book. First, we return to the first-wave postmodern luminaries and their significance for charting several new directions in the development of social theory and its application to various facets of institutional and civic life. Second, we reassess what this book endeavored to accomplish, mindful of its many suggestive, provocative, and novel approaches for rethinking a number of enduring debates in crime, law, and social justice. Third, we explore the relationship between theory and practice, emphasizing the dialectics of struggle in all social movement activities (e.g., prison resistance, victim offender mediation, intentional communities). Fourth, we ponder what work remains, especially if the disciplines of law and criminology are to promote meaningful and sustainable reform. In summary, then, this conclusion chapter represents a momentary step backward, enabling us to recall and to retrieve the future of change, of transpraxis, and of what could be. This is the postmodern legacy that awaits us all.

RECALLING THE FIRST WAVE

Motivated by the perennial desire to construct alternate political, economic, and cultural landscapes, generations of activists, philosophers, and educators have constructed ideal images of its people and their possibilities (Laclau 1990). Typically, these images have reflected a unifying signification of an idyllic past; one that promised to complete the grand human project. While often mythical, representations of the past through invented tradition (Hobsbawm and Ranger 1983) and nostalgic utopia (Benjamin 1969) spawned coalescent themes that propelled the Renaissance, the Enlightenment, and the considerable advance of science through positivism (Laclau 1990). Just as Marxist theory contemplated an evolutionary path to a more humane and just distribution of resources by ushering in a new mode of production (communism), modernist ideals articulated the emergence of an ever more reasonable, logical, and rational set of cultural relationships, institutions, and individuals. In short, human beings were "ever becoming." We were, as Jürgen Habermas (1984) suggests, the unfinished product of modernity. So, why fix it if it is not broken?

The collective intellectual effort presented in this book stands in stark contrast to the evolutionary views of human progress characteristic of the Enlightenment. Indeed, the first wave intellectuals discussed in the first two chapters signify the manifestation of an afterimage (Deleuze and Guatarri 1987); an event so important that it leaves an indelible mark on history. Represented in these first wave thinkers is a serious challenge to the momentum generated by theory, method, and policy promoting the free thinking, freely acting "individual." In fact, the idea of the individual itself has been dismissed as an artifact of the Renaissance. While a radical idea at the time, given its distinct cognitive and praxis-oriented separation from the powers of the king and church, the historical "individual," it turns out, is a far more complicated entity. Indeed, a new theory of the "subject" was needed to capture the constitutive, intersectional, and contingent aspects of identity; one that initially was built upon turn of the century phenomenology and symbolic interactionism to delve more deeply into the psychoanalytic, semiotic, and chaotic realms of organic composition.

The emergence of first wave postmodern scholarship signaled a challenge to theories driven by notions of evolutionary growth, human self-sameness, and the drive toward stasis, unity, and grand "Truth." To possess the Truth meant the construction of a discernible "inside" and "outside;" a complete and composite entity that was retrievable, quantifiable, knowable, and,

where necessary, correctable. These dualisms do a disservice to the understanding of the monistic subject (Grosz 1994). And while recognition of this
phenomenon for the constitution of group identity could be found in, among
others, Georg Simmel (1950), it took the work of Barthes (1974), Derrida
(1981), Baudrillard (1983a), and others to firmly establish what Connolly
referred to as the "politics of paradox." This expression of difference, as definitive of human consciousness and action, promotes a reenergized politic, especially, as we have seen, in the realm of crime, law, and social justice. For as
Laclau (1990, 20) has deftly claimed, "Contingency does not therefore mean
a set of merely external and [obligatory] relations between identities, but the
impossibility of fixing with any precision—that is, in terms of a necessary
ground—either the relations *or the identities*" (emphasis in original).

Like a meteor shooting through the tranquility of an ebony mountain
at twilight, the project first and second wave postmodern scholars set for
themselves was to probe the fluidity of identity as juxtaposed to organizational
and cultural expectations. Their elegant deconstruction of the institutions and
practices of social control, gender identity, power, and language promised to
destabilize long held theoretical and political conceptualizations of human
consciousness and desire. And while critics of French postmodernism derided
what appeared to be a narcissistic rejection of political challenges to oppressive
and alienating state apparatuses, affirmative and integrative applications of
their work materialized, generating innovative, though temporally and spatially bounded, praxis-oriented recommendations for many of our cultural ills.
We submit that the spirit of this activity is what promotes the possibility of a
truly transformative politics; one that can envision more genuine forms of
social justice. Indeed, once we acknowledge the myopia of a single path to the
one foundational expression of the "True" or the "Just," we are open to a new
phase space; one ignited by a liberating discourse of desire that acknowledges
contingent universalities and multiple renderings of the possible. Thus, the
value of the first and second wave postmodern theorists is their gift of deconstruction and reconstruction, and the promise associated with the total eclipse
of historically oppressive metanarratives.[1]

APPLYING THE POSTMODERN LEGACY TO CRIME, LAW, AND SOCIAL JUSTICE RESEARCH

Assimilating and consolidating the insights of the seminal, first wave French
postmodern thinkers represents a daunting task, especially given our additional call to apply their respective insights to various themes in crime, law,

and social justice. We are firmly committed to emancipatory transpraxis; one based on the politics of paradox. We believe that transpraxis can be realized through the application of affirmative and integrative forms of postmodern analyses. Indeed, our discursive reliance on postmodern inquiry was not built on despair, nihilism, or fatalism; rather, our vision advocated a more liberatory transpraxis including critique *and* transformative engagement.

This book was written to demonstrate through a series of applications chapters the many influences of first wave scholars on contemporary criminal and social justice practices. Each chapter constituted an aspect of justice studies where dominant cultural values erected barriers to the attainment of nonhierarchical social relations. In addition, these superordinate cultural values prohibited gender, sexual preference, race, class, and age equitable substantive justice. It is our hope that through the deconstruction of specific issues associated with crime, law, and social justice we stimulated researchers, activists, and educators to apply postmodern insights to the conceptualization of other socio-legal topics not addressed in this book.

In this sense, then, *The French Connection in Criminology,* is our contribution toward building a more just and diverse society where the measure becomes the unfolding, never linear to be sure, of human potential in a developing society. Admittedly, the occasions for conflict would probably increase (Unger 1987); but these would be opportunities for reflexive thought about what it means to be human in a complex society and about ossified COREL sets that contribute to conditions conducive for harms of reduction and harms of repression.

These periods of contestation and of reflection also would represent ongoing opportunities to reexamine structural forces. The presence of transformative (not restorative) justice programs would usher in new understandings about the other; about the self through the struggles and triumphs of the other; about the channeling of negative energy into a positive, life-affirming force; about the development of alternative discursive practices where the multiaccentual nature (Volosinov 1986) of the sign is recognized; and about reconstituted COREL sets where the full body without organs engages in ongoing "becoming."

Moreover, the "excessive investor" who participates in and manufactures harms of reduction and of repression would not signify the occasion where an increase in overall violence would prevail (here legitimized by the State); but rather, through the social judo metaphor, would be the moment where creative nonviolent responses would emerge that are transpraxis in form. From our perspective, these reflections of what would be and of social change indeed offer some challenges for critical thought.

SOME THOUGHTS ON THEORY AND PRACTICE

Previously (end of chapter 4), we addressed the issue of political resistance and the wherewithal of a replacement discourse. In this section, we want to conclude by addressing the relation of theory to practice and to the dialectics of struggle, including those found within social movements generally. A very useful starting point is found in Michael Hardt's book, *Gilles Deleuze: An Apprenticeship in Philosophy* (1993). He focuses specifically on Louis Althusser, Gilles Deleuze, and Hegelian logic. We add Michel Foucault, Jacques Derrida, topology, and constitutive theory to our commentary.

Following Deleuze, we advocate the Nietzschean ideal of an affirmative postmodern transpraxis and not the Hegelian logic of reaction-negation where the slave can only create value by a double negation. We note, too, Hegel's logic on the unfolding of the Absolute Spirit was also incorporated in Marx's dialectical materialism. In this analysis, modes of production and consciousness were understood to "evolve" implicating linear progression; thus, falling short of an affirmative postmodern social movement perspective.

Althusser (1969) prioritizes theory over practice (Hardt 1993, 105). He begins and ends on this subject with his quote from Lenin: "without theory, no revolutionary practice" (cited in Hardt 1993, 105; see also Althusser 1969, 166). Similarly, Foucault collapses theory into practice (1977a, 208): "theory does not express, translate or serve to apply practice: it is practice." Deleuze, however, inspired by Spinoza, argues: "practice is a set of relays from one theoretical point to another, theory is a relay from one practice to another. No theory can develop without eventually encountering a wall, a practice is necessary for piercing this wall" (Deleuze, cited in Hardt 1993, 105; see also Deleuze 1977, 206).

In contrast, Micheal Hardt's (1993, 106) reading of Deleuze is that "the relationship between theory and practice emphasizes that the two activities [theory and practice] remain autonomous and equal in principle . . . there is no synthesis of theory and practice, and no priority of one over the other." In other words, we cannot privilege, or prioritize, one over the other. As such, the mind, as connected to theory, and the body, as connected to practice, contribute, in their own way, to actual activity. For Hardt, the two are linked only in terms of "autonomy" and "equality." Thus, practice is not subsumable under theory and theory is not subsumable under practice. It is Hardt's (1993, 107) view to: "Bring the body out from the shadow of the mind, bring practice out from the shadow of theory, in all its autonomy and dignity, to try to discover what it can do." And thus, "the logic of constitution . . . accumulates its elements from below in open, nonteleological forms as original, unforeseeable, creative structures. The movement of a Hegelian practice is always recuperated within the logic of order, dictated from above, whereas a Deleuzian practice rises from below through an open logic of organization."

We build on Hardt's position. Following constitutive theory, we question whether there exists the "autonomy" between theory and practice. Instead, we argue that each already exists in the other. Separating the two has been the logic of creating dualisms, inspired by Cartesian and post-Enlightenment thought. Rather, following Derrida, any prioritization of the one already carries the trace of the other within it; the one is constituted by the other. In short, they are inseparable.

In addition, following Lacan's conceptualization of the subject in terms of the Moebius strip where the "inside" and "outside" communicate, we also can say that the dyad (theory/mind and practice/body) can be conceptualized by the traversing of the Moebius strip.[2] Theory (with practice always already being embedded within it) informs practice (with theory always already embedded within it); practice (with theory always already embedded within it) informs theory (with practice always already embedded within it). It is a disservice to stop this process, this flow, the dynamic in snapshot form, and then to say, "see, theory informs practice" or vice versa.

Given these observations, we want to conclude this section with a brief comment on struggles and social movements of various sorts (e.g., prison resistance, creating a jurisprudence of color, victim offender mediation, establishing intentional communities). Throughout this book we have been concerned with the dialectics of struggle. On occasion, committed and well-intended activists often inadvertently reconstitute hierarchies. We see this in Drucilla Cornell's (1999, 11, 139, 185) polemic on Catharine MacKinnon's work, citing it as often advocating the "politics of revenge," hate politics," and reversal of hierarchies. We see this in the form of schmarxism, whereby would-be reformers abide by a dogmatism that often translates into exorcism—going to great length to find, or to construct, the evil in the other and then attacking one's own constructions.[3] We see this in various forms of political correctness.

These constructions will not do. Activists must be informed by the historical literature on struggles and the dialectics often involved (see for example, Beirne 1990); theoreticians must expose their bodies to activities of the streets in encountering the diverse desires of disenfranchised peoples. At best, there can only exist "a plurality of contingent and partial emancipations" (Laclau 1996b, 101) found in an ever-emerging society marked by "structural dislocations." Unfortunately, those in struggle often privilege the one over the other. We argue that this posture can have negative, unintended consequences in social transformations.

BACK TO THE FUTURE: ON CRIME, LAW, AND SOCIAL CHANGE

There is still much more to do. However, this book has been a modest attempt at delineating the insights of the key first wave French scholars and at exploring how their contributions have been and can be relevant to law, criminology, and social justice. Indeed, what we demonstrated is that the novel conceptual and methodological tools offered by this first generation of social theorists profoundly resonate with the burning issues of our era.

Accordingly, we must have the conviction to theorize the alternative; to refrain from dogmatism, schmarxism, and the discourse of the *master*. Ours is a challenge for the new millennium. We must protect the "imaginary domain" (Cornell 1998a, 1998b), along with its creative suturing with the symbolic (Lacan 1977), so that new, discursive practices can emerge. These activities valorize the images of the other in all her/his complexity in more open, fluid, and dynamic social systems that approach far-from-equilibrium conditions. This is a place where orderly (dis)order, not stasis, prevails. In this realm, linear logic, the privileging of order, and Euclidean-based formulations and practices need to be tempered with the insights of dynamic systems theory (e.g., chaos theory). This is the path to transpraxis.

This book did not offer all the answers; however, it encouraged the reader to make use of the conceptual tools and the examples in application to both deconstruct and reconstruct human agency and social structure in more liberating ways. This volume has been about moving forward; however, this journey means embracing the challenge that is upon us. This bold invitation is nothing less than a call to develop a more humane society. Thus, the challenge that we face is to make a difference through the discourse on social change without, at the same time, doing so in ways that repress or reduce the other's humanity. This is a road that can transform the conditions and consciousness of people. This is a path that can lead us back to the future. This is a place where contingent, local, and relational expressions of crime, law, and social justice can be rediscovered again and anew.

Notes

INTRODUCTION

1.   Elsewhere, we describe this phenomenon as the "dialectics of struggle." This phenomenon challenges all of us to be cognizant of how closure to meaning can produce harm in unintended, unanticipated effects. In part, the application chapters (4–8) draw attention to where and how this can occur.

2.   We realize that an appeal to language alone cannot overcome the materialistic forces of oppression and alienation that people confront. The limits of such an undertaking produce idealism and sentimentalism, absent an understanding of material conditions. We argue, however, that material conditions take on meaning through language and it is this language itself that is the source of considerable controversy. Indeed, as we demonstrate in the subsequent application chapters exploring pressing crime, law, and justice topics, exposing the layered dimensions of marginalization is possible through an integrative and affirmative postmodern investigation. Thus, in brief, this book is designed to shed insight into the relationship between human agents and structural arrangements as they both shape and are shaped by language (Henry and Milovanovic 1996, 185–243).

CHAPTER 1: ESTABLISHING THE FIRST WAVE

1.   We note that the ordering of the social theorists, except for Jacques Lacan, is alphabetical. We explain our rationale for beginning with Lacan in note 2. Depending on one's scholarly orientation toward and intellectual proclivity for postmodern social theory, several ordering permutations could be suggested. Thus, for simplicity purposes, we adopted an alphabetical approach. Moreover, additional first-wave

French postmodernists contributing to our enterprise are certainly discernible (e.g., Benveniste, Jakobson), and, as such, we delineated several of their respective insights in the introduction to this book.

2.   Jacques-Marie-Émile Lacan was born in Paris, France in 1901. His early instruction was from the Jesuits at Stanislas College. After completing his baccalaureate, he studied medicine and subsequently received training in psychiatry. Lacan delivered a series of seminars in Paris in the 1950s until 1980, advancing his own version of psychoanalysis. Many of the prominent social theorists of Lacan's era (including most of the first-wave luminaries described in this text) were known to have attended his lectures, to have been trained in the Lacanian tradition, and/or to have incorporated several of his formulations into their own conceptualizations. Given Lacan's seminal contributions to the development of French postmodernist thought, our exploration of first-wave thinkers begins with reference to his considerable insights.

3.   As the application chapters explain, Lacan's insight here can be extended to other disenfranchised people who, because they must engage in semiotic production in the dominant Symbolic Order, also remain *pas-toute*, not-all, incomplete (for a feminist interpretation on this point see the sections on Cixous, Irigaray and Kristeva).

4.   Roland Barthes was born in Cherbough, Manche in 1915. He eventually moved to Paris, France and attended the Sorbonne where he received degrees in classical letters (1939), grammar, and philology (1943). The early work of Barthes (e.g., 1973a, 1967, 1968a) was heavily influenced by existentialism. Thus, themes of autonomy, choice, and freedom—all of which were anathema to the structuralist and poststructuralist enterprises—prevailed (Berman 1988, 145). It was not until the publication of *On Racine* (1964), *Elements of Semiology* (1968b), and *S/Z* (1974) that Barthes substantially reevaluated the form and structure of literary texts and the process of textual sense-making. He claimed that both author and the discourse of multiple readers fostered a "conflict" in interpretation. This insight was to form the basis for much of Barthes' subsequent literary criticism: an appraisal of classic books and novels that was to align him with much of the poststructural and semiotic thinking of his time (e.g., see, Barthes 1967, 1968a,, 1973a).

5.   Gilles Deleuze was trained as a philosopher and Felix Guattari was trained as a psychoanalyst in the Lacanian School. They began their joint projects in 1969, eventually publishing their first major collaboration: *Anti-Oedipus* (1983; originally, 1970). This was followed by *Kafka: Toward Minor Literature* (1986; originally 1975), *A Thousand Plateaus* (1987; originally 1980) and *What is Philosophy* (1994). Deleuze also single authored a number of prestigious books. In this section, we focus on their collaborations.

6.   Steven Best and Douglas Kellner (1991, 75) observe in their assessment of Deleuze and Guattari, "not only do [the theorists] not adopt the discourse of the postmodern . . . , [Guattari] even attacks it as a new wave of cynicism and conservatism . . ." Without question, however, the full force of Deleuze and Guattari's epistemology was a sustained rejection of stability, order, unity, thesis, form, hierarchy, identity, and concrete foundation. These are the cornerstones of modernist thought.

7.   See the popular TV show *Whose Line is it Anyway*, where the actors play out various animals and persons. In many ways, they are in the process of becoming.

8.   As a cultural artifact, *A Thousand Plateaus* (1987) signifies a true postmodern presentation of deterritorialization. Chapters can be read in any order (with the exception of the preface and conclusion), and each draws on different time frames, topics, and points of emphasis. Unlike *Anti-Oedipus* (1983) where Deleuze and Guattari consistently apply the concept schizoanalysis, multiple metaphors are invoked to stimulate association with ambulant, antiessentialist, and fractured conceptualizations of a new politics of desire (i.e., rhizomatic, pragmatic, diagrammatism, cartography, micropolitics).

9.   Michel Foucault was a philosopher, historian, and sexologist. He was a leading intellectual of his time and was Professor of the history of systems of thought, College de France (from 1970). He examined such wide-ranging themes as madness and its treatment in the seventeenth-century (see, *Madness and Civilization*, 1965), modern penality (*Discipline and Punish*, 1977), and the history of sexuality (published as a three volume set (1976–1984).

10.   Jean-François Lyotard was born in 1924 in Versailles, France. It is believed that much of what appears as Lyotard's postmodern criticism of meta-narrative emerged out of his 1960s activism. According to Schultz (1998), Lyotard was politically active in the left-wing organization *Socialism or Barbarism*. While Lyotard's critiques of capitalism continued into his mature writings, it is clear that he despaired of a form of political activism marked by modernism (strikes, complaints, etc.) when, with the ubiquitous profusion of technology, we were now living in postmodern times.

11.   "My excuse for writing has always been a political one; I've always considered that sufficient. Therefore, it is quite evident that I accept entirely that there is a prescriptive function in the ideal of paganism: it lies in the direction this idea indicates as necessary to follow" (Lyotard 1984).

12.   Lyotard was careful to position himself and his work in close juxtaposition with modernism. He stated: "I have said and will say again, that 'postmodern' signifies not the end of modernism" (1988a, 1988b). Like Derrida, Lyotard viewed postmodernism as a correction on modernist proclivities toward totalizing master narratives.

13.   "Truth," for Lyotard, was a less complicated and less relevant project since "that which is assigned the label of truth becomes, in a circular manner, true; it is true because it is truth. Truth is self-justificatory" (Drolet 1994, 261).

CHAPTER 2: SUSTAINING THE FIRST WAVE

1.   Jean Baudrillard was a professor of sociology at the University of Nanterre from the 1960s until 1987. He is Professor Emeritus at the University of Paris, and Professor of Philosophy of Culture and Media Criticism at the European Graduate College in Saas-Fee, Switzerland where he teaches an intensive Summer seminar. He was also associated with the radical group, *Socialism or Barbarism*. Best and Kellner (1991, 111) note that "Baudrillard's acolytes praise him as the 'talisman' of the new postmodern universe, as *the* commotion who theoretically energizes the postmodern

scene, as *the* supertheorist of a new postmodernity." The trajectory of Jean Baudrillard's social theory has undergone several permutations significantly influencing cultural theory, media studies, and contemporary society (Gane 1991; Best and Kellner 1997). These variations include: (1) a rejection of modernity's totalizing claims to truth, reason, and progress; (2) an effort to resituate the categories of Marx within the consumerism of a postmodern society; (3) an unequivocal break from Marxist political economy rationales; and (4) a wholesale endorsement of such noted Baudrillardian concepts as "simulation," "hyper-reality," and "simulacrum." In this section we draw on. Baudrillard's (1968, 1970 1981, 1983a, 1983b) voluminous body of work to trace the evolution of his thought to date.

2.   Mark Gottdiener (1995, 234) argues for the possibility of returning to "authentic cultural forms through the discovery of lost signifieds which counteract the superficial consumerist culture of postmodernism that privileges image, appearance, and disembodied signifiers." The concept of "lost signifieds" sounds question begging. This is similar in law to locating "original juridic positions" or the "original intent of the Constitution." Consistent with postmodernism, the question is from what contingent, local, and relational perspective do we engage in this search for original intent or lost signifieds? We contend that both notions seem to overlook the free play of the (legal) text. While our position is subject to debate, we suggest that Gottdiener's observations on lost signifieds might benefit from some additional conceptual refinement.

3.   Hélène Cixous, was born in Oran, Algeria in 1937 of two very diverse parents (mother, German/Jewish; father, Spanish/French/Jewish), moved to France for her formal studies, completing her doctoral thesis (1968) on an analysis of James Joyce's writings. Her father died when she was a small girl; this event and her colonial environment in Algiers left a profound influence on her writing forever after. In 1974, she founded *the Centre d'Etudes Feminines* (Center for Feminine Studies) at the University of Paris V111. This offered the first doctoral program in women's studies in Europe. This provided her an opportunity to develop a more independent program of thinking about feminine subjectivity. She is a novelist, philosopher, dramatist, playwright, literary critic, poet, and professor.

4.   Hélène Cixous is the author of over forty books and over one hundred articles. Among her most important books are: *Angst* (1985), *The Newly Born Woman* (1986), *The Book of Promethea* (1991), *Three Steps on the Ladder of Writing* (1993*)*, *Reading With Clarice Lispector* (1990), *Authorship, Autobiography and Love* (1996). See also the collection, *The Helene Cixous Reader* (Sellers 2000). Even though she is more noted as a theoretician, about thirty-four of her books are fiction. In an interview, she states "for me, theory does not come before, to inspire, it does not precede, does not dictate, but rather it is a consequence of my text, which is at its origin philosophico-poetical. . . ." (O'Grady 1996, 1).

5.   Jacques Derrida was born in El Biar, Algeria in 1930. He moved with his family to France in 1949 to pursue *Normale Supérieure* studies in philosophy, language, and literature. He received his doctorate in philosophy in 1954 from *Ecole*. Derrida founded the International College of Philosophy in Paris and the International Group for Research into the Teaching of Philosophy in 1975. Currently, he is affiliated with the *Etudes des Hautes en Sciences Sociales*, Paris. Among his many works are *Speech and*

Other Phenomena (1973), *Of Grammatology* (1977), *Writing and Difference* (1978), *Positions* (1981), and *Spectres of Marx* (1994).

6.   The concept "radical democracy" is being used consistent with Ernesto Laclau and Chantal Mouffe's (1985) articulation of it. As M. Calarco (2000) has demonstrated, Laclau and Mouffe's rejection of essentialist hegemonic expressions of justice and their emphasis on nodal points of agreement struck between adversaries, closely parallel's Derrida's tenuous positioning between tradition and differentiation.

7.   This theme emerges in M. Walzer (1994) commenting on international peace activism, Bruce Arrigo and Robert Schehr (1998) discussing restorative justice for juveniles, and Robert Schehr and Dragan Milovanovic (1999) assessing critical approaches to conflict mediation.

8.   In philosophy, logocentrism refers to the privileging of speech over writing. It found its most famous progenitor in Plato (*Phaedrus*). For Derrida, to adopt a logo-centric position is to practice the "metaphysics of presence," where "Truth" is only delivered by speaking. To demonstrate the contradictions in logocentric thought, Derrida points out that in order for Plato to make his point, "Truth" could only be told by speaking, he was forced to juxtapose it to writing. Thus, speaking is dependent on writing (Newman 2001).

9.   Luce Irigaray was born in Belgium but moved to France in the early 1960s. She trained in psychoanalysis at the Louvain and holds a doctorate (1968) degree in linguistics and philosophy. Her second doctorate, *Speculum of the Other Woman*, was subsequently published. She has written extensively on feminism. Although she attended many of Lacan's Seminars in 1974, she was attacked by a number of Lacanians because of her disagreement and reinterpretation of psychoanalytic social theory. She was dismissed from the University of Vincennes shortly after completing her second Doctorate. Her main books are *Speculum of the Other Woman* (1985b), *This Sex Which is Not One* (1985a), *Je, Tu, Nous: Toward a Culture of Difference* (1993a), *An Ethics of Sexual Difference* (1993b), *Sexes and Genealogies* (1993c), and *Thinking the Difference: For a Peaceful Revolution* (1994).

10.   Julia Kristeva was born and raised in communist Bulgaria and was the student of Roland Barthes. She has written several works focused on linguistics and psychoanalysis. Among her main books are *About Chinese Women* (1977, orig. 1974), *Revolution in Poetic Language* (1984, orig. 1974; this was her Ph.D. dissertation), *Desire in Language* (1980, orig. 1977), *Powers of Horror* (1982), *Tales of Love* (1987), *Black Sun* (1989), *New Maladies of the Soul* (1995), *Time and Sense* (1996), *The Sense and Non-sense of Revolt* (2000, orig. 1996).

11.   The *Concise Oxford Dictionary* defines "abject" as: "brought low, miserable; craven, degraded, despicable, self-abasing." For "abjection": "state of misery or degradation."

12.   Consider some expressions of "abjections" (Pentony 1996, 1): bodily waste, death, murder, decay, women's bodies. Elizabeth Grosz (1994, 81, 192–94, 205–206), building on Mary Douglas (1980), adds bodily fluids, bodily by-products, or various "detachable parts of the body.

13.   "The metaphor leads to a view of criminals as diseased and contagious and to a policy requiring segregation of contaminated criminals from uncontaminated non-criminals" (Duncan 1996, 122).

14.   Ironically, Kristeva's personal connections with feminism have been ambiguous. She views feminism as undergoing three phases (Oliver 1998, 3): the first phase argued for formal equality and is rejected because it downplays sexual difference; the second phase advocated a unique feminist language (*écriture féminine*) as a replacement to patriarchal forms and is rejected because it is not attainable and because language and culture are constituted by both women and men; the third phase, which Kristeva endorses, argues for multiple identities. This would include varieties of sexual identities.

CHAPTER 3. THE SECOND WAVE: INTERPRETING THE PAST

1.   Our purpose here is to identify important sociological, epistemological, and cultural themes that inform the postmodern agenda and to situate them within the domain of law and criminology. For an accessible review of these notions see Dragan Milovanovic, "Dueling Paradigm," *Humanity and Society* 19: 19–44. For applications to crime and justice studies see Bruce Arrigo, "The Peripheral Core of law and Criminology," *Justice Quarterly* 12: 452–463.

2.   As others have argued, we may also read Lacan prescriptively, offering the possibility of a more liberated form of desire in the idea of *jouissance* of the body, of the Other, an inexpressible and indescribable form of desire (see e.g., Milovanovic 1992, 1997; Arrigo, 2002a).

3.   COREL sets (constitutive interrelational sets) are historically constituted grouping of relatively stabilized constellations of coupled iterative loops demonstrating extreme sensitivity to environmental conditions (Henry and Milovanovic, 1996: 170-180).

4.   For an analysis of the connection between philosophy and quantum mechanics, see Christopher Norris, *Quantum Theory and the Flight from Realism* (New York: Routledge and Kegan Paul, 2000).

5.   Constitutive criminology draws from a number of areas: topology theory, discourse analysis, phenomenology, chaos theory, Marxist theory, structuration theory, to name some of the more prominent contributors.

6.   See David Matza (1969), Steven Lyng (1990), Jack Katz (1988). See also the integration by Pat O'Malley and S. Mugford, "Crime, Excitement, and Modunity,: in Variety of Ciminology, ed., Gregg Barak (Westport, CT: Praeger, 1994); and the ethnography of Jeff Ferrell, Dragan Milovanovic, and Steven Lying, "Edgework, Media Practice and the Elogation of Meaning," *Theoretical Ciminology* 5: 177–202, 2001.

7.   Take a rectangular piece of paper, place one twist in it and reglue the ends. Now trace a movement along the surface and you will see that a complete circuit can take place without any negotiation of borders.

8.   In this sense, too, COREL sets could be examined as to their harmful contributions.

CHAPTER 4. CONFINEMENT LAW AND PRISON RESISTANCE

1.   Of course, other grass roots struggles, appearing individual in nature, defying capture within the prevalent discourse of those in struggle, await more politically con-

stituted discursive framing and interventionist practices that may transform what appears as individual to collective struggle. For example, how does one come to an understanding of a hunger strike by a prisoner? How does one address the layers of issues that are its constitutive elements?

2. Ostensibly, condemned prisoners are to appreciate what is about to happen to them and those who place a high premium on law and order at all costs are to content themselves in knowing that restored-to-competency death row prisoners appreciate what is about to happen to them. This also indicates the high value placed on circumscribed notions of responsibility, order, predictability, and stasis.

3. We note that our position is consistent with sociolegal scholars such as Austin D. Sarat (1993), Austin D. Sarat and Thomas Kearns (1991, 1992, 1996), Alison Young and Sarat (1994), Austin D. Sarat and William L. Felstiner (1995), Patricia Ewick and Susan S. Silbey (1995), and William M. O'Barr (1982). They have shown how the language of law, in different contexts, produces certain effects, including the marginalization of various constituencies where resistance to the cultural power of the law is essential (Merry 1995). What we suggest, however, is a deeper understanding of the sociological, psychological, and symbolic dynamics activated and at work through the selection of words and expressions whose contents represent the perspective of some and silence or dismiss the perspective of others.

4. For example, several meanings for the sign of mental illness include "sick," "crazy," "psychiatric survivor," "deficient," "mental health systems user," "mad," "troubled," "differently abled." These meanings convey various intents, values, and assumptions about persons identified as psychiatrically disordered; however, only certain values are selected out and are understood to represent the "true" or "real" meaning for the sign of mental illness. These "true" and "real" meanings can be subsequently linked to the interests of specific collectives invested in the sustained legitimacy of their particular values over and against others (for a detailed exploration of these matters in civil and criminal mental health law see e.g., Arrigo 1993, 1996c).

5. The text of executing the mentally ill is repeatedly simulated through conspicuously consumed mass mediated images (e.g., film documentaries chronicling the lives of mentally disordered offenders, news magazines describing the behavior of "crazed" sociopaths, television crime dramas exploring the thought processes of dangerous and psychotic killers). These images are the counterfeit of the real but become more factual than the reality upon which they are based. However, the more-real-than-real representations are themselves illusory. Form and substance, appearance and reality, counterfact and fact collapse and collide through simulations: meaning is conveyed through the pseudo sign values (i.e., simulacra) of the hypertext.

6. In the discourse of the *master*, speech is used (i.e., psycholegal discourse), consciously or unconsciously, in ways that oppress or marginalize individuals or groups (e.g., the psychiatrically disordered). Receivers or listeners of this speech (e.g., mentally ill offenders and/or their defense lawyers) respond by utilizing the same or similar speech responsible for victimization in language. Thus, they reconstitute and relegitimize the very knowledge that oppresses.

7. In the discourse of the *hysteric*, the repressed subject (i.e., the psychiatrically disordered offender) seeks recognition and legitimacy, through discourse, on his or her own terms. The person offers words and phrases (i.e., replacement values and assump-

tions) that convey the subject's truth and experience about "mental illness," "execution," "dangerousness," "competency." The other (i.e., the psycholegal system and its agents) is not receptive to these alternative vocabularies of sense-making, because the established method of communicating permits only certain expressions consistent with the parameters of meaning constituting what is already defined as psychiatric justice.

8.   In the discourse of the *analyst,* the despairing subject's truth and experience is validated by another (e.g., a social activist, an insurgent lawyer, a cultural revolutionary, Lacan's analyst) who begins to speak from the perspective of the alienated individual (i.e., the mentally disordered offender). The other attempts to expand and develop the subject's language and knowledge, mindful that "true words" (Freire 1972) must be spoken. Thus, the other searches for ways in which the subject's identity can be embodied in words that communicate his or her unique experiences and felt longing.

9.   Interestingly enough, the majority also did say in passing that if it was a question of political or religious expression that was attached to the hunger-strike prisoner, that that would represent a different case. Thus, it does seem that the Court is providing future hunger-strikers with possible signifiers out of which to have a legal case. However, activists who embrace this reconstructed political or religious discourse only face a new round of "balancing" in which a majority could restate the importance of the correctional interests in any "balancing" test. Here, too, the rule of law gains additional legitimacy, both allowing convicts an avenue to redress grievances, but only to deny reconstituted discursive frameworks. Indeed, this represents a case of repressive formalism.

10.   For example, college, art, alternative religious, and other programs all have been diminished from the 1980s well into the 1990s. This has led to fewer activists in the prison system engaging in possible alternative discursive productions with prisoners. Consequently, more and more activists speak from outside the prison on behalf of the kept.

11.   Howe's preference is poststructuralist rather than postmodern.

12.   H. Giroux, *Border Crossings* (New York: Routledge and Kegan Paul, 1992); A. R. Jan Mohamed, "Some Implications of Paulo Freire's Border Pedagogy," in *Between Borders,* eds. H. Giroux and P. MacLaren (New York: Routledge and Kegan Paul, 1994); Paul McLaren "Multiculturalism and the Postmodern Critique," in *Between Borders,* eds., H. Giroux and P. McLaren (New York: Routledge and Kegan Paul, 1994).

13.   Stuart Henry and Dragan Milovanovic, *Constitutive Criminology* (London: Sage Publications, 1996).

14.   See particularly the work of critical race theorists, border crossers, and the literary and cinematic work of T. m-ha Trinh, *Framer Framed* (New York: Routledge and Kegan Paul, 1992.

15.   Jim Thomas, Prisoner Litigation (Totawa, N.J. Rowman and Littlefield, 1988); Dragan Milovanovic, "Jailhouse lawyers and Jailhouse Layering," *International Journal of the Sociology of Law* 16 (1988); Jim Thomas and Dragan Milovanovic, "Overcoming the Absurd," *Social Problems* 36 (1989); Jim Thomas and Dragan

Milovanovic, "Revisting Jailhouse Lawyers," in *Constitutive Criminology at Work*, eds., S. Henry and D. Milovanovic (New York: State University of New York Press, 1999.

16.   This echoes the reservations of critical race theorists with postmodern analysis (see chapter 5).

17.   Some of the following comments draw from Dragan Milovanovic, "'Rebellions Lawyering,'" *Legal Studies Forum* 20 (1996a) analysis of "rebellious lawyering."

18.   We draw from chaos theory which indicates how trajectories can be plotted. Phase spaces are multidimensional and map the various attractors that can be located in nonlinear dynamic systems.

19.   Here, for example, we could conceive of a reconstruction of the "molar structures" in stasis (Deleuze and Guattari 1987). And with this reconstruction, striated space, Euclidean geometrical forms, and more rigid dominant master signifiers materialize.

20.   For example, we do see the usefulness of applying chaos theory's notion of the "strange attractor." In this configuration, one wing represents dominant master signifiers of law while the other wing represents alternative forms and the logic of switching from one to the other. Perhaps, too, one might theorize an intersectional discourse or signifiers that may develop.

21.   A handful of studies exist in the theory and application of constitutive penology (See Milovanovic and Henry 1991; Milovanovic and Henry 2002; see also the applications by Bosworth 1999b; Thomas and Milovanovic 1999; Arrigo 1997b, 2001b).

22.   Consider, too, Richard Sparks (2001, 207): "however much penologists have historically claimed to stand on the progressive side of every engagement, the subject cannot evade complicity in or responsibility for the disciplinary apparatuses erected in its name and especially their regressive consequences for stigmatized and disposed people."

23.   See for example, Martha Duncan's *Romantic Outlaws, Beloved Prisons*, (New York: New York University Press, 1996). She argues that we, as non lawbreakers, both have an attraction to the lawbreaker as well as a revulsion. The prisoner, too, is both attracted to and repulsed by the prison.

24.   See Lacan (1977); for an explanation of the algorithm of metaphor, see J. Dor, *(Introduction to the Reading of Lacan* (London: Jason Aronson, 1997); and Dragan Milovanovic, *Critical Criminology at the Edge* (Westport, CT: Prager, 2002), pp. 143–151.) and Milovanovic (2002: 143-151). Lacan's algorithm pointing out the unconscious movement of signifiers in metaphor is: $f(S'/S) S \sim S (+) s$. What this represents is that the original signifier, S, is replaced by another, S', and the + sign represents the "crossing of the bar" which provides the "poetic spark" in the creation of sense, of the meaning of the metaphor. The original "S" falls below the bar, but remains in connected form to chains of signifiers within the unconscious. The bar represents the separation of the conscious from the unconscious. For example, if one says, "she is a dynamo," one shows how the signifier, "dynamo," now comes to represent the person, S. The "s" represents the new sense constructed. Thus, in Duncan's (1996) analysis of lawbreakers seen as "slime," the metaphor now takes on

life and force within a hyperreal created. Slime, for example, suggests particular methods of cleansing. If the metaphor, "problems of living" existed, this would call out different responses. Much like Marxist analysis of commodity production, use-value is now transformed into exchange-value, the concrete is transformed into an abstraction.

25.   Consider Malcolm X's conversion from a "common" criminal to one with a revolutionary consciousness. Consider various prison writings from Gramsci to Solzenietzian.

26.   "To the barricades!" surely is a summoning of forces to say "no." And indeed it may very well be, in the end, that the "sufficient" conditions for the development of replacement discourses emerge in the crucible of street encounters against State control, as "molar structures" (Deleuze and Guattari 1987) give way to "molecular structures," a deterritorialization that provides the grounds for epiphanies, new identi-tites, and momentary insights of what could be; occasions in which a full body without organs shows momentary appearances where visions abound; moments in which a becoming other is provided a space in which to take form.

27.   Hobbsbawm's "primitive rebels," similar to Thomas and Milovanovic's (1989, 1999) jailhouse lawyers are more doers, not "thinkers" in so far as the developers of a full-blown political agenda that systematically relates their struggles to the advancement of the subaltern. On the other hand, in the 1960s some prisoner rebellion was developing based on a political agenda, for example, the Black Muslim convicts. And some conscientization did occur, as presented in Malcolm X and Alex Haley's classic autobiography, *Malcolm X*.

28.   Similarly, Judith Butler's (1990, 145–148) call for "subverting repetition" is a necessary condition; however, it requires more.

29.   It could be argued that the emerging society, even, one in a more ideal form, would increase the occasion for conflict as Roberto Unger (1987) suggests. But these moments could, conceivably, be occasions for: (1) reevaluation of harmful COREL sets and the prevalence of excessive investors in doing harm; (2) more fully understanding and appreciating differences; and (3) the basis for new accommodations with the other. In this sense, revised forms of VOM (see chapter 7) might further produce more organic bonds of solidarity as Émile Durkheim has suggested.

30.   Drucilla Cornell (1998b, 8) defines the imaginary domain as "the space of the 'as if' in which we imagine who we might be if we made ourselves our own end and claimed ourselves as our own person." And elsewhere (1998b, 24): "The effort to chal-lenge, engage with, and imagine who we are sexually demands that we have the courage to look into the crevices in ourselves to see things frightening indeed. We need to sink ourselves into our dreams. We need to play with metaphor to undercut the rigidity of engendered meanings that embed themselves in the images and symbols by which we can represent ourselves."

CHAPTER 5: CRITICAL RACE THEORY . . .

1.   Mari Matsuda, Charles Lawrence, Richard Delgado, and Kimberle Crenshaw, *Words that Wound* (San Francisco: Westview Press, 1993); Richard Delgado

and Jean Stefancic, *Critical Race Theory* (New York: New York University Press, 2001); Kimberle Crensaw, Neil Gotanda, Gary Pellerm, and Kendall Thams eds., *Critical Race Theory* (New YorK: New Press, 1995).

2.   Many CRT scholars reject the critical legal studies agenda of "trashing" law and "rights discourse," arguing that it "relinquishes too much, since [an] appeal to legal ideology represents one of the only strategies that ha[s] effectively elicited a response to the desperate needs of subordinate people" (Goldfarb 1992: 696). And, as Crenshaw (1988, 1357–58) argues, "the most troubling aspect of the Critical program, therefore, is that 'trashing' rights consciousness may have the unintended consequence of disempowering the racially oppressed while leaving white supremacy basically untouched . . ."

3.   Other good summaries have been delineated by Matsuda et al (1993, 6). In addition, see the notion of petit apartheid and a typology of its various forms as described by Dragan Milovanovic and Katheryn Russell, *Petit Apartheid in the US Criminal Justice System* (Durham, NC: Carolina Academic Press, 2001).

4.   The other camp argues that it is the economic structure and hierarchies that reduce the life chances of African-Americans (Delgado and Stefancic 2001, 17, 120). Our view is that it is both. Space limitations do not allow us to fully develop this theme here.

5.   There have been a number of law journal articles that have argued for narrative practices (see Alfieri 1991; Delgado 1989, 1999; Matsuda 1990; Martinez 1999; Olivas 1990; White 1990; see also Symposium, 1989). We wish only to add a more postmodern oriented theoretical component to each of these, arguing that this heterodox orientation could provide even further momentum for this radically inspired direction.

6.   Recall, the discourse of the *analyst*:

$$\frac{a}{S2} \rightarrow \frac{\$}{S1}$$

and the discourse of the *hysteric*:

$$\frac{\$}{a} \rightarrow \frac{S1}{S2}$$

7.   Historical stages exist in devising alternative strategies: from reversal of hierarchies, to standpoint epistemology, to the notion of "contingent universalities."

8.   Further useful integration from first wave postmodern scholars includes Judith Kristeva (1984) with her notion of "semanalysis" (the strategy of disruption, subversion, transgression, dislocation of texts and stable identities and in their reconstruction in more liberating forms), and Deleuze and Guattari's (1987) notion of "schizoanalysis" (the strategy of deterritorialization—breaking down of unities and ossified stabilities ["molar structures"]—and in alternative expressions of desire ["molecular structures"] in the full body without organs (BwO).

9.   Consider national discussions on the issue of the necessity of diversity on campus as a replacement to "affirmative action." More recently, this has been connected to the necessity of a diverse work place. Hence, by their coupling, the notion of "diversity," as an ingredient for college and law school admissions, is becoming more accepted by the dominant classes.

10.   For example, see, Milovanovic (2002, 143–155) where the metaphor for crime as a "virus" and the metaphor for the criminal as "slime" undergo transformations whereby the initial phenomena (crime, lawbreaker) are suppressed and a new connectedness is established. This new connectedness then precludes certain responses to crime and to the criminal (e.g., retribution rather than restorative justice).

See also Lacan's algorithm of metaphor and how substitutions take place, chapter 4, note 24.

11.   M. Tushnet has been a long involved member of the Critical Legal Studies movement. Randal Kennedy was an African American colleague of Bell and in his 1989 article strongly criticized Bell, Matsuda, and Delgado in their analysis of African-Americans. They claimed that African-Americans assumed "unique voices" (see commentary, see Delgado and Stefancic 2001, 87–88).

12.   P. Lather's (1993) notion of "ironic" validity (legitimation) indicates the diversity of possible representations of the real whereby none is dominant; whereas "voluptuous" validity (legitimation) focuses on the suppressed female voices and alternative discursive constructions that may exist (also see, Lather 1986, for additional observations on ideology and validity).

CHAPTER 6: CINEMA AND LITERARY TEXTS . . .

1.   Perhaps breaking away from Lacan is Deleuze's post-Lacanian work on cinema. We have declined to include a fully developed explanation of Deleuzian thought on cinema. There are three reasons for this decision. First, Deleuze has published two books on the subject (1986, 1989) and, as such, this does not necessarily represent the manifestation of a new "cinema theory." For an insightful commentary, see D. N. Rodowick (1997). Second, our attention to Deleuze's work principally has been in relation to his collaborations with Guattari. Their joint philosophical endeavors form the basis of compelling scholarship, consistent with other first-wave French postmodernists canvassed in this book who theorize the possible. Third, the sheer volume of insights found in over six hundred pages of Deleuze's work on cinema renders a detailed exposition of this material necessary before any application to law, criminology and social justice meaningfully can occur. Thus, in our analysis of Deleuze's cinema work, we merely wish to suggest some possible linkages, integrations, and inroads awaiting future investigation.

2.   As R. Ericson (1991, 219) has said, "media do not merely report on events but rather participate directly in processes by which events are constituted and exist in the world."

3.   We say nonlinear because the iterative effects remain somewhat unpredictable. In one form, it may lead to an exaggerated portrayal of the offender that takes on a life on its own in the hyperreal.

4.   See Umberto Eco and Thomas Sebeok (1983) potraying Peirce as a detective compared to Sherlock Holmes as a semiotician.

5.   The mirror stage of Lacan is discussed in DeLauretis, PUB, 1990); Kaja Silverman, *The Acoustic Mirror* (Bloomington, IN: Indiana University Press, 1988), "Dis-Embodying the Female Voice," in *Issues in Feminist Film Criticisms*, ed. P. Erens

(PLACE: PUB, 1990); Tina Chanter, "Viewing Abjection," www.women.it/ 4thfemcmf/worshops/spectaclos2/tinachanter.htm.

6.   For a recent, much-discussed, and litigated parody, see Alice Randall's, *The Wind Done Gone* (PLACE: PUB, 2001), parody of Margaret Mitchell's, *Gone With the Wind*.

7.   Trinh's films include: *Reassemblage* (1982), *Naked Spaces—Living Is Round* (1985), *Surname Viet Given Name Nam* (1989), and *Shoot for the Contents* (1991).

8.   Gilles Deleuze's two-volume set (1986, 1989) on cinema has not offered direct material for analysis of class, gender, race, and sexual preference. He also does not directly deal with feminist film theory. Future work, however, could productively engage this complex *ouvre* in law, criminology, and social justice.

9.   A starting point for an application of Deleuze's challenging work on cinema would be in his likening political cinema to "minor cinema" or "minor literature." However, with Deleuze, "by addressing a (minority) people already assumed to exist, identity politics falls prey to a schema of reversal that reifies or essentializes the sub-altern subject no less than that of the cultural hegemony it is trying to combat" (Rodowick 1997, 153–54; Deleuze, 1989: 219–20, 286). Therefore, Third World cinema, in the form of postcolonial directors, are posed with the dilemma: to assume undiscovered identity already in existence, or to open up dialogue hoping that what has been repressed will emerge on its own terms by creative directorship. According to Rodowick (1997, 156), then, "a minority discourse must create strategies for mapping becoming without immobilizing it." A case in point: former colonies of France witness not only the imposition of francophonic tendencies, but also have colonized peoples alienated from their own myths and language (1997, 159). In Lacanian discourse, this is the imposition of the discourse of the *master*. For Deleuze, the key is the intervention of "intercessors" (see especially Rodowick's lucid presentation, 1997, 162–69). Here the representer and represented interchange in narratives and thereby begin the process of a more authentic becoming. Only in this way can a deterritorialization within a linguistic space take place followed by a reterritorialization in new, noncolonizer languages. A case in point where the director does encourage the "intercessors" and the production of alternative master signifiers is in Ousmane Sembene's short film, *Borom Sarret* (1963). See D. N. Rodowick Gilles Deleuzes' Time Machine (Durham, NC: Duke University Press, 1997), 1962–69, for additional commentary.

CHAPTER 7: RESTORATIVE JUSTICE AND VICTIM OFFENDER . . .

1.   Mark Umbreit, *The Handbook of Victim Offender Medication* (San Francisco: Jossey-Bass, 2001); Daniel Van Ness and K. Strong, 1997); Howard Zehr, *Changing Lenses* Scottsdale, PA: Herald Press, 1990); Brian Galaway and J. Hudson, *Restorative Justice* (Monsey, NY: Criminal Justice Press, 1996).

2.   Mark Umbreit, *Victim Meets Offender* (Monsey, NY: Criminal Justice Press, 1994), *Mediating Interpersonal Conflicts* (West Concord, MN: CPI Publishing, 1995); M. Wright, *Justice for Victims and Offenders* (Philadelphia: Open University Press, 1991); M. Wright and B. Galaway ed., *Mediation and Criminal Justice* (Newbury, CA:

Sage Publications, 1989); Sara Cobb, "The Domesticaion of Violence in Mediation," *Law and Society Review* 31 91997): 397–440.

3.   A typology of justice policy could be constructed by ranging levels of intervention (agent/person, social relational/community, and structural/societal) and by an accusatory or remedial philosophical style (Henry and Milovanovic 1996, 189) providing six ideal types of responses to harm. Restorative justice, and Black's (1976) closely connected conciliatory style, would fall within the intersections of social relational/remedial style. In neither case is a structural/accusatory or a structural/remedial style of sufficient concern. The radical accusatory model would implicate macro factors as major determinants of harm and, hence, call for the transformation of the whole political economic structure, whereas the reformist remedial style would work within the given political economy but radically alter some key elements. This is what Roberto Unger (1987) referred to as an "empowered democracy" and "superliberalism." In the latter sense, Unger's analysis stands out as a model that could be consistent with, and also be amenable to, various integrations with first and second wave scholars, as well as contemporary critics of restorative justice programs. Space limitations do not permit us to develop this stream of thought more completely. However, critical scholars are encouraged to pursue this line of inquiry further.

4.   Sara Cobb (1997) asserts that VOM diversion primarily functions to differentiate "rights" based adjudication from "needs" based restitution. In the latter instance, victims experience the denial of their status as victims when the violence that has been perpetrated against them is diluted and reframed by mediators in critical moments of discursive communication.

5.   John Braithwaite's (2002) recent book on restorative justice, arguably one of the most solid in terms of theoretical analysis on the dynamics themselves, is almost entirely rooted in modernist assumptions. His claim that "regulatory theory . . . is advanced as more useful . . . than explanatory theory," and that "regulatory theory delivers superior and more general explanations than criminological theory" (2002, vii, viii), is devoid of alternative assumptions in terms of subjectivity, nonlinearity, iterative effects, multiplicity of discourses, intersectional standpoints, effects of dominant discourses, and so forth.

6.   Two earlier contributions to alternative responses suggestive of a restorative justice model were presented by Morris (1974, 53–57), in his notion of a "pre-trial hearing," and J. Griffith (1970), with his "family model." For Morris, the pretrial hearing would include the judge, prosecutor, defense counselor, accused and victim. This would provide for an opportunity to work out some settlement prior to trial on which the victim and accused could agree. It would also provide psychological advantages for the victim and would personalize the harm done by the offender and provide an opportunity to acknowledge guilt. Griffith's model was an alternative to the "battle model." It argued for the reintegration of the offender back into society much as an errant child would be accepted back into the family with love and support.

7.   Umbreit (2001, xxxvii) estimates the number of victim offender mediation programs in the United States to be approximately three hundred.

8.   In 1997, one of the authors (Schehr) received training as a Victim Offender Mediator. During the weeklong training, he had the opportunity to interview the founder of the Vermont Reparative Probation Community Boards. Since considerable authority and latitude has been granted to the citizen volunteers on the Boards, the question was asked, "Do you have a mechanism for removing volunteers should they show a proclivity for retribution rather than restitution?" The answer at that time was a surprising, "No." Schehr suggested that this was a serious problem, especially since citizens might not possess the values articulated by the restorative justice paradigm as necessary to promote healing, and might be ignorant of class, race, age, and gender dynamics that influence speech situations. Interestingly, the planners had not considered the matter. A year later, a subsequent meeting indicated that a policy to remove "troublesome" members had been established. Indeed, as the interviewer (Schehr) was informed, this very scenario occurred on one of the large Boards. Apparently, a citizen volunteer was motivated to participate as a member of the Board principally as a way to punish offenders.

9.   To create a "community" is to differentiate those who belong to it from those who do not. Sociological studies of geographically situated class, religious, ethnic, and age groupings with respect to formal and informal marginalization raise considerable questions about what the concept of "community" signifies (e.g, Worsley 1992; Bauman 2001; Seelye and Wasilewski 1996; Simmel 1950; Rorty 1989; Melucci 1996; Benhabib 1992, 1996; Walzer 1994). In other words, when determining the normative order of things, certain less desirable groups (i.e., those who do not possess the sought after qualities) are cast out. By juxtaposing those marginalized against those who are not (i.e., the dominant group), the identity of the latter entity (in this case, the community) is solidified. Unfortunately, clarification concerning the meaning of "community" is absent in D. Maloney and D. Holcomb's (2001) articulation of "community justice." This conspicuous deficiency also is apparent within every discussion of restorative justice and victim offender mediation available to date.

10.   Consider Micheal Foucault (1978, 61–62): "The confession is a ritual of discourse in which the speaking subject is also the subject of the statement; it is also a ritual that unfolds within a power relationship, for one does not confess without the presence (or virtual presence) of a partner who is not simply the interlocutor but the authority who requires the confession, prescribes and appreciates it, and intervenes in order to judge, punish, forgive, console, and reconcile."

11.   One of us (Dragan Milovanovic) recently was invited to present his work at another university. One evening, he, another visiting faculty member, and two faculty from the department got into a three-hour discussion brought about by a conflict between the two otherwise friendly faculty members within the department. As outsiders, we found ourselves in the position of unplanned "mediators" to the dispute. As the differences came out, layers and layers of complexities emerged at every moment. After three hours of sometimes quite emotional pleas, close empathizing, and even suggesting certain directions for a possible settlement, a resolution only then began to emerge.

12.   For a summary of data on the effectiveness of VOM and restorative justice, see Daniel Van Ness and K. Strong, Restoring Justice (Cincinnati, OH: Anderson,

2002); John Braithwaite, Restorative Justice and Responsive Regulation (New York: Oxford University Press, 2002), pp 45–71.

13.   Schehr's point is strikingly apparent in the "community justice" approach espoused by Maloney and Holcomb, "In Pursuit of Community Justice," *Youth and Society* 33 (2001): 296–313.

14.   Critical race theory (Delgado and Stefancic 2001: 44) offers an example: "when contemporary Euro-Americans resist even discussing reparations for Blacks on the grounds that no black living today has been a slave and so lacks standing, nor has any white person alive today been a slaveholder, the black who wishes to discusss the question, and is shunted aside, suffers the differand."

15.   As Norman Denzin (1997, 266) argues, "In contrast to the realist regime, the new writers seek a model of truth that is narrative, deeply ethical, open-ended, and conflictual, performance, and audience based, and always personal, biographical, political, structural, and historical."

16.   Suggestive in this direction is Dragan Milovanovic's (1996) application of chaos theory, psychoanalytic semiotics, and Paulo Freire's dialogical pedagogy to Gerald Lopez's *Rebellious Lawyering* (1994). He first argues that the mediator should be better situated within the discourse of the *analyst and* the discourse of the *hysteric*, and then shows how Lopez's "dialogical problem solving" approach between lawyer and client could provide the space within which alternative master signifiers emerge that become the basis of meaning constructions that better reflect the conflict or issues at hand. Chaos theory was suggested as being able to map the nonlinear developments.

17.   See especially conflict theory which argues that contestation is often functional and not necessarily undermining. Roberto Unger's (1987) admirable suggestion for a "superliberalism" also indicates that there will be an increase in contestations but that these conflicts will be the basis of reconsiderations of given social formations and identities. They are occasions for the acknowledgement of the other and the necessity of reconciling differences. In short, conflicts, in a maximalist position, could be seen as occasions for the reestablishment of even closer bonds of solidarity while assuming differences.

18.   In Jacque Lacan's (1975–1976; see also Milovanovic 2002, 44–47, 1996b) very late work, he developed the notion of the borromean knots and *le sinthome* to represent the subject and sense production. Here, three interconnected circles representing the Real, Symbolic and Imaginary provide the framework for sense production and *jouissance*. However, they can be undone. It is *le sinthome* that reestablishes some unity or constancy for the psychic apparatus. Therefore, meaning can always be otherwise. First wave French postmodern social theorists and second-wave thinkers and their integrators/appliers have offered various insights on how alternative, more liberating configurations can indeed emerge or have the potential to do so.

19.   See chapter 3.

20.   In the second edition of Daniel Van Ness and K. Strong's *Restoring Justice* (Cincinnati, OH: Anderson, 2002, chapter 12), there seems to be movement in the direction of a transformative, as opposed to a restorative, justice model. However, the

authors still equate restorative with transformative justice (2002, 241), even as they acknowledge the need to integrate "structural factors" in their analysis (2002, 246, 249). In so much as they do, Van Ness and Strong diminish the discussion for a possible integration of dimensions advancing a more holistic response to harm. This is the challenge for more critical thinkers: how to integrate a dimension in VOM such that existing ossified COREL sets can be continuously reexamined and transformed where necessary.

21.   In calling for "destabilization rights" in his vision of an empowered democracy, Roberto Unger (1987, 530) has said that these rights "protect the citizen's interest in breaking open the large-scale organizations or the extended areas of social practice that remain closed to the destabilizing effects of ordinary conflict and thereby sustain insulated hierarchies of power and advantage." In our integration, this is quite compatible with chaos theory's position on far-from-equilibrium conditions and dissipative structures that emerge in this milieu. Many of Unger's other suggestions also are compatible and include: role jumbling; establishing a rotating capital fund accessible by workers for investment; assuring giving form to the emergent "solidarity rights"; recognizing that in the coming orderly (dis)order more occasions for conflict will emerge, but productively could be the basis of new understandings; the acceptance in an empowered democracy of a broader range of conflict without threat to being (1987, 579); a greatly expanded imagination of being and becoming, and so forth. In short, conflict management is indeed a central value.

22.   See John Braithwaite's (2002, 85–90) useful discussion about how neutralizations are offset in restorative justice.

CHAPTER 8. SOCIAL MOVEMENTS AND NONLINEARITY . . .

1.   As R. Schehr (1997, 158) observes, "Social movement theory can generally be said to comprise one of the three contemporary paradigms: collective behavior, resource mobilization, and from Europe . . . new social movement theory (NSM). . . . For purposes of our inquiry, we focus principally on the NSM literature, sometimes termed the identity paradigm (Jamison and Eyerman 1991).

2.   For a more detailed presentation of NSM theory, see A. Touraine, "An Introduction to the Study of Social Movements," *Social Research* 52 (1985): 775–787; J. Cohen, "Strategy or Identity," *Social Research* 52 (1986): 664–716; A. Melucci, "Getting Involved," *International Social Movement Research* 1 (1998): 124–154, *Nomads of the Present* (Philadelphia, PA: Temple University Press, 1990), "The Process of Collective Identity," in *Social Movements and Culture*, ed. B. Klandermans, 41–63 (Minneapolis, MN: University of Minnesota Press, 1995).

3.   We preface our treatment of the wrongful conviction section with a substantive comment on the dialectics of struggle. Living social movement activities and embracing the dialectics of struggle can be difficult to reconcile. Each of us, in our own ways, has worked for and advocated change in different institutional contexts. Innocence projects, as an exemplar of movement potential, also illustrate the need for

ongoing reflexivity and transparency. Perhaps what is most difficult to reconcile is how well intended, progressive social reformers can unintentionally produce effects that undo or compromise prospects for fuller articulations of justice and humanism. Indeed, sometimes in the rush for change, we overlook how our words and actions can become the basis for exclusion. Affirmative and integrative postmodern inquiry rejects these tendencies. It calls for the inclusion of all voices, even those who, on occasion, are responsible for oppression and victimization (e.g., attorneys, judges, police officers social change agents). To the extent that innocence project workers seek to promote this vision of a better, more complete existence for all concerned, they support and nurture the postmodern call for transpraxis.

   4.   We recall Ernesto Laclau and Chantal Mouffe (1985, 161) concerning "the multiplicity of social relations from which antagonisms and struggles may originate." They reject notions of an objective universal class, and argue for a "plurality of antagonisms" (1985, 167–690).

   5.   We are mindful of the difference Laclau and Mouffe (1985, 189) suggest between strategies of opposition versus strategies of construction. For the former: "the element of negation of a certain social or political order predominates, but this element of negativity is not accompanied by any real attempt to establish different nodal points from which a process of different and positive reconstructions of the social fabric can be instituted—and as a result the strategy is condemned to marginality." For strategies of construction, "the elements of social positivity predominates, but this very fact creates an unstable balance and a constant tension with the subversive logic of democracy."

   6.   For a more elaborate discussion of chaos theory see, Katherine Hayles, *Chaos Bound* (London: Cornell University Press, 1990); Ilya Prigogine and Isabella Stengers, *Order Out of Chaos* (New York: Bantam Books, 1984); I. Steward, *Does God Play Dice?* (New York: Blackwell, 1989); J. Gleick, *Chaos,* (New York: Penguin, 1987); E. Porter and J. Gleick, *Nature's Chaos* (New York: Penguin, 1990); J. Briggs and D. Peat, *Turbulent Mirror* (New York: Harper and Row, 1989 or 1980?),

   7.   For an accessible and informative explanation of Deleuze's use of dynamic nonlinear systems theory, see Delanda, *Intensive Science and Virtual Philosophy* (New York: Continuum, 2002).

   8.   For Deleuze's appropriation of bifurcation and symmetry-breaking, see Manuel Delanda, *Intensive Science and Virtual Philosophy* (New York: Continuum, 2002), 18–21.

   9.   Self organization is most significant in environments identified by chaologists as "far-from-equilibrium." These are dynamic conditions rather than those we find celebrated in talk of homeostasis, order, and structural functionalism, with perhaps its most visible form manifested in the rigid bureaucracy. Within far-from-equilibrium conditions we find the ubiquity of "dissipative structures." These represent the idea of only relatively stable "structures" very susceptible to perturbation; that is, small inputs may produce profound disproportionate effects. Structures are always both dissipating and reforming. In this sense, we have orderly disorder.

   10.   For references to actions of interest groups see, H. Mawhinney, "Theoretical Approaches to Understanding Interest Groups," *Educational Policy* 15 (2001):

187–215; F. R. Baumgartner and B. L. Leech, *Basic Instincts* (Princeton, NJ: Princeton University Press, 1988); V. Gray and D. Lowery, *The Population Ecology of Interest Representation* (Ann Arbor, MI: University of Michigan Press, 1996); A. McFarland, "Interest Groups and Theories of Power in America," *British Journal of Political Science* 17 (1998): 129–147. P. Sabatier and U. Perkey, "Incorporating Multiple Actors and Guidance Instruments Into Models of Regulatory Policymaking," *Administration and Society* 19 (1887): 236–263; M. Diane, "The Concept of Social Movement," *The Sociological Review* 40 (1992) 1–25; D. Kubler, "Understanding Policy Change with the Advocacy Coalition Framework," *Journal of European Public Policy* 8 (2001): 623–641.

11.   While it is true that contemporary attempts to generate state-by-state changes in due process, police investigation procedures, compensation statutes, and Innocence Commissions, appear somewhat unlike conventional social movements, they are, nonetheless, activities that parallel many of the same criteria while grafting activities from other less obviously associated organization strategies.

12.   In Canada and England Innocence Commissions review cases to develop detailed knowledge of problems that may have produced a wrongful conviction. These postmortum evaluations represent a significant institutional response to the problem of wrongful conviction in that they not only recommend immediate remedies for cases under review, but they also promote changes in problem areas in the due process systems of each country.

13.   The question of motivation to participate can be raised. Indeed, motivation could vary considerably. On one end of the continuum it could reflect genuinely concerned activist students, to those concerned who prioritize attaining better experience of "the other side," to variously sought psychic rewards. On the other end of the continuum, it could include those finding a momentary space within which to practice their newly learned skills in preparation for future employment. Notwithstanding these observations, researching this question more thoroughly is beyond the scope of our investigation.

14.   The most obvious example of movement success comes in the form of exonerations. Relatedly, however, is the dramatic influence of the Center for Wrongful Convictions and their success in the Anthony Porter case. It was Porter's case that influenced Illinois governor, George Ryan, leading him to sign a death penalty moratorium and establish the Illinois Death Penalty Commission. The state of Maryland followed in its wake. Moreover, in the summer of 2002, federal judges in New York and Vermont ruled the death penalty unconstitutional. The reasons they cited speak to the overwhelming evidence of wrongful conviction, and to the realization that by March of 2000, eighty-seven death row inmates had been exonerated (thirteen in Illinois), and that twenty-three had already been executed (Radelet and Bedout 1992).

15.   Emphasis on the end product is more typical of conventional social movement literatures (Smelser 1962; Zablocki 1980; Kanter 1972). However, in this section of the chapter, we argue that the sheer existence of innocence projects produces certain but unanticipated changes at the structural level.

16.   State steering mechanisms can, within certain limits, absorb social movement activity. Following Bertramsen et. al. (1991), the state exists at the nodal point between the accumulation regime and hegemonic block to promote coherent

regulation. Six sectors are identified for regulation: (1) industry, (2) agriculture, (3) education, (4) finance, (5) the workforce, (6) the relation between central and local government (Delorme 1984). Schehr (1999) has argued that the ability of the state to absorb social movement activity is in part dependent on the number of social movement organizations emerging at a specific point in time. Consistent with fractal geometry and the Feigenbaum number, the ability of the system to regulate the relationship between accumulation and hegemony using the state steering mechanisms applied to each of the six sectors indicated above requires three or fewer large-scale movements. Should civil society experience the emergence of three or more movement actions at one fixed point in time, considerable systemic would instability emerge leading to a greater likelihood of structural transformations.

17.   As B. Moyer (2001, 18) notes, in order to be successful, grand strategies must accomplish the following four goals: (1) social movements must focus directly on the power-holders' policies and institutions to expose their societal secrets and challenge their actual policies and programs. This involves developing critical analyses, presentations, and publications and using the normal channels available to the public; (2) Social movements put a public spotlight on the problem and on the power-holders' actual policies and practices in order to alert, educate, win over, involve, and inspire the general public to become involved in the movement. These activities are not intended to get policymakers to change their policies at this point; (3) social movements mobilize the general public to put tremendous pressure on the power-holders and social institutions to change their policies and, at the same time, create a new peaceful culture and democratic political conditions; and (4) these activities attract additional members of the general public to become social activists and either join existing movement organizations and activities or create their own.

18.   "Truths," desire, and discourse could also be studied productively by reference to Lacan's late work (early to late 1970s) on the Borromean knots and *le sinthome*. Here the psychic structure was depicted in terms of three interconnected rings, representing the Real, Imaginary and Symbolic Order. At the center is *objet petit a*, or objects of desire. At the intersection of the Imaginary and Symbolic is *sens*, meaning. However, there are times when the stability of the three is undermined (depicted by the cutting of one circle and the others becoming undone). Laclau and Mouffe's (1985) work and Laclau's (1996) on structural dislocations in late society could be connected with this development. This is overcome by *le sinthome*, a reknotting of the three in the form of a supplement. *Le sinthome* provides a new basis of stability for the psychic apparatus, and is the basis of an alternative discursive production, since new master signifiers become the basis of narrative construction. *Le sinthome* often appears in dominant ideologies and dictums. For activists, being sensitive to the development of alternative discourses that do not reproduce hierarchical forms becomes central to their task of individual and social change.

19.   "Attractors" are designated by the number of parameters existing in a given phase space. With few parameters; that is, with few opportunities for generating options to dominant patterns, the number of attractors is limited, or "fixed." Fixed and "cycle" attractors tend to appear when opportunities for articulating alternate modes of existence are minimized.

20.   See also Laclau and Mouffe's (1985, 139) discussion of "hegemonic nodal points" or conventional anchorings of signifiers to signified and their disruptions due to "structural disclocations" (1985, 167–171, 176). See also note 18 above.

21.   Wood Street Commons (WSC) was a former YMCA that provided safe and affordable housing to 259 adult men and women. The facility addressed the problem of urban homelessness characteristic of many cities around the country during the mid-1980s and early 1990s. The presence of crime, drug use, illiteracy, poverty, unemployment, and health/mental health-related difficulties were stable features of the building's internal ecology and residential makeup. However, during a seven-year period, one of the authors (Bruce Arrigo) worked closely with residents, city developers, a property management team, and human service specialists to establish a sense of community that was least restrictive, peer supportive, and personally empowering. As a vertical neighborhood composed of ten floors with twenty-six single rooms occupied by tenants, prospects for establishing a intentional community presented many difficulties linked to new social movement and non-linear social movement theory. For more on Wood Street Commons see, Bruce Arrigo "Dimensions of Social Justice Win the SRO (Single Room Occupancy)," in *Chaos, Criminology and Social Justice,* ed. D. Milovanovic (Westport, CT: Prager, 1997c), 179–194; "Constitutive Theory and the Homeless Identity," in *Constitutive Criminology at Work,* eds. S. Henry and D. Milavanovic (Albany, NY: State University of New York Press, 1999c), 67–85.

CONCLUSION: BACK TO THE FUTURE

1.   Nietzsche refers to the metaphor of the total eclipse of the sun as a way to exemplify the ideological influence of the ideas of the powerful. If the sun is eclipsed thereby darkening the sky, the enumerable stars are more brilliantly illuminated. The sun signifies the dominant metaphysic operating in any historical epoch. The stars signify the many alternative ways of being that are "always already," but because of the oppressive power of the state, are unable to be fully realized.

2.   Elizabeth Grosz (1994) suggests how to reconceptualize the dualism found in the Cartesian subject of post-Enlightenment thought by the use of the Moebius strip. The Moebius strip indicates a unification of the body and mind by the traversal of this single sided topological figure. Similar to Grosz, our previous conceptualization of the "edgeworker" (see chapter 3) in terms of the Moebius strip, indicates the wherewithal of a momentary emergence of the monistic subject.

3.   As Ernesto Laclau (1996, 100) informs us, "a democratic society is not one in which the 'best' content dominates unchallenged but, rather, one in which nothing is definitely acquired and there is always the possibility of challenge." And further, "there is democracy only if there is the recognition of the positive value of a dislocated identity." There exists, in a word, the impossibility of an "ultimate grounding."

Bibliography

Achilles, M., and Zehr, Howard. 2001."Restorative Justice for Crime Victims: The Promise, The Challenge." In *Restorative Community Justice: Repairing Harm and Transforming Communities*. Edited by G. Bazemore and M. Schiff, 87–99. Cincinnati, OH: Anderson Publishing Co.

Agger, Ben. 1991. "Critical Theory, Post-structuralism, Post-modernism: Their Sociological Relevance. In *Annual Review of Sociology*. Edited by W. R. Scott and J. Blake. Palo Alto: Annual Reviews.

Alfieri, Anthony. 1991. "Reconstructive Poverty Law Practice: Learning Lessons of Client Narrative." *Yale Law Journal* 100 (1991): 2107–2146.

Althusser, Louis. 1969. *For Marx*. New York: Vintage Books.

———. 1971. *Lenin and Philosophy and Other Essays*. New York: New Left Books.

Arrigo, Bruce. "The Logic of Identity and the Politics of Justice: Establishing a Right to Community Based Treatment for the Institutionalized Mentally Disabled." *New England Journal on Criminal and Civil Confinement* 18 (1992): 1–31.

———. 1993. *Madness, Language, and the Law*. New York: Harrow and Heston.

———. "(De)constructing Classroom Instruction: Theoretical and Methodological Contributions of the Postmodern Sciences for Crimino-Legal Education." *Social Pathology* 1 (1995a): 113–148.

———. "New Directions in Crime, Law, and Social Change: On Psychoanalytic Semiotics, Chaos Theory, and Postmodern Ethics." *Studies in the Social Sciences* 33 (1995b): 101–129.

———. "The Peripheral Core of Law and Criminology: On Postmodern Social Theory and Conceptual Integration." *Justice Quarterly* 12 (1995c): 447–472.

———. "The Behavior of Law and Psychiatry: Rethinking Knowledge Construction and the Guilty-But-Mentally-Ill Verdict." *Criminal Justice and Behavior* 23 (1996a): 572–592.

————. Desire in the Psychiatric Courtroom: On Lacan and the Dialectics of Linguistic Oppression." *Current Perspectives in Social Theory* 16 (1996b): 159–187.

————. 1996c. *The Contours of Psychiatric Justice: A Postmodern Critique of Mental Illness, Criminal Insanity and the Law.* New York/London: Garland.

————. 1996d. "Media Madness as Crime in the Making: On O. J. Simpson, Consumerism, and Hyper-reality." In *Representing O. J.: Murder, Criminal Justice, and Mass Culture.* Edited by G. Bara, 123–135. New York: Harrow and Heston.

————. "Insanity Defense Reform and the Sign of Abolition: Revisiting Montana's Experience." *International Journal for the Semiotics of Law* 29 (1997a): 121–211.

————."Transcarceration: Notes on a Psychoanalytically Informed Theory of Social Practice in the Criminal Justice and Mental Health Systems." *Crime, Law, and Social Change: An International Journal* 27 (1997b): 31–48.

————. 1997c. "Dimensions of Social Justice in an SRO (Single Room Occupancy): Contributions for Chaos Theory, Policy, and Practice." In *Chaos, Criminology, and Social Justice: The New Orderly (Dis)Order.* Edited by D. Milovanovic, 179–194. Westport, CT: Praeger.

————. "Reason and Desire in Legal Education: A Psychoanalytic Semiotic Critique." *International Journal for the Semiotics of Law* 31 (1998): 3–24.

————. "Critical Criminology's Discontent: The Perils of Publishing and the Call to Action." *The Critical Criminologist* 10 (1999a): 10–15.

————. "Martial Metaphors in Medical Justice: Implications for Law, Crime, and Deviance." *Journal of Political and Military Sociology* 24 (1999b): 307–322.

————. 1999c. "Constitutive Theory and the Homeless Identity: The Discourse of a Community Deviant." In *Constitutive Criminology at Work: Applications to Crime and Justice.* Edited by S. Henry and D. Milovanovic, pp. 67–85. Albany, NY: State University of New York Press.

————. "Social Justice and Critical Criminology: On Integrating Knowledge." *Contemporary Justice Review* 3 (2000): 7–37.

————. "Critical Criminology, Existential Humanism, and Social Justice: Exploring the Contours of Conceptual Integration." *Critical Criminology: An International Journal* 10 (2001a): 83–95.

————. "Transcarceration: A Constitutive Ethnography of Mentally Ill 'Offenders'." *The Prison Journal* 81 (2001b): 162–86.

————. 2002a. *Punishing the Mentally Ill: A Critical Analysis of Law and Psychiatry.* Albany, NY: State University of New York Press.

————. "The critical perspective in psychological jurisprudence: Theoretical Advance and Epistemological Assumptions." *International Journal of Law and Psychiatry* 25 (2002b): 151–172.

————. "Psychology and the Law: The Critical Agenda for Citizen Justice and Radical Social Change." *Justice Quarterly* 20 (2003a).

————. "Justice and the Deconstruction of Psychological Jurisprudence: The Case of Competency to Stand Trial." *Theoretical Criminology: An International Journal* 7 (2003b): 55–88.

Arrigo, Bruce, and Robert Schehr. "Restoring Justice for Juveniles: Toward a Critical Analysis of Victim Offender Mediation." *Justice Quarterly* 15 (1998): 629–666.

Arrigo, Bruce, and T. R. Young. "Theories of Crime and Crime of Theorists: On the Topological Construction of Criminological Reality." *Theory and Psychology* 8 (1998): 219–252.

Arrigo, Bruce, and Jeffrey Tasca. "Right to Refuse Treatment, Competency to be Executed, and Therapeutic Jurisprudence." *Law and Psychology Review* 23 (1999): 1–47.

Arrigo, Bruce, and Christopher Williams. "Law, Ideology, and Critical Inquiry: The Case of Treatment Refusal for Incompetent Prisoners Awaiting Execution." *New England Journal On Criminal and Civil Confinement* 25 (1999a): 367–412.

———. "The (Im)possibility of Democratic Justice and the 'Gift' of the Majority: On Derrida, Deconstruction, and the Search for Equality." *Journal of Contemporary Criminal Justice* 16 (1999b): 321–343.

———. "Chaos Theory and the Social Control Thesis: A Post-Foucauldian Analysis of Mental Illness and Involuntary Civil Confinement." *Social Justice* 26 (1999c): 177–207.

———. "Victim Vices, Victim Voices, and Impact Statements: On the Place of Emotion and the Role of Restorative Justice in Capital Sentencing." *Crime and Delinquency* 49 (2003): 603–626.

Arrigo, Bruce, Dragan Milovanovic, and Robert Schehr. "The French Connection: Implications for Law, Crime, and Social Justice." *Humanity & Society* 24 (2000): 162–203.

Ashe, Marie. "Minds' Opportunity." *Syracuse Law Review* 38 (1987): 1129.

———. "The Doubly-Prized World: Myth, Allegory, and the Feminine." *Cornell Law Review* 75 (1990): 644–99.

Bae, I. 1992. "A Survey on Public Acceptance of Restitution as an Alternative to Incarceration for Property Offenses in Hennepin County, Minnesota, U. S. A." In *Restorative Justice on Trial: Pitfalls and Potentials of Victim Offender Mediation—International Research Perspectives*. Edited by H. Messmer and H. U. Otto, pp. 291–308. Dordrecht, Netherlands: Kluwer Academic.

Baker, P. "Chaos, Order and Sociological Theory." *Sociological Inquiry* 62 (1993): 123–149.

Balkin, Jack M. "Deconstructive Practice and Legal Theory." *Yale Law Journal* 96 (1987): 743–786.

Banks, Cynthia. "Victims in the Village: Aspects of Restorative Justice in Papua New Guinea." *International Review of Victimology* 6 (1999): 377–405.

Barak, Gregg, and Stuart Henry. 1999. "An Integrative-Constitutive Theory of Crime, Law, and Social Justice." In *Social Justice/Criminal Justice: The Maturation of Critical Theory in Law, Crime, and Deviance*. Edited by B. Arrigo, pp. 152–175. Belmont, CA: West/Wadsworth.

Barak, Gregg. "Newsmaking Criminology." *Justice Quarterly* 5 (1988): 565–87.

———. Ed. 1994. *Media, Process, and the Social Construction of Crime: Studies in Newsmaking Criminology*. New York: Garland.

———. 1998. *Integrating Criminologies*. Boston, MA: Allyn and Bacon.

Barthes, Roland. 1964. *On Racine*. New York: Hill and Wang.

———. 1967. *System de la Mode*. Paris: Seuil.

————. 1968a. *Writing Degree Zero*. New York: Hill and Wang.

————. 1968b. *Elements of Semiology*. New York: Hill and Wang.

————. 1973a. *Mythologies*. England: Paladin.

————. 1973b. *The Pleasure of the Text*. New York: Hill and Wang.

————. 1974. *S/Z*. New York: Hill and Wang.

————. 1988. *The Semiotic Challenge*. New York: Hill and Wang.

Barton, S. "Chaos, Self-organization, and Psychology." *American Psychologist* 49 (1994): 5–14.

Baudrillard, Jean. 1968. *Le Systeme des Objets*. Paris: Denoel-Gonthier.

————. 1970. *La Societe de Consommation*. Paris: Gallimard.

————. 1981. *For a Critique of the Political Economy of the Sign*. St Louis: Telos Press.

————. 1983a. *Simulations*. New York: Semiotext(e).

————. 1983b. *In the Shadow of the Silent Majorities*. New York: Semiotext(e).

Bauman, Z. 2000. *Liquid Modernity*. Malden, MA: Blackwell Publishers.

————. 2001. *Community*. London: Polity Press.

Baumgartner, F. R., and B. L. Leech. 1988. *Basic Instincts: The Importance of Groups in Politics and Political Science*. Princeton, NJ: Princeton University Press.

Beirne, Pierce ed. 1990. *Revolution in Law: Contributions to the Development of Soviet Legal Theory, 1917–1938*. New York: M. E. Sharpe.

Bell, Derrick. "*Brown v. Board of Education* and the Interest-Convergence Dilemma." *Harvard Law Review* 93 (1980): 518.

Bell, Derrick. 1987. *And We Are Not Saved*. New York: Basic Books.

Bell, Vicki. "Beyond the 'Thorny Question': Feminist, Foucault, and the Desexualization of Rape." *International Journal of the Sociology of Law* 19 (1991): 83–100.

————. 1993. *Interrogating Incest: Feminism, Foucault, and the Law*. London: Routledge and Kegan Paul.

Benhabib, S. 1992. *Situating the Self: Gender, Community and Postmodernism in Contemporary Ethics*. New York: Routledge and Kegan Paul.

————. 1996. *Democracy and Difference: Contesting the Boundaries of the Political*. Princeton, NJ: Princeton University Press.

Benveniste, E. 1971. *Problems in General Linguistics*. Coral Gables, FL: University of Miami Press.

Berman, Art. 1988. *From the New Criticism To Deconstructionism: The Reception of Structuralism and Post-Structuralism*. Urbana, IL: University of Illinois Press.

Bertramsen, R., J. Thomsen, and J. Torfing. 1991. *State, Economy, and Society*. London: Unwin Hyman.

Besley, A. C. "Foucault and the Turn to Narrative Therapy." *British Journal of Guidance and Counseling* 30 (2002): 125–143.

Best, Steven. "The Commodification of Reality and the Reality of Commodification: Jean Baudrillard and Postmodernism." *Current Perspectives in Social Theory* 9 (1989): 23–51.

Best, Steven, and Douglas Kellner. 1991. *Postmodern Theory: Critical Interrogations*. New York: Guilford Press.

————. 1997. *The Postmodern Turn*. New York: Guilford Press.

Binder, G., and Weisberg, R. 2000. *Law as Literature: Literary Criticisms of Law*. Princeton, NJ: Princeton University Press.

Black, Donald. 1976. *The Behavior of Law*. San Diego, CA: Academic Press.

Bogue, Ronald. 1989. *Deleuze and Guattari*. New York: Routledge and Kegan Paul.

Bosworth, Mary. 1999a. *Engendering Resistance: Agency and Power in Women's Prisons*. Sydney: Ashgate.

———. 1999b. "Agency and Choice in Women's Prisons." In *Constitutive Criminology at Work*. Edited by S. Henry and D. Milovanovic, pp. 205–226. New York: State University of New York Press.

Bracher, Mark. 1993. *Lacan, Discourse, and Social Change*. Ithaca, NY: Cornell University Press.

Braithwaite, John. 1989. *Crime, Shame and Reintegration*. New York: Cambridge University Press.

———. 2002. *Restorative Justice and Responsive Regulation*. New York: Oxford University Press.

Brigg, M. "Post-Development, Foucaul and the Colonisation Metaphor." *Third World Quarterly*, 23 (2002): 421–436.

Briggs, J., and D. Peat. 1989. *Turbulent Mirror*. New York: Harper and Row.

Brion, Dennis. 1991. "The Chaotic Law of Tort." In *Peirce and Law*. Edited by Roberta Kevelson. New York: Peter Lang.

Britt, T. "Narrative Pragmatics and the Genius of the Law in Lyotard's Just Gaming." *College Literature* 25 (1998): 190–200.

Brown, Wendy. 1995. *States of Inquiry: Power and Freedom in Late Modernity*. Princeton, NJ: Princeton University Press.

Butler, Judith. 1990. *Gender Trouble*. New York: Routledge and Kegan Paul.

———. 1992. "Contingent Foundations: Feminism and the Question of 'Postmodernism.'" In *Feminists Theorize the Political*. Edited by J. Butler and J. W. Scott. London: Routledge and Kegan Paul.

———. 1993. *Bodies That Matter*. New York: Routledge and Kegan Paul.

———. 1997a. *Excitable Speech*. New York: Routledge and Kegan Paul.

———. 1997b. *The Psychic Life of Power*. Stanford, CA: Stanford University Press.

———. 1999. *Subjects of Desire*. New York: Columbia University Press.

Butz, M. 1997. *Chaos and Complexity: Implications for Psychological Theory and Practice*. Bristol, PA: Taylor and Francis.

Calarco, M. "Derrida on Identity and Difference: A Radical Democratic Reading of The Other Heading." *Critical Horizons* 1 (2000): 51–70.

Carter, A. 1985. *The Bloody Chamber*. New York: Vintage Books.

———. 1990. The Tiger's Bride. New York: Vintage Books.

Caputo, John ed. 1998. *Deconstruction in a Nutshell: A Conversation with Jacques Derrida*. New York: Fordham University Press.

Caudill, David. 1997. *Lacan and the Subject of Law*. Atlantic Highland, NJ: Humanities Press.

Cavender, G. 1998. "In The Shadow of Shadows." In *Entertaining Crime*. Edited by M. Fishm and G. Cavender. Hawthorne, New York: Aldine.

Chanter, Tina. 2002. "Viewing Abjection: Film and Social Justice." *http://www. women. it/4thfemconf/workshops/spectacles2/tinachanter. htm*

Chilton, P. "Metaphor, Euphemism and the Militarization of Language." *Journal of Peace Research* 23 (1986): 7–20.

Cixous, Helene. "The Laugh of the Medusa." *Signs* 1–4 (1976): 875–93.

———. 1985. *Angst*. Jo Levy. London: John Calder.

———. 1986. *The Newly Born Woman*. Translated by Betsy Wing. Minneapolis, MN: University of Minnesota Press.

———. 1990. *Reading with Clarice Lispector*. Minneapolis, MN: University of Minnesota Press.

———. 1991. *The Book of Promethea*. Lincoln: University of Nebraska Press.

———. 1993. *Three Steps on the Ladder of Writing*. Translated by Catherine MacGillivray. Minneapolis, MN: University of Minnesota Press.

———. 1996. *Authorship, Autobiography and Love*. Cambridge: Polity Press.

Clough, Patricia Ticineto. 2000. *Autoaffection*. Minneapolis, MN: University of Minnesota Press.

Cobb, Sara. "The Domestication of Violence in Mediation." *Law and Society Review* 31 (1997): 397–440.

Cohen, J. "Strategy or Identity: New Theoretical Paradigms and Contemporary Social Movements." *Social Research* 52 (985): 664–716.

Cohen, Stanley. "The Punitive City: Notes of the Dispersal of Social Control." *Contemporary Crisis* (3) 1979: 339–363.

———. 1988. *Visions of Social Control: Crime, Punishment, and Classification*. Cambridge: Polity Press.

Cole, David. 1999. *No Equal Justice*. New York: The New Press.

Collins, Barry. "Where Have All the Canaries Gone?" *International Journal for the Semiotics of Law*. 34 (199?).

Collins, Patricia. "Toward a New Vision: Race, Class, and Gender as Categories of Analysis and Connection." *Race, Sex and Class* 1 (1993): 25–45.

Conklin, William. 1998. *The Phenomenology of Modern Legal Discourse*. Aldershot, England: Dartmouth Publishing Company.

Conley, Verena. 1994. "Hélène Cixous. 1937–)." [http://prelectur. stanford. edu/lecturers/cixous/conley. html].

Connolly, William. 1991. *Identity/Difference: Democratic Negotiations of Political Paradox*. Ithica: Cornell University Press.

Conrad, Clay. 1998. *Jury Nullification: The Evolution of a Doctrine*. Durham, NC: Carolina Academic Press.

Coombs, Mary. "Outsider Scholarship." *University of Colorado Law Review* 63 (1992): 683.

Cornell, Drucilla. 1991. *Beyond Accommodation: Ethical Feminism, Deconstruction, and the Law*. New York: Routledge and Kegan Paul.

———. 1992. "The Philosophy of the Limit: System Theory and Feminist Legal Reform." In *Deconstruction and the Possibility of Justice*. Edited by D. Cornell, M. Rosenfeld, and D. Carlson. New York: Routledge and Kegan Paul.

———. 1993. *Transformations*. New York: Routledge and Kegan Paul.

———. 1998a. *At the Heart of Freedom*. Princeton, NJ: Princeton University Press.

———. 1998b. *The Imaginary Domain*. New York: Routledge and Kegan Paul.

———. 1999. *Beyond Accommodation*. Lanham, MD: Rowman and Littlefield.

Cornell, Drucilla., M. Rosenfeld, and D. Carlson, eds. 1992. *Deconstruction and the Possibility of Justice*. New York: Routledge and Kegan Paul.

Couzens, David H., ed. 1992. *Foucault: A Critical Reader*. New York: Basil Blackwell.

Creed, Barbara. 1993. *The Monstrous Feminine, Film, Feminism and Psychoanalysis*. London: Routledge and Kegan Paul.

Crenshaw, Kimberle. "Race, Reform and Retrenchment." *Harvard Law Review* 101 (1988): 1356–1387.

———. "Demarginalizing the Intersection of Race and Sex: A Black Feminist Critique of Antidiscrimination Doctrine." *University of Chicago Legal Forum* (1989): 139–167.

———. 1993. "Beyond Racism and Misogyny: Black Feminism and 2 Live Crew." In *Words That Wound*. Edited by M. Masuda, C. Lawrence, R. Delgado, and K. Crenshaw, pp. 111–132. Oxford: Westview Press.

Crenshaw, Kimberle, Neil Gotanda, Gary Peller, and Kendall Thomas, eds. 1995. *Critical Race Theory: The Writings That Formed the Movement*. New York: New Press.

Critchley, S. "Remarks on Derrida and Habermas." *Constellations: An International Journal of Critical and Democratic Theory* 7 (2000): 455–467.

Culler, Johnathan. 1975. *Structural Poetics*. Ithaca, NY: Cornell University Press.

———. 1981. *The Pursuit of Signs: Semiotics, Literature, and Deconstruction*. Ithaca, NY: Cornell University Press.

———. 1982. *On Deconstruction*. Ithaca: Cornell University Press.

Cummins, J. "Refashioning the Disparate Treatment and Disparate Impact Doctrines in Theory and in Practice." *Howard Law Journal* 41 (1998): 455.

Currie, Dawn, Brian MacLean, and Dragan Milovanovic. 1991. "Three Traditions of Critical Justice Inquiry: Class Gender and Discourse." In *Re-Thinking the Administration of Justice*. Edited by Dawn Currie and Brian MacLean. Halifax, Nova Scotia: Fernwood.

Delanda, Manuel. 2002. *Intensive Science and Virtual Philosophy*. New York: Continuum.

DeLauretis, Teresa. 1990. The Practice of Love. Bloomington, IN: Indiana University Press.

Deleuze, Gilles. 1983. *Nietzsche and Philosophy*. New York: Columbia University Press.

———. 1986. *Cinema 1: The Movement-Mage*. Minneapolis, MN: University of Minnesota Press.

———. 1989. *Cinema 2: The Time-Image*. Minneapolis, MN: University of Minnesota Press.

Deleuze, Gilles, and Felix Guattari. 1983. *Anti-Oedipus*. Minneapolis, MN: University of Minnesota Press.

———. 1986. *Kafka: Toward a Minor Literature*. Minneapolis, MN: University of Minnesota Press.

———. 1987. *A Thousand Plateaus*. Minneapolis, MN: University of Minnesota Press.

———. 1994. *What is Philosophy?* Minneapolis, MN: University of Minnesota Press.

Delgado, Richard, and Jean Stefancic. 2001. *Critical Race Theory*. New York: New York University Press.

Delgado, Richard. "Storytelling for Oppositionists and Others: A Plea for Narrative." *Michigan Law Review* 87 (1989): 2411.

———. "On Telling Stories in School: A Reply to Farber and Sherry." *Vanderbilt Law Review* 46 (1993): 665–674.

———. "Rodrigo's Thirteenth Chronicle: Legal Formalism and Law's Discontents." *Michigan Law Review* 95 (1997): 1105–1149.

———. 1999. *When Equality Ends: Stories About Race and Resistance.*

Delphy, Christine. "The Invention of French Feminism." *Yale French Studies* 87 (1995): 199?.

Delorme, R. 1984. "New View on the Economic Theory of the State: A Case Study of France." Paris: CEPREMAP, memo no. 8401.

Denzin, Norman. 1997. *Interpretive Ethnography.* Thousand Oaks, CA: Sage Publications.

Derrida, Jacques. 1968. "The Ends of Man." In *Margins of Philosophy.* Translated by A. Bass. Chicago: University of Chicago Press.

———. 1973. *Speech and Other Phenomena.* Evanston, IL: Northwestern University Press.

———. 1977. *Of Grammatology.* Baltimore, MD: Johns Hopkins University Press.

———. 1978. *Writing and Difference.* Chicago, IL: University of Chicago Press.

———. 1981. *Positions.* Chicago, IL: University of Chicago Press.

———. 1991. *The Other Heading: Reflections on Today's Europe.* Bloomington, IN: Indiana University Press.

———. 1992. "Force of Law: The Mystical Foundation of Authority." In *Deconstruction and the Possibility of Justice.* Edited by Cornell, M. Rosenfeld, and D. Carlson. New York: Routledge and Kegan Paul.

———. 1994. *Spectres of Marx: The State of Debt, the Work of Mourning, and the New International.* Translated by P. Kamuf. New York: Routledge and Kegan Paul.

———. 1994. *Politics of Friendship.* New York: Verso.

———. 1997. "The Villanova Roundtable." In *Deconstruction in a Nutshell: A Conversation with Jacques Derrida.* Edited by J. Caputo. New York: Fordham University Press.

Diani, M. "The Concept of Social Movement." *The Sociological Review* 40 (2001): 1–25

Dienst, Richard. 1994. *Still Life in Real Time.* Durham, NC: Duke University Press.

Doane, M. "Film and Masquerade: Theorizing the Female Spectator." *Screen* 23 (1987): 74–87.

———. 1988. *The Desire to Desire: The Woman's Film of the 1940s.* Bloomington, IN: Indiana University Press.

Dor, J. 1997. *Introduction to the Reading of Lacan.* London: Jason Aronson.

Douglas, Mary. 1980. *Purity and Danger.* London: Routledge and Kegan Paul.

Doyle, A. 1998. "Cops." In *Entertaining Crime.* Edited by M. Fishman and G. Cavender, pp. 37–58. New York: Aldine de Gruyter.

Dreyfus, Harold, and Paul Rabinow. 1982. *Michel Foucault: Beyond Structuralism and Hermeneutics.* Chicago: University of Chicago Press.

Drolet, M. "The Wild and the Sublime: Lyotard's Post-Modern Politics." *Political Studies* 42 (1994): 259–273.

Duncan, Martha. 1996. *Romantic Outlaws, Beloved Prisons: The Unconscious Meaning of Punishment*. New York: New York University Press.

Dupont, D., and F. Pearce. "Foucault contra Foucault: Rereading the 'Governmentality' Papers." *Theoretical Criminology* 5 (2001): 123–158.

Eco, Umberto, and Thomas Sebeok. 1983. *The Sign of Three: Dupin, Holmes, Peirce*. Bloomington, IN: University of Indiana Press.

Edge, Sarah. "'Women are Trouble, Did You Know that Fergus?': Neil Jordan's 'The Crying Game'." *Feminist Review* 50 (1995): 175–186.

Einstadter, Werner, and Stuart Henry. 1996. *Criminological Theory*. Fort Worth, TX: Harcourt Brace.

Ericson, R. "Mass Media, Crime, Law, and Justice," *British Journal of Criminology* 31 (1991): 219–49.

Etzioni, A. 1995a. *Rights and the Common Good: The Communitarian Perspective*. New York: St. Martins Press.

———. 1995b. *New Communitarian Thinking: Persons, Virtues, Institutions, and Communities*. Charlottesville, NC: University of Virginia Press.

Ewick, Patricia, and Susan S. Silbey. "Subversive Stories and Hegemonic Tales: Toward a Sociology of Narrative." *Law and Society Review* 29 (1995): 197–226.

Farber, Daniel, and Suzanna Sherry. Telling Stories Out of School: An Essay on Legal Narratives." *Stanford Law Review* 45 (1993): 807–45.

Farnsworth, Margaret. 1989. "Theory Integration Versus Model Building." In *Theoretical Integrations in the Study of Deviance and Crime*. Edited by Stephen Messner, Marvin Krohn, and Allen Liska, pp. 93–100. Albany, NY: State University of New York Press.

Ferguson, Margaret, and Jennifer Wicke eds. 1994. *Feminism and Postmodernism*. London: Duke University Press.

Ferrell, Jeff. 1996. *Crimes of Style: Urban Graffiti and the Politics of Criminality*. Boston: Northeastern University Press.

Ferrell, Jeff, Dragan Milovanovic, and Steven Lyng. "Edgework, Media Practices, and the Elongation of Meaning." *Theoretical Criminology* 5 (2001): 177–202.

Forker, Allison. 1997. " Chaos and Modelling Crime." In *Chaos, Criminology and Social Justice*. Edited by Dragan Milovanovic, pp. 55–76. Westport, CT: Praeger.

Foucault, Michel. 1965. Madness and Civilization. New York: Vintage.

———. 1972. *Archeology of Knowledge*. New York: Pantheon.

———. 1973. *The Order of Things*. New York: Vintage.

———. 1977. *Discipline and Punish*. New York: Pantheon.

———. 1977a. "Intellectuals and Power." *In Language, Counter Memory, Practice*. Edited by D. F. Bouchard. Ithaca: Cornell University Press.

———. 1980a. *Power/Knowledge: Selected Interview and Other Writings, 1972–1977*. London: Harvester.

———. 1980b. *History of Sexuality, Vol 1: An Introduction*. London: Allen Lane.

———. 1986a. *Use of Pleasure*. New York: Vintage.

———. "Of Other Spaces." *Diacritics* 16 (1986b): 22–27.

———. 1988. The Care of the Self. New York: Vintage.

Fraser, Nancy. 1997. *Justice Interruptus*. New York: Routledge and Kegan Paul.

Freire, Paulo. 1972. *Pedagogy of the Oppressed*. South Hadley, MA: Herder and Herder.

————. 1985. *The Politics of Education*. South Hadley, MA: Bergin and Garvey.

Freivalds, P. "Balanced and Restorative Justice Project." *Office of Juvenile Justice and Delinquency Fact Sheet* July (1996).

Freud, Sigmund. 1965. *The Interpretation of Dreams*. New York: Avon Books.

Frug, Mary Joe. "A Postmodern Feminist Legal Manifest." *Harvard Law Review* 105 (1992): 1045.

Fuchs, Stephan, and Steven Ward. "What is Deconstruction, and Where and When Does It Take Place: Making Facts in Science, Building Cases in Law." *American Sociological Review* 59 (1994): 481–503.

Galaway, Brian, and J. Hudson. 1996. *Restorative Justice: International Perspectives*. Monsey, NY: Criminal Justice Press.

Gamman, L., and M. Marshment 1988. *The Female Gaze: Women as Viewers of Popular Culture*. London: Women's Press.

Gane, Michael. 1991. *Baudrillard: Critical and Fatal Theory*. New York: Routledge and Kegan Paul.

Gardam, J. 1995. *The Queen of The Tambourine*.

Garland, David. 1990. *Punishment and Modern Society*. Oxford: Clarendon Press.

Georges-Abeyie, Daniel. 1990. "The Myth of a Racist Criminal Justice System?" In *Racism, Empiricism and Criminal Justice*. Edited by Brian MacLean and Dragan Milovanovic. Vancouver: Collective Press.

Gibbons, Don. 1994. *Talking About Crime and Criminals*. Englewood Cliffs, NJ: Prentice-Hall.

Giddens, Anthony. 1984. *The Constitution of Society*. Cambridge: Polity Press.

————. 1991. *Modernity and Self-Identity*. Cambridge: Polity Press.

Giroux, H. 1992. *Border Crossings*. New York: Routledge and Kegan Paul.

Gleick, J. 1987. *Chaos: Making a New Science*. New York: Penguin.

Godel, K. 1962. *On Formally Undecidable Propositions in 'Principia Mathematica' and Related Systems*. Edited by R. B. Braitewaite. New York: Basic Books.

Goffman, Irving. 1961. *Asylums*. London: Penguin Books.

Goldfarb, P. "From the Worlds of 'Others': Minority and Feminist Responses to Critical Legal Studies." *New England Law Review* 26 (1992): 683–710.

Goodrich, Peter. 1990. *Languages of Law*. London: Weidenfeld and Nicolson.

Gottdiener, Mark. 1995. *Postmodern Semiotics*. Oxford, UK: Blackwell.

Gray, V., and D. Lowery. 1996. *The Population Ecology of Interest Representation*. Ann Arbor, MI: University of Michigan Press.

Grbich, Judith. 1996. "The Taxpayer's Body." In *Thinking Through the Body of Law*. Edited by Pheng Cheah, David Fraser, and Judith Grbich. New York: New York University Press.

Greatbatch, R., and R. Dingwall. "Selective Facilitation: Some Preliminary Observations on a Strategy Used by Divorce Mediators." *Law and Society Review* 23 (1989): 613–643.

Gregerson, H., and L. Sailer. "Chaos Theory and its Implications for Social Science Research." *Human Relations* 46 (1993): 777–802.

Griffith, J. "Ideology in Criminal Procedure or a Third 'Model' of the Criminal Process." *Yale Law Journal* 79 (1970): 359–89.

Grosz, Elizabeth. 1990. *Jacques Lacan: A Feminist Introduction*. New York: Routledge and Kegan Paul.

———. 1994. *Volatile Bodies*. Bloomington, IN: Indiana University Press.

Habermas, Jorgen. 1975. *Legitimization Crises*. Boston, MA: Beacon Press.

———. 1984. *Theory of Communicative Action, Volume 1*. Boston, MA: Beacon Press.

———. 1987. *Theory of Communicaive Action, Volume II*. Boston, MA: Beacon Press.

Halper, Louise. "Tropes of Anxiety and Desire: Metaphor and Metonymy in the Law of Takings." *Yale Journal of Law and the Humanities* 8 (1995): 1–101.

Handler, Joel. "The Presidential Address, 1992 Law and Society: "Post modernism, Protest, and the New Social Movement." *Law and Society Review* 26 (1992): 697–731.

Hardt, Michael. 1993. *Gilles Deleuze: An Apprenticeship in Philosophy*. Minneapolis, MN: Minnesota University Press.

Harrington, Christine. 1985. *Shadow Justice: The Ideology and Institutionalization of Alternatives to Court*. Westport, CT: Greenwood Press.

Harris, Angela. 1991. "Race and Essentialism in Feminist Legal Theory." In *Feminist Legal Theory*. Edited by Katharine Bartlett and Rosanne Kennedy. Oxford: Westview Press.

Harris, M. Kay. 1989. "Alternative Visions in the Context of Contemporary Realities." In *New Perspectives on Crime and Justice: Occasional Papers of the MCC Canada Victim Offender Ministries Program and the MCC U. S. Office of Criminal Justice*, Issue 7. Elkhart, IN: Mennonite Central Committee U. S. Office of Criminal Justice.

Hayles, Katherine. 1990. *Chaos Bound: Orderly Disorder in Contemporary Literature and Science*. London: Cornell University Press.

Henry, Stuart. 1983. *Private Justice*. London: Routledge and Kegan Paul.

Henry, Stuart, and Mark Lanier. "The Prism of Crime: Arguments for an Integrated Definition of Crime." *Justice Quarterly* (1998): 609–629.

Henry, Stuart, and Dragan Milovanovic. 1996. *Constitutive Criminology: Beyond Postmodernism*. London: Sage Publications.

———. 2001. "Constitutive Definition of Crime: Power as Harm." In *What is Crime?*. Edited by Stuart Henry and Mark Lanier, pp. 165–178. New York: Rowman and Littlefield.

Higgins, Tracey. "By Reason of their Sex: Feminist Theory, Postmodernism and Justice." *Cornell Law Review* 80 (1995): 1536.

Hirsch, Elizabeth, and Gary Olson. "'Je—Luce Irigaray': A Meting with Luce Irigaray." *Hypatia* 10 (1995): 93–114.

Hobsbawm, Eric. 1965. *Primitive Rebels*. New York: W. W. Norton & Company.

Hobsbawm, Eric, and Terrence Ranger. 1983. *The Invention of Tradition*. New York: Cambridge University Press.

Holmund, Chris. 1993. "Masculinity as Multiple Masquerade." In *Screening the Male: Exploring Masculinities in Hollywood Cinema*. Edited by S. Cohen and I. Hark, pp. 213–229. New York: Routledge and Kegan Paul.

hooks, bell. 1990. *Yearning: Race, Gender, and Cultural Politics*. Boston, MA: South End Press.

————. 1994. "Seduction and Betrayal: The 'Crying Game' Meets the Bodyguard." In *Outlaw Culture: Resisting Representations*. New York: Routledge and Kegan Paul.

Howe, Adrian. "Sentencing Women to Prison in Victoria." *Law in Context* 8 (1990): 32–53.

————. 1994. *Punish and Critique*. New York: Routledge and Kegan Paul.

Hulme, K. 1986. *The Bone People*. ???: Picardor.

Hunt, Alan. 1993. *Explorations in Law and Society*. New York: Routledge and Kegan Paul.

Hunt, Alan, and Gary Wickham. 1995. *Foucault and the Law: Towards a Sociology of Law as Governance*. New York: Pluto Press.

Irigaray, Luce. 1985a. *This Sex Which is Not One*. Ithaca, NY: Cornell University Press.

————. 1985b. *Speculum of the Other Woman*. Ithaca, NY: Cornell University Press.

————. 1993a. *Je, Tu, Nous: Toward a Culture of Difference*. New York: Routledge and Kegan. Paul.

————. 1993b. *An Ethics of Sexual Difference*. Ithaca, NY: Cornell University Press.

————. 1993c. *Sexes and Genealogies*. New York: Columbia University Press.

————. 1994. *Thinking the Difference: For a Peaceful Revolution*. New York: Routledge and Kegan Paul.

James, Joy. "Black Femmes Fatales and Sexual Abuse in Progressive 'White' Cinema: Neil Jordan's Mona Lisa and 'The Crying Game'." *Camera Obscura* 36 (1995): 33–45.

Jameson, Frederick. 1981. *The Political Unconscious*. Ithaca, NY: Cornell University Press.

Jamison, Andrew, and Ronald Eyerman. 1991. *Social Movements: A Cognitive Approach*. University Park, PA: Penn State University Press.

JanMohamed, A. R. 1994. "Some Implications of Paulo Freire's Border Pedagogy. In *Between Borders*. Edited by H. Giroux and P. MacLaren, pp. 242–52. New York: Routledge and Kegan Paul.

Jessop, Bob. 1991. *State Theory: Putting the Capitalist State in Its Place*. State College, PA: Pennsylvania State University Press.

Johnson, Sheri. 2001. "Racial Derogation in Prosecutor's Closing Arguments." In *Petit Apartheid in the U. S. Criminal Justice System*. Edited by D. Milovanovic and K. Russell, pp. 79–102. Durham, NC: Carolina Academic Press.

Johnston, H., and B. Klandermans 1995. *Social Movements and Culture*. Minneapolis, MN: University of Minnesota Press.

Jordon, Neil. *The Crying Game*. Artisan Entertainment.

Joseph, R. "Denial, Acknowledgement and Peace Building Through Reconciliatory Justice." *Journal of Waikato University College* 1 (2001): 63–79.

Kairys, David ed. 1982. *The Politics of Law: A Progressive Critique*. New York: Pantheon Books.

Kanter, R. M. 1972. *Commitment and Community*. Cambridge, MA: Harvard University Press.

Katz, Jack. 1988. *Seductions of Crime*. New York: Basic Books.

Kelman, Mark. 1987. *A Guide to Critical Legal Studies*. Cambridge, MA: Harvard University Press.

Kellner, Douglas. 1989. *Jean Baudrillard: From Marxism to Postmodernism and Beyond.* Cambridge: Polity Press.

Kennedy, Randal. "Racial Critiques of Legal Academia." *Harvard Law Review* 102 (1989): 1745.

Kennedy, Duncan. 1997. *A Critique of Adjudication: Fin de Siecle.* Cambridge, MA: Harvard University Press.

Kevelson, Roberta. 1988. *The Law as a System of Signs.* New York: Plenum.

Klages, Mary. 1997. "Hélène Cixous: 'The Laugh of the Medusa." [http://www. Colorado. edu/English/ENGL2012Klages/cixous. html].

Kozeny, G. 1995. "Intentional Communities: Lifestyles Based on Idelas." In *Communities Direcotry,* pp. 18–24. Langley, WA: Fellowship for Intentional Community.

Kozol, J. 1985. *Illustrate America.* New York: Doubleday.

Kristeva, Julia. "Signifying Practice and Mode of Production." *Edinburgh Review* (1976): 1.

———. 1977. *About Chinese Women.* London: Marion Boyars.

———. 1980. *Desire in Language.* New York: Columbia University Press.

———. 1982. *Powers of Horror.* New York: Columbia University Press.

———. 1984. *Revolution in Poetic Language.* New York: Columbia University Press.

———. 1986. "A New Type of Intellectual: The Dissident." In *The Kristeva Reader.* Edited by T. Moi. Oxford: Blackwell.

———. 1987. *Tales of Love.* New York: Columbia University Press.

———. 1989. *Black Sun.* New York: Columbia University Press.

———. 1995. *New Maladies of the Soul.* New York: Columbia University Press.

———. 1996. *Time and Sense.* New York: Columbia University Press.

———. 2000. *The Sense and Non-Sense of Revolt.* New York: Columbia University Press.

Kübler, D. "Understanding Policy Change With the Advocacy Coalition Framework: An Application to Swiss Drug Policy." *Journal of European Public Policy* 8 (2001): 623–641.

Lacan, Jacques. 1975–1976. Seminar 23, *Le Sinthome.* Ornicar 6: 30–29; 7: 3–18; 8: 6–20; 9: 32–40; 10: 5–12; 11: 2–9.

———. 1977. *Ecrits: A Selection.* Translated by A. Sheridan Trans. New York: W. W. Norton.

———. 1981. *The Four Fundamental Concepts of Psychoanalysis.* New York: W. W. Norton.

———. 1985. *Feminine Sexuality.* New York: W. W. Norton and Pantheon.

———. 1988. *The Seminars of Jacques Lacan, Book 2: The Ego in Freud's Theory and in the Techniques of Psychoanalysis, 1954–55.* Cambridge: Cambridge University Press.

———. 1991. *L'envers de la Psychanalyse.* Paris: Editions du Seuil.

Laclau, Ernesto. 1990. *New Reflections on the Revolution of Our Time.* London: Verso.

———. 1996a. "Deconstruction, Pragmatism, Hegemony." In *Deconstruction and Pragmatism* Edited by C. Mouffe, pp. 47–68. London: Routledge and Kegan Paul.

———. 1996b. *Emancipation(s).* London: Verso.

Laclau, Ernesto, and Chantal Mouffe. 1985. *Hegemony and Socialist Strategy*. London: Verso.

Lash, Scott, and John Urry. 1994. *Economies of Signs and Space*. London: Sage Publications

Lather, P. "Issues of Validity in Openly Ideological Research." *Interchange* 17 (1986): 63–84.

———. "Fertile Obsession: Validity after Poststructuralism." *Sociological Quarterly* 34 (1993): 673–94.

Lauritis, T. de. "Eccentric Subjects." *Feminist Studies* 16 (1990): 115–50.

Lawrence, Charles. "The Id, Ego, and Equal Protection: Reckoning with Unconscious Racism." *Stanford Law Review* 39 (1987): 317–388.

Legendre, Pierre. "Id Efficeit, Quad Figurat. It is the Symbol Which Produces Effects." *Legal Studies Forum* 20 (1996): 247–263.

Lem, Stanislaw. "Metafantasia." *Science-Fiction Studies* 8 (1981): 54–71.

Lerman, L. "Mediation of Wife-Abuse Cases: The Adverse Impact of Informal Dispute Resolution on Women." *Harvard Law Review* 7 (1984): 57–113.

Leverant, S., F. Cullen, B. Fulton, and J. Wozniak. "Reconsidering Restorative Justice: The Corruption of Benevolence Revisited?" *Crime and Delinquency* 45 (1999): 1.

Leviton, S., and Greenstone, J. 1997. *Elements of Mediation*. Pacific Grove, CA: Brooks/Cole.

Lippens, Ronnie. "Critical Criminologies and the Reconstruction of Utopia." *Social Justice*, 22 (1995): 32–50.

———.Border-Crossing Criminology. *Theoretical Criminology* 2 (1997): 119–151.

———. "Hypermodernity, Nomadic Subjectivities, and Radical Democracy: Roads Through Ambivalent Clues." *Social Justice* 24 (1998a): 16–43.

———. "Hybrid Hopes Ltd.: Reflections on Hybrid Hopes for Rhizologists." *Humanity and Society* 22 (1998b): 386–410.

———. "Alternatives to What Kind of Suffering?: Toward a Border-Crossing Criminology." *Theoretical Criminology* 3 (1998c): 311–343.

———. "Into Hybrid Marshlands: Thirdspatial Notes on Postcolonial Theory and Feminist Legal Theory." *International Journal for the Semiotics of Law* 12 (1999): 59–89.

Litowitz, Douglas. 1997. *Postmodern Philosophy and Law*. Lawrence, KS: University Press of Kansas.

Lopez, Gerald. 1994. *Rebellious Lawyering*. San Francisco, CA: Westview Press.

Lorraine, Tamsin. 1999. *Irigaray and Deleuze: Experiments in Visceral Philosophy*. Ithaca, NY: Cornell University Press.

Lynch, Mona. "Pedophiles and Cyber-Predators as Contaminating Forces." *Law and Social Inquiry* 27 (2002) 529– 57.

Lyng, Steven. "Edgework." *American Journal of Sociology* 95 (1990): 876–921.

Lyotard, Jean-Francois. 1971. *Discourse, Figure*. Paris: Klincksieck.

———. 1974. *Economie Libidinale*. Paris: Minuit.

———. 1984. *The Postmodern Condition*. Minneapolis, MN: University of Minnesota Press.

———. 1988a. *Perigrinations*. New York: Columbia University Press.

———. 1988b. *The Differend*. Minneapolis, MN: University of Minnesota Press.

MacKinnon, Catherine. 1987. *Feminism Unmodified: Discourses on Life and Law.* Cambridge, MA: Harvard University Press.

———. 1989. *Towards a Feminist Theory of the State.* Cambridge, MA: Harvard University Press.

———."Symposium on Unfinished Business: Points Against Postmodernism." *Chicago-Kent Law Review* 75 (2000): 687.

Malcolm X., and Alex Haley. 1965. *The Autobiography of Malcolm X.* New York: Ballantine Books.

Maloney, D., and Holcomb, D. "In Pursuit of Community Justice." *Youth and Society* 33 (2001): 296–313.

Manderson, D. "Transgender Jurisprudence." *Sydney Law Review* 24 (2002): 442.

Manning, Peter. 1988. *Symbolic Communication: Signifying Calls and the Police Response.* Cambridge, MA: MIT Press.

Martin, Rux. 1988. "Truth, Power, Self: An Interview With Michel Foucault." In *Technologies of the Self.* Edited by L. Martin, H. Gutman, and P. Hutton. Amherst, MA: University of Massachusetts Press.

Martinez, George. "A Philosophical Consideration and the Use of Narrative in the Law." *Rutgers Law Journal* 30 (1999): 683.

Matsuda, Mari. "Pragmatism Modified and the False Consciousness Problem." *Southern California Law Review* 63 (1990): 1763–1782.

———. 1996. *Where is Your Body.* Boston, MA: Beacon Press.

Matsuda, Mari, Charles Lawrence, Richard Delgado, and Kimberle Crenshaw. 1993. *Words That Wound: Critical Race Theory, Assaultive Speech, and the First Amendment.* San Francisco, CA: Westview Press.

Matsuda, Mari, and Charles Lawrence. 1993. "Epilogue: Burning Crosses and the R. A. V. Case." In *Words That Wound.* Edited by Matsuda et al. San Francisco, Ca: Westview Press.

Matza, David. 1969. *Becoming Deviant.* Englewood Cliffs, NJ: Prentice-Hall.

Mawhinney, H. "Theoretical Approaches to Understanding Interest Groups." *Educational Policy,* 15 (2001): 187–215.

McAdam, D., J. McCarthy, and M. Zald. 1996. *Comparative Perspectives on Social Movements.* London: Cambridge University Press.

McFarland, A. "Interest Groups and Theories of Power in America." *British Journal of Political Science* 17 (1998): 129–147

McGraw, B. "Jean-François Lyotard's Postmodernism: Feminism, History, and the Question of Justice." *Women's Studies* 20 (1992): 259–272.

McKinney, D. "Violence: The Strong and the Weak." *Film Quarterly* 46 (1984): 16–22.

McLaren, Paul. 1994. "Multiculturalism and the Postmodern Critique." In *Between Borders. Edited by* H. Giroux and P. McLaren, pp. 1992–222. New York: Routledge and Kegan Paul.

Melucci, A. "Getting Involved: Identity and Mobilization in Social Movements." *International Social Movement Research* 1 (1988): 124–154.

———. 1990. *Nomads of the Present: Social Movements and Individual Needs in Contemporary Society.* Philadelphia, PA: Temple University Press.

———. 1995. "The Process of Collective Identity." In *Social Movements and Culture*. Edited by B. Klandermans, pp. 41–63. Minneapolis, MN: University of Minnesota Press.

———. 1996. *The Playing Self. Person and Meaning in the Planetary Society*. New York: Cambridge University Press.

Merry, Sally Engle. "Resistance and the Cultural Power of Law." *Law and Society Review* 29 (1995): 11–26.

Metz, C. 1981. *Imaginary Signifier*. Bloomington, IN: Indiana University Press.

Milovanovic, Dragan. "Jailhouse Lawyers and Jailhouse Lawyering." *International Journal of the Sociology of Law* 16 (1988): 455–75.

———."Schmarxism, Exorcism, and Transpraxis." *The Critical Criminologist* 3 (1991): 5–6, 11–12.

———. 1992. *Postmodern Law and Disorder*. Merseyside, UK: Deborah Charles Publications.

———. "Dueling Paradigms: Modernist versus Postmodernist Thought." *Humanity and Society*, 19 (1995): 19–44.

———. "'Rebellious Lawyering:' Lacan, Chaos, and the Development of Alternative Juridico-Linguistic Forms." *Legal Studies Forum* 20 (1996a): 295–322.

———."Postmodern Criminology: Mapping the Terrain." *Justice Quarterly* 13 (1996b): 567–609.

———. 1997. *Postmodern Criminology*. New York: Garland.

———. 1999. "Catastrophe Theory, Discourse, and Conflict Regulation." In *Social Justice/Criminal Justice: The Maturation of Critical Theory in Law, Crime, and Deviance*. Edited by Bruce Arrigo, pp. 203–223. Belmont, CA: Wadsworth.

———. 2002. *Critical Criminology at the Edge: Postmodern Perspectives, Integration, and Applications*. Westport, CT: Praeger.

———. 2003. "Edgework: A Subjective and Structural Model of Negotiating Boundaries." In *Edgework: The Sociology of Voluntary Risk Taking*. Edited by Steve Lyng. New York: Routledge and Kegan Paul.

Milovanovic, Dragan, and Stuart Henry. "Toward a New Penology: Constitutive Penology." *Social Justice*. 18 (1991): 204–223.

———. 2002. "Constitutive Penology Revisited." Forthcoming, *Postmodern Criminology*. http://www. tryoung. com/journal-pomocrim/pomocrimindex. html

Milovanovic, Dragan and Katheryn Russell eds. 2001. *Petit Apartheid in the US Criminal Justice System: The Dark Figure of Racism*. Durham, NC: Carolina Academic Press.

Minow, Martha. "Interpreting Rights: An Essay for Robert Cover." *Yale Law Journal* 96 (1987): 1860–1915.

Moi, Toril. 1985. *Sexual/Textual Politics* London: Methuen.

———. 1988. Peregrinations. New York: Columbia University Press.

———. ed. 1990. *The Kristeva Reader*. New York: Columbia University Press.

Morris, Norval. 1974. *The Future of Imprisonment*. Chicago, IL: University of Chicago Press.

Morris, Ruth. 1994. *A Practical Path to Transformative Justice*. Toronto: Tittenhouse.

———. 2000. *Stories of Transformative Justice*. Toronto: Canadian Scholarly Press.

Mouffe, Chantal. 1992. "Feminism, Citizenship and Radical Democratic Politics." In *Feminists Theorize the Political*. Edited by Judith Butler and Joan Scott. New York: Routledge and Kegan Paul.

Moyer, B. 2001. *Doing Democracy: The MAP Model For Organizing Social Movements*. Gabriola Island, B. C.: New Society Publishers.

Mulvey, Laura. "Visual Pleasure and Narrative Cinema." *Screen* 16 (1990/1975): 3.

Naffine, Ngaire. 1996. *Feminism and Criminology*. Philadelphia, PA: Temple University Press.

Newman, S. "Derrida's Deconstruction of Authority." *Philosophy and Social Criticism* 27 (2001): 1–20.

Nielsen, M. "Navajo Nation Courts, Peacemaking and Restorative Justice Issues." *Journal of Legal Pluralism* 44 (1999): 105–126.

Norris, Christopher. 2000. *Quantum Theory and the Flight from Realism*. New York: Routledge and Kegan Paul.

Nugent, W. R., M. Umbreit, L. Wiinamaki, and J. B. Paddock. "Participation in Victim Offender Mediation and Re-offense: Successful Replications? *Journal of Research on Social Work Practice* 11 (2001): 5–24.

O'Barr, William M. 1982. *Linguistic Evidence: Language, Power, and Strategy in the Courtroom*. San Diego, CA: Academic Press.

O'Grady, Kathleen. 1996. "Guardian of Language: An Interview with Helen Cixous." [http://bailiwick. lib. uiowa. edu/wstudies/cixous/]. Originally in Cixous, Hélène.*Women's Education des Femmes* 12, No. 4 (1996–7): 6–10.

Olivas, Michael. "The Chronicles, My Grandfather's Stories and Immigration: The Slave Trader's Chronicle as Racial History." *St. Louis University Law Journal* 34 (1990): 425.

Oliver, Kelly. 1993. *Reading Kristeva*.

———. 1998. "Kristeva and Feminism." *http://www. cddc. vt. edu/feminism/Kristeva. html*

O'Malley, Pat, and S. Mugford. 1994. "Crime, Excitement, and Modernity." In *Varieties of Criminology*. Edited by Greg Barak, pp. 189–211. Westport, CT: Praeger.

Palmer, B. D. 1990. *Descent into Discourse: The Reification of Language and the Writing of Social History*. Philadelphia, PA: Temple University Press.

Patterson, D. The Theory of Law as Literature: Literary Criticisms of Law. *Buffalo Law Review*, 49 (2001): 544.

Pavlich, George. "The Power of Community Mediation: Government and Formation of Self-identity." *Law and Society Review* 30 (1996): 707–733.

———."Justice in Fragments: The Political Logic of Mediation in "New Times." *Critical Criminologist* 8 (1998): 20–23.

———. "Criticism and Criminology." *Theoretical Criminology* 3 (1999): 29–51.

Peller, Gary. "The Discourse of Constitutional Degradation." *Georgia Law Journal* 81 (1992): 313–332.

Pentony, Samantha. "How Kristeva's Theory of Abjection Works in Relation to the Fairy Tale and Post Colonial Novel." *Deep South* 3 (1996): 1–6. Reproduced at *http://www. otago. ac. nz/DeepSouth/vol2no3/pentony. html*.

Pfohl, Stephen. "Twilight of the Parasites: Ultramodern Capital and the New World Order." *Social Problems* 40 (1993): 125–151.

Porter, E., and J. Gleick. 1990. *Nature's Chaos*. New York: Penguin.

Poster, Mark ed. 1988. *Jean Baudrillard: Selected Writings*. Stanford, CA: Stanford University Press.

Pranis, K., and M. Umbreit. 1992. *Public Opinion Research Challenges Perception of Widespread Public Demand for Harsher Punishment*. Minneapolis, MN: Citizens Council.

Price, Mark. "Comparing Victim Offender Mediation Program Models." *Victim Offender Mediation Journal* 6 (1995): 1–6.

Prigogine, Ilya., and Isabella Stengers. 1984. *Order Out of Chaos*. New York: Bantam Books.

Questenberry, D. 1995. "Who Are We: An Exploration of What 'Intentional Community' Means." In *Communities Directory*, pp. 33–38. Langley, WA: Fellowship for International Community.

Quinney, Richard. 1977. *Class, State, and Crime*. New York: David Mackay.

Rabinow, Paul. 1997. *Michel Foucaul: Ethics, Subjectivity and Truth*. New York: New Press.

Radelet, M., and H. Bedout. 1992. *In Spite of Innocence*. Boston, MA: Northeastern University Press.

Randall, Alice. 2001. *The Wind Done Gone*. New York, Mariner.

Rodowick, D. N. 1997. *Gilles Deleuzes' Time Machine*. Durham, NC: Duke University Press.

Rorty, Richard. "Philosophy as a Kind of Writing: An Essay on Derrida." *New Literary History* 10 (1978): 141–157.

———. 1989. *Contingency, Irony, and Solidarity*. Cambridge: Cambridge University Press.

Rossi-Landi, F. 1977. *Linguistics and Economics*. Netherlands: Mouton.

Rubin, Edward. "On Beyond Truth: A Theory for Evaluating Legal Scholarship." *California Law Review* 80 (1992): 889–940.

Russell, Katheryn. "The Critical Legal Studies Challenge to Contemporary Mainstream Legal Philosophy." *Ottawa Law Review* 18 (1986): 1–24.

———. 1998. *The Color of Crime*. New York: New York University Press.

Sabatier, P., and N. Pelkey. "Incorporating Multiple Actors and Guidance Instruments Into Models of Regulatory Policymaking: An Advocacy Coalition Framework." *Administration and Society* 19 (1987): 236–263

Salecl, Renata. 1994. *The Spoils of Freedom*. New York: Routledge and Kegan Paul.

Sarat, Austin D. "Speaking of Death." *Law and Society Review* 27 (1993): 19–58.

Sarat, Austin, and Thomas Kearns. 1991. "A Journey through Forgetting: Toward a Jurisprudence of Violence." In *The Fate of Law*. Edited by A. Sarat and T. R. Kearns. Ann Arbor, MI: University of Michigan Press.

———. 1992. *Law's Violence*. Ann Arbor, MI: Michigan University Press.

———. 1996. *The Rhetoric of Law*. Ann Arbor, MI: Michigan University Press.

Sarat, Austin D., and William L. Felstiner. 1995. *Divorce Lawyers and Their Clients: Power and Meaning in the Legal Process*. New York: Oxford University Press.

Sarup, Michael. 1989. *An Introductory Guide to Post-Structuralism and Postmodernism.* Athens, GA: University of Georgia Press.

Saussure, Ferdinand de. 1966. *Course in General Linguistics.* New York: McGraw-Hill.

Scarry, E. 1985. *The Body in Pain: The Making and Unmaking of the World.* New York: Oxford University Press.

Schehr, R. "Divarications of Employee Drug Testing Through Deconstruction and Discourse Analysis." *Humanity and Society* 19 (1995): 45–64

————. *Dynamic Utopia.* Westport, CT: Praeger.

————. 1997. "Surfing the Chaotic." In *Chaos, Criminology and Social Justice: The New Orderly (Dis)Order.* Edited by Dragan Milovanovic, pp. 157–178. Westport, CT: Praeger.

————. 1999. "Intentional Communities, The Fourth Way: A Constitutive Integration." In *Constitutive Criminology at Work.* Edited by S. Henry and D. Milovanovic, pp. 249–274. New York: State University of New York Press.

————. Martial Arts Films and the Action-Cop Genre: Ideology, Violence and Spectatorship." *Journal of Criminal Justice and Popular Culture* 7 (2000a): 102–118.

————."From Restoration to Transformation: Victim Offender Mediation as Transformative Justice." *Mediation Quarterly* 18 (2000b): 151–169.

Schehr, Robert, and Dragan Milovanovic. "Conflict Mediation and the Postmodern." *Social Justice* 25 (1999): 208–232.

Scheppele, K. L. "The Revisioning of Rape Law." *University of Chicago Law Review* 54 (1987): 1095–1116.

Schroeder, Jeanne. "The Vestal and the Fasces." *Cardoza Law Review* 16 (1995): 805.

————. "The Hysterical Attorney: The Legal Advocate Within Lacanian Discourse Theory." *International Journal for the Semiotics of Law* 13 (2000): 181–213.

Schulman, Caren. 1997. "Chaos, Law, and Critical Legal Studies." In *Chaos, Criminology and Social Justice.* Edited by Dragan Milovanovic. Westport, CT: Praeger.

Schwartz, Martin, and David O. Friedrichs. "Postmodern Thought and Criminological Discontent: New Metaphors for Understanding Violence." *Criminology* 32 (1994): 221–246.

Schwendinger, Herman, and Julia Schwendinger. 1985. *Adolescent Subcultures and Delinquency.* New York: Praeger.

Seelye, H., and J.Wasilewski. 1996. *Between Cultures.* New York: McGraw-Hill.

Sellers, Susan. 1994. *The Hélène Cixous Reader.* New York: Routledge and Kegan Paul.

————. 2000. *The Hélène Cixous Reader.* London: Routledge and Kegan Paul.

Sembene, Ousmane. 1963. Borom Sarret. Produced and directed by Ousmane Sembene.

Sheehan, Katherine. "Caring for Deconstruction." *Yale Journal of Law and Feminism* 12 (2000): 85.

Shepherdson, Charles. "The Concept of Race." *Journal for the Psychoanalysis of Culture and Society* 1(1996): 173–178.

Shiach, Morag. 1990. "Their 'Symbolic' Exists, It Holds Powe5r—W, the Sowers of Disorder, Know it Only Too Well." In *Between Feminism and Psychoanalysis.* Edited by Teresa Brennan, 153–67. London: Routledge and Kegan Paul.

Shon, Phillip Chong Ho. "'Hey You C'me Here!': Subjectivization, Resistance, and the Interpellative Violence of Self-Generated Police-Citizen Encounters." *International Journal for the Semiotics of Law* 13 (2000): 159–179.

———."Hey You C'me Here!" *International Journal for the Semiotics of Law* 13, No. 2 (1999): 159–79.

Shreve, G. "Fact, Value and Action in Nonconceptual Jurisprudence." *American Journal of Comparative Law* 50 (2002): 33.

Silbey, Susan. "'Let Them Eat Cake': Globalization, Postmodern Colonialism, and the Possibility of Justice." *Law and Society Review* 31 (1996): 207–235.

Silbey, Susan, and Austin Sarat. "Dispute Processing in Law and Legal Scholarship: From Institutional Critique to the Reconstruction of the Juridic Subject." *Denver Law Review* 66 (1989): 437–498.

Silverman, Kaja. 1983. *The Subject of Semiotics.* New York: Oxford University Press.

———. 1988. *The Acoustic Mirror: The Female Voice in Psychoanalysis and Cinema.* Bloomington, IN: Indiana University Press.

———. 1990. "Dis-Embodying the Female Voice." In *Issues in Feminist Film Criticism.* Edited by P. Erens, pp. 309–327.

———. 1992. *Male Subjectivity at the Margins.* New York: Routledge and Kegan Paul.

Simmel, Georg. 1950. *The Sociology of Georg Simmel.* Translated by K. Wolff. London: The Free Press.

Slaughter, Marty. "Fantasies: Single Mothers and Welfare Reform." *Columbia Law Review* 95 (1995): 301.

Smart, Carol. 1989. *Feminism and the Power of the Law.* London/New York: Routledge and Kegan Paul.

Smelik, Anneke. 1998. *And the Mirror Cracked.* New York: St. Martin's Press.

Smelser, N. 1962. *Theory of Collective Behavior.* New York: Free Press.

Snow, D., and R. Benford. 1988. "Ideology, Frame Resonance, and Participant Mobilization." In *International Social Movement Research: From Structure to Action.* Edited by B. Klandermans, H. Kriesi, and S. Tarrow. Greenwich, CT: JAI Press.

Snow, D., E. B. Rockford, S. K. Wordenand, and R. Benford. "Frame Alignment Processes, Micromobilization, and Movement Participation." *American Sociological Review* 51 (1986): 464–481.

Sorensen, Inge Ejbye. "Abjection in the Bone People and The Queen of the Tambourine." *Deep South* 2 (1996): 3. Reproduced in: *http://www. otago. ac. nz/DeepSouth/vol2no3/inge. html*

Sparks, Richard. 2001. "Penology" In *The Sage Dictionary of Criminology.* Edited by E. McLaughlin and J. Muncie, pp. 206–207. London: Sage Publications.

Spivak, Gayatri Chakravorty. 1987. "French Feminism in an International Frame." In *In Other Worlds.* Edited by Gayatri Spivak, pp. 134–153. New York: Methuen.

———. 1991. "Can the Subaltern Speak" In *Marxism and the Interpretation of Culture.* Edited by C. Nelson and L. Grossberg. London: Macmillan.

———. 1992. "French Feminists Revisited." In *Feminists Theorize the Political.* Edited by J. Butler and J. Scott, pp. 54–85. New York: Routledge and Kegan Paul.

Stacey, Helen. "Lacan's Split Subjects: Raced and Gendered Transformations." *Legal Studies Forum* 20 (1996): 277–294.

Stacey, J. 1994. *Star Gazing: Hollywood Cinema and Female Spectatorship.* London: Routledge and Kegan Paul.

Stanford Law School. "Critical Legal Studies Symposium." *Stanford Law Review* 36 (1984): 1–674.

Stanley, Christopher. 1996. *Urban Excesses and the Law.* Wharton Street, London: Cavendish Publishing.

Stewart, I. 1989. *Does God Play Dice?* New York: Blackwell.

Stockdill, Brett. 1999. "Queer Theory and Social Justice." In *Social Justice/Criminal Justice.* Edited by B. Arrigo, pp. 226–250. Belmont, CA: Wadsworth.

Sullivan, Dennis, and Larry Tifft. 2001. *Restorative Justice: Healing the Foundations of Our Everyday Lives.* Monsey, NY: Willow Tree Press.

Sutherland, Kate. "Legal Rites: Abjection and the Criminal Regulation of Consensual Sex." *Saskatchewan Law Review* 63 (2000): 119–37.

Symposium: Legal Storytelling. *Michigan Law Review* 87 (1989): 2073.

Thomas, Jim. 1988. *Prisoner Litigation: The Paradox of the Jailhouse Lawyer.* Totawa, NJ: Rowman and Littlefield.

Thomas, Jim, and Dragan Milovanovic. "Overcoming the Absurd: Prisoner Litigation as Primitive Rebellion." *Social Problems* 36 (1989): 48–60.

———. 1999. "Revisiting Jailhouse Lawyers." In *Constitutive Criminology at Work: Applications to Crime and Justice.* Edited by S. Henry and D. Milovanovic, pp. 227–248. New York: State University of New York Press

Thorton, M. "Feminist Jurisprudence: Illusion or Reality?" *Australian Journal of Law and Society* 3 (1986): 5–29.

Tiefenbrun, Susan. "Legal Semiotics." *Cardozo Arts and Entertainment Law Review* 5 (1986): 89–156.

Touraine, A. "An Introduction to the Study of Social Movements. *Social Research* 52 (1985): 775–787.

———. 1988. *The Return of the Actor.* Minneapolis, MN: The University of Minnesota Press.

Trinh, T. M-ha. 1989. *Woman, Native, Other: Writing Postcoloniality and Feminism.* Bloomington, IN: Indiana University Press.

———. *Surname Viet Given Name Nam.* Jean-Paul Bourier, Associate Producer. Directed by Trinh T. Minh-ha.

———. 1991. *When the Moon Waxes Red: Representation, Gender and Cultural Politics.* New York: Routledge and Kegan Paul.

———. 1992. *Framer Framed.* New York: Routledge and Kegan Paul.

Tushnet, M. "Critical Legal Studies: An Introduction to Its Origins and Underpinnings." *Journal of Legal Education* 36 (1986): 505–517.

———. "The Degradation of Constitutional Discourse." *Georgia Law Journal* 81 (1992): 251.

Umbreit, Mark. 1994. *Victim Meets Offender: The Impact of Restorative Justice on Mediation.* Monsey, NY: Criminal Justice Press.

———. 1995. *Mediating Interpersonal Conflicts: A Pathway to Peace.* West Concord, MN: CPI Publishing.

———. 2001. *The Handbook of Victim Offender Mediation: An Essential Guide to Practice and Research.* San Francisco: Jossey-Bass.

Umbreit, Mark, R. Coates, and A. Roberts. "Cross National Impact of Restorative Justice Through Mediation and Dialogue." *The ICCA Journal of Community Corrections* 8 (1997): 46–50.

Unger, Roberto. 1986. *The Critical Legal Studies Movement.* Cambridge, MA: Harvard University Press.

———. 1987. *False Necessity.* New York: Cambridge University Press.

Van Ness, Daniel, and K. Strong. 1997. *Restoring Justice.* Cincinnati, OH: Anderson.

Van Ness, Daniel, and K. Strong. 2002. *Restoring Justice.* Cincinnati, OH: Anderson.

Velan, Y. 1972. "Barthes." In *Modern French Criticism.* Edited by J. Simon. Chicago, IL: University of Chicago Press.

Volosinov, V. 1986. *Marxism and the Philosophy of Language.* Cambridge, MA: Harvard University Press.

Voruz, Veronique. "Psychosis and the Law: Responsibility and the Law of Symbolization." *International Journal for the Semiotics of Law* 13 (2000): 133–158.

Walzer, M. 1994. *Thick and Thin: Moral Arguments at Home and Abroad.* Notre Dame, IN: Notre Dame University Press.

Wandel, T. "The Power of Discourse: Michel Foucault and Critical Theory." *Cultural Values* 5 (2001): 368–382.

Wexler, P. 1992. *Becoming Somebody: Toward a Social Psychology of School.* London: Falmer Press.

White, Lucie. "Subordination, Rhetorical Survival Skills, and Sunday Shoes." *Buffalo Law Review* 38 (1990): 1.

Whitford, Margaret. 1991. *Luce Irigaray: Philosophy in the Feminine.* London/New York: Routledge and Kegan Paul.

Wijeyeratne, Roshan D. "Deconstruction, Semiotics and Justice." *International Journal for the Semiotics of Law* 31 (1998): 105–112.

Williams, Christopher. "Inside the Outside and Outside the Inside: Negative Fusion From the Margins of Humanity." *Humanity and Society* 23 (1998): 49–67.

Williams, Christopher, and Bruce Arrigo. "The Philosophy of the Gift and the Psychology of Advocacy: Critical Reflections on Forensic Mental Health Intervention." *International Journal for the Semiotics of Law* 13 (2000): 215–242.

———."Anarchoas and Order: On the Emergence of Social Justice." *Theoretical Criminology: An International Journal* 5 (2001): 223–252.

———. 2002. *Law, Psychology, and Justice: Chaos Theory and the New (Dis)Order.* Albany, NY: State University of New York Press.

Williams, Joan. 1991. "Deconstructing Gender." In *Feminist Legal Theory.* Edited by Katharine Bartlett and Rosanne Kennedy. Oxford: Westview Press.

Williams, L. 1990. *Hardcore: Power, Pleasure and the Frenzy of the Visible.* London: Paladin.

Williams, P. R. "Taking Rights Aggressively: The Perils and Promise of Critical Legal Theory for People of Color." *Law and Inequality* 5 (1987): 103–118.

Williamson, Judith. 1987. *Decoding Advertisement.* New York: Marioin.

Willis, S. 1991. *A Primer for Daily Life.* New York: Routledge and Kegan Paul.

Winick, Bruce. "Competency to be Executed: A Therapeutic Jurisprudence Perspective." *Behavioral Sciences and the Law* 10 (1992): 317–338.

————. 1997. *The Right to Refuse Mental Health Treatment.* Washington, DC: American Psychological Association.

Wittgenstein, Ludwig. 1953. *Philosophical Investigations.* Oxford: Basil Blackwell.

Woodhull, Winifred. 1988. "Sexuality, Power, and the Question of Rape." In *Feminism and Foucault: Reflections on Resistance.* Edited by I. Diamond and I. Quinby. Boston, MA: Northeastern University Press.

Worsley, P. 1992. The New Introducing Sociology. New York: Penguin Books.

Wright, M. 1991. *Justice for Victims and Offenders.* Philadelphia, PA: Open University Press.

Wright, M., and B. Galaway eds. 1989. *Mediation and Criminal Justice: Victims, Offenders, and Community.* Newbury, CA: Sage Publications.

Young, Allison. 1996. *Imagining Crime.* London: Sage Publications.

Young, Alison, and Austin D. Sarat. "Beyond Criticism: Law, Power, and Ethics," *Social and Legal Studies* 3 (1994): 323–331.

Young, Iris. 1990. *Justice and the Politics of Difference* Princeton, NJ: Princeton University Press.

Young, M. 1995. *Restorative Community Justice: A Call to Action.* Washington, DC: National Organization for Victim Assistance.

Young, R. 1995. *Colonial Desire: Hybridity in Theory, Culture, and Race.* London: Routledge and Kegan Paul.

Young, T. R. "Chaos Theory and Human Agency." *Humanity and Society* 16 (1992): 441–60.

————. 1997. "The ABCs of Crime." In *Chaos, Criminology and Social Justice.* Edited by Dragan Milovanovic, 77–96. Westport, CT: Praeger.

————. 1999. "A Nonlinear Theory of Justice: Affirmative Moments in Postmodern Criminology." In *Social Justice/Criminal Justice: The Maturation of Critical Theory in Law, Crime, and Deviance.* Edited by B. Arrigo, 190–200. Belmont, CA: West/Wadsworth.

Zablocki, B. 1980. *Alienation and Charisma.* New York: Free Press.

Zehr, Howard. 1985. *Restorative Justice, Retributive Justice.* Akron, PA: Mennonite Central Committee, Office of Criminal Justice.

————. 1990. *Changing Lenses.* Scottsdale, PA: Herald Press.

CASES CITED

Brown v Board of Education, 347 US 483 (1954).
Ford v Wainwright, 477 US 399 (1986).
State v Perry, 610 S. 2d 746 (La. 1992).
Washington v Harper, 494 US 210 (1990).

Name Index

Subject Index